GLOBALIZATION AND TECHNOCAPITALISM

Globalization and Technocapitalism
The Political Economy of Corporate Power and Technological Domination

LUIS SUAREZ-VILLA
University of California, Irvine, USA

Routledge
Taylor & Francis Group

LONDON AND NEW YORK

First published 2012 by Ashgate Publishing

Published 2016 by Routledge
2 Park Square, Milton Park, Abingdon, Oxfordshire OX14 4RN
711 Third Avenue, New York, NY 10017, USA

First issued in paperback 2016

Routledge is an imprint of the Taylor & Francis Group, an informa business

British Library Cataloguing in Publication Data
Suarez-Villa, Luis.
   Globalization and technocapitalism : the political economy
   of corporate power and technological domination.
   1. Corporate power. 2. Technocracy. 3. Capitalism--
   History--21st century. 4. Globalization--Social aspects.
   5. Globalization--Economic aspects. 6. High technology
   industries--Influence.
   I. Title
   338'.064-dc23

Library of Congress Cataloging-in-Publication Data
Suarez-Villa, Luis.
   Globalization and technocapitalism : the political economy of corporate
power and technological domination / by Luis Suarez-Villa.
      p. cm.
   Includes bibliographical references and index.
   ISBN 978-1-4094-3915-8 (hardback)
   1. Globalization--Economic aspects. 2. Economics--Political aspects.
3. Corporations--Social aspects. 4. Technology--Social aspects.
I. Title.
   HF1365.S843 2011
   337--dc23

ISBN 13: 978-1-138-27166-1 (pbk)
ISBN 13: 978-1-4094-3915-8 (hbk)

Contents

Introduction

Globalization is one of the most complex and long-running phenomena in human history. It has transcended diverse social, political and economic systems in ways that few other phenomena were able to. Today, globalization is platform and vehicle for the spread of a new version of capitalism that is deeply grounded in technology and corporate power. It is a new version of capitalism with a global projection that is likely to become a hallmark of the twenty-first century, as it transforms our existence, the way we relate to life and nature, our governance, and our survival as a species.

At no prior time in history was the long-term future of human existence, of life and nature as dubious as it is in our time. Technology and science are being harnessed to penetrate our lives, our existence, our social relations and our planet's ecology as never before. No aspect of human existence, of life and nature is likely to be spared by the global reach of a new capitalism whose global quest for greater profit and power respects no boundaries, social restraints or cultural features. Its global reach reflects the ethos of a new era in which corporate power, technology and science have become deeply entwined and all-encompassing, moved by a seemingly unstoppable drive for control over everyone and over all of the earth's resources.

This book provides an understanding of globalization's role as enabler and supporter of this new capitalist era, of the fundamental phenomena involved in its worldwide reach, and of the social pathologies and injustices it generates. The premises of this book are forthright and unequivocal. One premise is that social, economic and political systems that generate social injustice are nefarious to human advancement. The systemic realities they impose are major obstacles to a just and sustainable global society, and deserve to be exposed and opposed. Another premise is that theories that are indifferent or apologetic toward social injustice are wrong. They are wrong because they help justify the exploitive domination of some nations, social classes and cultures over others, and because they help perpetuate social injustices and pathologies that diminish our human condition.

Exposing the global dimensions of *technocapitalism*, its social pathologies and injustices, and its connection with corporate power, is a major objective of this book. This objective is made urgent by the fact that the new era of capitalism that technocapitalism represents will impose new global realities upon us and upon future generations of humanity, that can only be countered at great human cost. Those realities, imposed through the global spread of new technologies and of a new form of corporate power, are likely to transform most every facet of human existence, of life and nature in potentially irreversible ways. New sectors closely associated with the emergence of technocapitalism, such as nanotechnology, diverse branches of biotechnology such as genomics, synthetic bioengineering, proteomics and agro-biotech, the related fields of bioinformatics, biopharmacology and biomedicine, the transformation of robotics through the emerging field of biomimetics, and major changes in computing and communications through intelligent software, nanotech sensors and transmitters, and molecular or bioengineered processors, among other technologies, are intimately tied to technocapitalist corporate power and to its global reach.

These new sectors are providing the technologies that the twenty-first century will most likely be associated with. Corporations that live or die by their global research capabilities, where research is far more important than any other function, and where corporate appropriation of research results is the key to profit, control of these new sectors. Turning research creativity into a commodity thereby acquires fundamental importance in the global drive for greater corporate profit and power, in much the same way that turning raw materials and factory labor into commodities was fundamental for the corporations of industrial capitalism.

Creativity, an intangible global resource that is inherently qualitative and practically impossible to program, is the lifeblood of this new capitalist era. Capitalism thus enters a new global phase where intangibles—rather than tangible resources—are most valuable, where research and intellectual appropriation—rather than industrial or service production—are most important for corporate profit, and where the global power of corporations depends not so much on raw materials or the capacity to use labor in production, but on conceiving new inventions and innovations. No aspect of human existence, life or nature can be considered safe from the global reach of this new capitalist era, so long as it has the potential to advance the quest for greater corporate profit and power.

Although not representative of the larger global economy at this time, the new sectors and corporations are the vanguard of a new version of capitalism that promises to spread and take up a much larger profile. When they began, prior capitalist eras seemed largely irrelevant to their context and to the larger social panorama. At the outset of industrial capitalism, for example, the factory system and the new sectors associated with it seemed foreign to most every existing socioeconomic framework then in existence, and to the larger social reality of the nations where it was taking root. Nonetheless, the operational modes of the new sectors eventually spread to the rest of society and to the world at large, redefining the relations of power and most aspects of the social order. Today, the new corporations and sectors associated with technocapitalism are influencing how we view human existence, life and nature, and are well on their way to impose new realities.

Signs of some of the new global realities that technocapitalism and its corporate apparatus (referred to as *corporatism* in this book) impose through these new sectors are already upon us, and are becoming visible in many aspects of our everyday existence. For example, human nutrition and global food production are increasingly dependent on the use of bioengineered seeds and related new herbicides in farming, that destroy the food chain of numerous species. Their long-term effects on human health and on nature are largely unknown, and the ecological damage they cause may become irreversible. In synthetic bioengineering, corporate entities are creating living organisms out of non-living matter, patenting them as their property, and are moving fast along the pathway to engineer diverse forms of life from scratch. Their operations will very likely lead to the creation of myriad living organisms, from viruses that can generate disease to microbes that produce fuels, to human organs for replacement, to new animal species and possibly humanoids, all created as corporate property. A new industry and a vast new market may thus be created for synthetic life, affecting most any aspect of human existence and of nature.

With genomics and genetic engineering, the ever present human desire to produce offspring that are economically successful may turn the genetic design of fetuses into an industry. Engineering genetic specifications that can be related to economic success, or at least to traits that are highly desirable to corporate power, may thus come to the fore as a major aspect of human reproduction in the twenty-first century. Corporations typically recruit and screen personnel on the basis of traits they consider desirable, and it may be possible to associate those traits with genetic features that can be introduced in the human genetic make-up before birth. This kind of genetic design has already been extensively practiced on numerous animal and plant species by corporate entities seeking to profit from their use. By and large, the knowledge required to make human genetic design a reality is already available.

Nanotechnology, combined with advances in computing, telecommunications, intelligent software and biomimetics, promises to turn many nations into surveillance societies, where most every personal activity can be monitored and archived. The end of individual privacy may thereby be coupled with greater social, political and economic control, where powerful corporate entities play a fundamental role as providers of technology, executors of surveillance, and controllers of public governance. The future use of new surveillance technology based on nanotechnology, biomimetics, advanced software, computing and telecommunications in espionage should not be underestimated, given their profit potential and the global political imperative for greater control.

A new kind of warfare may be made possible by the new technologies created by technocapitalist corporate power. The creation of new technologies of warfare is part of an emerging techno-military-corporate complex that is likely to be a hallmark of the twenty-first century, more technologically capable than the military-industrial complex of the second half of the twentieth century. The new tools of warfare are likely to involve genomics and genetic engineering, synthetic bioengineering, nanotechnology, biomimetics, intelligent software and advances in computing and communications, to produce diverse war machines, animal-like war robots, cyberwarfare, and possibly genetically engineered humanoid soldiers that can more effectively kill and be expendable.

These examples reflect underlying phenomena that are closely associated with the globalization of technocapitalism and its corporate apparatus. It is a central objective of this book to consider those phenomena, given their importance for understanding the global reach of technocapitalism, the power of the corporate apparatus that sustains it, and the social pathologies they generate. Those social pathologies are derived from the contradictions that pervade technocapitalist corporate power and its global projection. They are unlike any social pathologies that humanity has dealt with before, because of their deep grounding in technology and science, and because of their global scope. One set of pathologies, for example, is grounded in corporate predation of intellectual property, a rapidly growing global phenomenon that is driven by the overarching need to appropriate creativity and all related intangibles. The rapid global increase in corporate litigation over intellectual property is one symptom of this phenomenon, which now encompasses every creative activity in the corporate domain. The all-encompassing character of technocapitalism and of its corporate apparatus extrapolates this and other pathologies to the world, imposing new realities that influence vital aspects of social existence such as our governance, how we view social justice, and how we deal with life and nature.

The phenomena to be considered in this book are abstract and complex, they defy simplification and their full profile is still largely unknown, but they are fundamental for understanding the globalization of technocapitalism. They are *macro* in scope and scale, in contrast with the micro-level, organizational phenomena that were at the core of my previous book, *Technocapitalism*. Because there is so little knowledge about those phenomena and the new realities they create, the discussions of this book may at times seem tentative or speculative. Understanding the global scope of technocapitalism is therefore in many ways a work in progress, because of the dynamic character of globalization and also because the trajectory of technocapitalism is still largely uncharted.

The approach taken by this book emphasizes wholeness, connection and contradiction, along with the multifaceted character of the phenomena to be considered. The technological rationality of technocapitalism and of its globalization will be addressed in a critical way, in contrast with the functionalist perspectives that populate the literature on technology, society and corporations. It is therefore assumed that the technological rationality of technocapitalism and of its globalization combines *technique*—the rational character of technology—with the *relations of power*—the global projection of corporate power in this case— and with the *ideological dimension* of technocapitalist corporate power. This latter element manifests itself through the corporate drive for global domination over most any facet of society, such as its governance, the regulatory apparatus, and its institutions. These three elements—technique, relations of power and ideological dimension—are abstract and complex, and they comprise major contradictions within and between themselves that influence technocapitalist globalization, its pathologies, and the new global realities that are imposed on us.

The perspective of this book is at odds with the overwhelming reductionist bent of contemporary social science literature on technology and corporations. It is also at odds with academic work that lacks a critical perspective on corporate power and social injustice. Its perspective is likewise at odds with the extensive management literature on technology and corporations, and in particular the large number of how-to manuals that purport to show how to exploit and compete ever more ruthlessly, or how to maximize profits in ever more clever ways that often incur great social cost. Because of these characteristics and because of its perspective, it can be expected that this book's reception among those who support the predominant global order, or are apologetic toward social injustice, may be rather negative. It may also be expected that the contents of this book might be seen as threatening by those heavily invested in reductionist constructs that exclude social injustice.

In the experience of this and other authors, exposing social injustice, breaking with the reductionist mold and with status quo apologetics often carry personal costs in this day and age, in the form of subtle discrimination, pejorative opinions or demeaning attitudes, as academia and academics become ever more dependent on corporate power and on corporate capital. Authors who choose the critical path must take account of this reality, and it is to their awareness and struggles that this work is dedicated. No work of social criticism can be considered effective or complete unless it compels others to change reality, and most of all to work for a just social order in our global society. It is hoped that this book will encourage readers to work for a just global order, by providing a better understanding of the phenomena and pathologies that underlie the spread of technocapitalism.

During the past decade, many scholars have offered comments and criticism that have benefited the elaboration of this book and, more generally, my work on technocapitalism. They are far too numerous to name here, but their feedback and concerns are deeply appreciated. To my spouse, I owe much gratitude for her support in difficult times, despite her illness. Her philosophical perspective, her moral rectitude in the face of adversity, and her personal concern for justice and fairness provided inspiration throughout the writing of this book.

I would also like to express my gratitude to Dr Neil Jordan, my Commissioning Editor at Ashgate Publishing, for his understanding and his diligence in all matters related to the completion of this work. The production and marketing staff at Ashgate, and in particular Pamela Bertram, also deserve special gratitude for their work, and for their efforts in all aspects related to the final preparation, printing and distribution of this book. In this day and age, with all the challenges faced by academic book publishers, to have the support of such talented people is most valuable.

Technocapitalism on a Global Scale

The globalization of technocapitalism is grounded in the expansion of corporate power and its deep-seated domination over technology and science. It is a domination that is spawning new economic sectors and activities which promise to be hallmarks of the twenty-first century, but that nonetheless continue the long historical evolution of capitalism. Technocapitalism, its globalization, its corporate apparatus, its new sectors and technologies, and the new phenomena they encompass therefore have much in common with past versions of capitalism, yet at the same time they impose new realities that intrude into most every aspect of human existence, of life and nature as no prior socioeconomic system ever could.

The new sectors that technocapitalism and its corporate apparatus have spawned are global in scope and reach. In biotechnology, for example, agro-biotech corporations are active in most nations around the world, and are affecting the ecologies of crops in irreversible ways. In nanotechnology, corporations that cater to intelligence services and the military are developing miniature engines, cameras, processors and transmitters to perform pervasive surveillance or spying practically anywhere in the world, aided by intelligent software, biomimetics and advanced telecommunication satellites. Corporations engaged in bioinformatics and genomics are deciphering the genetic code of practically all animal, plant, microbe and marine life on earth, thereby enabling large-scale genetic engineering that can irreversibly transform life and nature. Corporations engaged in biopharmacology, agro-biotech and biomedicine are utilizing such genetic data to radically transform medicine and nutrition, with limited understanding of its long-term effects on human wellbeing and survival. All of these and many other developments that characterize the emerging technocapitalist era have a common denominator—they are undertaken by corporate entities to further their self-serving quest for greater profit and power, above everything else.

The globalization of these new sectors and corporate domains is advancing at a fast pace, mainly because their effects on human existence, life and nature can occur anywhere, even in nations that lack the technological and corporate capability to contribute to them. This is all too obvious, for example, in the case of bioengineered seeds for agricultural crops, which have already spread to all corners of the globe, or in biopharmacology and biomedicine, where corporate testing of new treatments is now undertaken in poor nations, recruiting vulnerable populations to become human guinea pigs. Animal cloning can now be undertaken most anywhere, using limited equipment and following procedures that are available online. Nanotechnology and biomimetic gadgets for spying and surveillance may be used most anywhere, regardless of sovereignty, justice or legality, whenever military or intelligence strategies dictate it. We therefore increasingly live in a world that has no boundaries for technocapitalism's new technologies and sectors, or for the corporate powers that appropriate them.

And the creation of those new technologies and sectors is systematic. It is systematic because research programs are set by corporations to suit their quest for profit and power above everything else. It is systematic because research in the corporate domain is systematized in order to try to make it less risky and uncertain, and to generate as continuous and rapid a flow of new inventions and innovations as possible. And it is systematic because creativity—the most precious resource of the technocapitalist era—has to be turned into a commodity for corporate appropriation of its results to occur, and for any profit to be extracted from those results. Clearly, the systematic character of these key aspects is also a *systemic* feature of technocapitalism and of its corporatism, much as production and labor processes were systemic features of industrial capitalism.

The systemic dimension of technocapitalism and of its corporate apparatus is also global, mainly because boundaries and restraints to the global reach of technocapitalism either do not exist or are being collapsed, for reasons that will be explored in this chapter and later throughout this book. Among those reasons is the rising influence of corporate power over public governance around the world—an influence that now seems to be all-encompassing and that co-opts, corrupts or otherwise induces compliance with corporate priorities, often at great cost to the public and to society at large. Another reason is the increasingly authoritarian control that corporatism exercises over technology—control that spares nothing that can contribute to the overarching quest for profit and power, anywhere and everywhere. It is a form of systemic control that places profit over people whenever extracting profit conflicts with human priorities.

This chapter will consider the historical context of technocapitalism and of its globalization, along with the ideological framework and politico-economic circumstances that influenced its emergence and worldwide reach. Technocapitalism, like all prior capitalist eras, emerged out of specific historical circumstances that have influenced its associated phenomena and its globalization. Technocapitalism's global reach depends on a new ethos of corporate control over technology and science, and on the unfettered expansion of corporate power, with consequences for humanity, life and nature that are all too often irreversible. The ethos of this new capitalist era and its association with technocapitalism's globalization will therefore draw our attention as well. Finally, the premises that promote technocapitalism's globalization, its ethos, its relations of power and its societal impacts will be considered, along with the component phenomena that define the global reach of this new era.

Historical Panorama

The globalization of technocapitalism is part of the centuries-old evolution of capitalism and comprises the general contradictions, exploitive character and social pathologies that have long characterized this socioeconomic system. Despite the common elements, the globalization of this new phase of capitalism nonetheless exhibits features that are markedly different from those of prior phases of capitalism. Those features have much to do with technocapitalism's deep grounding in technology and science, with its dependence on intangible resources, among which creativity is most precious, and with its need for new forms of corporate organization to exploit and appropriate this most important resource. As we will see later in this book, those features are part of a new reality of global power and domination that are becoming a hallmark of the twenty-first century, and that are likely to affect us for many generations.

Although globalization did occur in pre-capitalist times, its support for capitalism has been vital for this socioeconomic system's sustenance and expansion. The growth and sustenance of mercantile capitalism depended on its globalization, executed mostly through imperial conquest, the exploitation of labor or slavery, and the extraction of commodities. Commercial exchange, through markets or by other means, and the accumulation of commercial capital were major features of mercantile capitalism. Mercantile exchange regimes ensured the flow of commodities for exchange, the imposition of standards, and the exploitation or capture of labor to sustain commodity flows. Globalization expanded not only the quantum of exchange and accumulation, but also the profit and power of mercantile companies associated with imperial administration and colonization.

The globalization of industrial capitalism followed the paths opened by mercantile capitalism, but was based instead on the extraction of mineral raw materials for factory production, the exploitation of labor through factory production regimes and labor processes, and the accumulation of industrial capital. Imperialism played a vital role in the global reach of industrial corporate power during the incipient stages of industrialization, in the eighteenth and nineteenth centuries, whenever raw materials had to be extracted in diverse parts of the world due to insufficient domestic supply in the richer industrializing nations.[1]

---

1 Although it must be noted that availability of raw materials at home was not the only consideration. At times, imperial relations of power dictated that raw materials be extracted from the colonized as a means to establish greater control over territories and peoples, even when the commodities in question were available in the imperial power's home market. See, for example, Eric Hobsbawm, *Industry and Empire: From 1750 to the Present Day* (London: Penguin, 1999) and his *Industry and Empire: An Economic History of Britain* (London: Weidenfeld and Nicolson, 1968); Michel Beaud, *A History of Capitalism: 1500–2000*, transl. T. Dickman and A. Lefebvre (New York: Monthly Review Press, 2001).

Later, by the middle of the twentieth century, the expansion of industrial corporate power into the multinational arena to take advantage of low-cost labor, new markets, and greater access to raw materials spawned a new stage of globalization, as factory production regimes and labor processes spread around the world.[2] This globalization of industrial corporate power and factory production regimes was one of the most important features of the twentieth century, particularly in its second half. Even though in some nations industrialization occurred outside the control of corporate power, by the last quarter of the twentieth century the global spread of industrial and services-based corporate capitalism was a distinctive phenomenon.

Stagnation and Crisis

Understanding the emergence and globalization of technocapitalism requires a broad perspective on the dynamics of late twentieth century capitalism. After the second World War, cyclical economic downturns coupled with limited growth finally gave way to stagnation with inflation in the 1970s. Clearly, the liberal economic policies that had long guided governance in the rich capitalist nations were exhausted.[3] The global oil crisis that started in 1973, a deep recession, and the emergence of "stagflation" (stagnation with inflation) that followed through the 1970s and the early 1980s exacerbated fears about the sustenance of capitalism. Such fears were most prominent among the corporate elites and the richer classes of that time in the wealthier nations of the planet, and were reflected in the deliberations of numerous think-tanks and policy formulation bodies.[4] Cold War tensions and the revolutionary trajectories of numerous nations in Asia, Africa and Latin America added to those fears, prompting a search for new ways to generate economic growth and provide jobs for an increasingly restive population.

Mechanisms were therefore sought to allow governments in the wealthier capitalist nations to spend more, to try to stave off high unemployment and the rising discontent of the population. This approach followed long-established Keynesian ideas on the need for government to boost its spending during economic crises.[5] In the US, however, the cost of the Vietnam war and the American worldwide military machine was rapidly increasing along with Cold War tensions. This limited the possibility for additional government spending at a time when it was

---

2   See Richard J. Barnet's *Global Reach: The Power of the Multinational Corporations* (New York: Simon and Schuster, 1974).

3   An alarming prospect to followers of Keynesian policies; see John Maynard Keynes' *The General Theory of Employment, Interest and Money* (London: Macmillan, 1936); Michel Beaud and Gilles Dostaller, *Economic Thought Since Keynes*, transl. V. Cauchenez and E. Litwack (London: Routledge, 1997).

4   Among which were, for example, the Trilateral Commission, the Council on Foreign Policy, and the Brookings Institution, all in the United States.

5   See Keynes, *General Theory*.

needed to boost domestic social programs, to cover the cost of new weapons, and to support American global military expansion. A way therefore had to be found to allow government to spend more without damaging the currency or triggering an international monetary crisis.

A major obstacle was posed by the so-called Bretton Woods Agreement of the late 1940s. This agreement had fixed currency exchange rates (based on gold reserves) between the richer nations of the planet, to try to ensure currency stability and to support international trade.[6] Given the fixed exchange rates, a government that sought to spend more to cover military costs or domestic social programs would be in danger of driving itself into a currency devaluation or into insolvency. In many ways, therefore, the fixing of exchange rates by the Bretton Woods Agreement was a safety measure that held government spending in check.[7] One of its effects, however, was that it implicitly limited government spending during times of crisis, thereby potentially compromising the stability of capitalist regimes.

The Bretton Woods Agreement was therefore scrapped in 1971 at the behest of the US. Doing so was important to expand American political and military power at a time of rising Cold War rivalry. Floating currency exchange rates thus became a reality, allowing certain governments (most of all the US) to spend more and incur large budget deficits. The floating of exchange rates by opening them to financial market speculation, was seen by many as a victory for "free market" ideology. Many neoclassical economists then thought that market speculation would provide better monetary management than governments could, with the markets imposing discipline on governments through changes in the floating value of currencies.[8] This ideologically laden view of currencies and government finance marked the beginning of what some authors would later refer to as free-market fundamentalism.

Much overlooked in this ideological justification, however, was the fact that the supply of currencies and monetary instruments is typically decided through governments' monopoly over money supply and legality, rather than through any play of markets. A cartel of central banks, rather than any market process,

---

6   Setting fixed exchange rates, based on the US dollar's convertibility into gold (with the price of gold also set at a fixed price) were key aspects of the Bretton Woods Agreement. David Harvey's *A Brief History of Neoliberalism* (New York: Oxford University Press, 2005) considers the abrogation of this agreement to be an important step that later allowed neoliberal policies to become global.

7   The General Agreement on Tariffs and Trade, set up after the Bretton Woods Agreement, tried to ameliorate the effects of fixed exchange rates on trade, but became a vehicle to sustain industrialized capitalist nations' advantages in key sectors; see Douglas A. Irwin, Petros C. Mavroidis and Alan O. Sykes, *The Genesis of the GATT* (New York: Cambridge University Press, 2009).

8   See, for example, Milton Friedman, *The Balance of Payments: Free Versus Fixed Exchange Rates* (Washington: American Enterprise Institute for Public Policy Research, 1967).

issues currencies, fixes interest rates and otherwise sets the conditions upon which speculation and trade occur. To think that markets would actually rule currency exchange and monetary management on their own was a great fallacy that many nations and peoples came to experience at great economic cost and social pain.

In the case of the US, the fact that the dollar was the world's standard currency provided the possibility of reducing the national debt by printing money, with the resulting inflation eroding the value of government debt to anyone who purchased it (usually in the form of treasury bonds). This was a luxury not available to other nations, of course, and it worked to cement American financial power over the rest of the world. The move to create in western Europe a common currency that might compete with the US dollar as a world standard currency, was part of an effort to offset the American advantage in this vital aspect. For the European nations that joined this effort, having their own common currency and making it a potential global alternative to the US dollar was also a way to secure freer government spending of their own.

The global economic crisis of the middle and late 1970s, however, brought up the need for greater government outlays in a very powerful way, as the wealthier nations sought to cope with social unrest and unemployment by spending more, thereby incurring larger deficits and higher debt. The results were meager and worrisome, however, as inflation rose while economies stagnated. At a time when most every government in every rich nation was spending more and incurring greater debt, Keynesian economic policies were thus generating few results, with stagnant performance, persistently high unemployment, and much higher inflation becoming part of daily economic reality. New ideas, if not a new ideology, therefore had to be found if capitalism was to have a new lease on life.

Neoliberalism

Neoliberalism provided capitalism with that new lease on life, by redefining public governance and the political projection of corporate power. The emergence of neoliberalism as a global economic, political and social doctrine therefore provided the ideological platform for a change in governance and in government's role in society. The first target of neoliberal economic management was inflation, with monetary policy becoming a major economic and political tool. Tighter monetary supply and a higher cost of capital (achieved largely by setting higher interest rates) were used to subdue inflation, despite the unemployment they generated.[9] Reducing the power of labor unions, by scrapping laws that protected employee rights, also became an important component of the neoliberal agenda. The resulting containment of wages and labor costs proved to be a boon to corporate

---

9   Inflation was also reduced by an oversupply of oil in the early 1980s, which led to much lower prices for this commodity. OPEC member nations and other (non-OPEC) oil-producing nations had incurred considerable debts during the 1970s, and increasing the supply of oil was their main vehicle to deal with high debt loads.

power, eventually leading to some growth in employment albeit at the low end of the wage and skill spectrum.

This new framework started to be implemented in the US in 1979 with the installation of a new Federal Reserve regime, and in Britain after the election of Margaret Thatcher. In 1980, the election of Ronald Reagan in the US gave political impetus to the neoliberal project, with the elaboration of policies that were wide-ranging in scope and that went beyond monetary recipes and the attempt to control inflation.[10] Curiously, the measures adopted in the US and Britain had by and large earlier been implemented in Chile by the Pinochet regime after the 1973 military coup. The Pinochet regime had provided the earliest test of neoliberal dogma, an experiment that was hypocritically disowned by neoliberals because of the regime's brutality, despite the valuable lessons it provided them with.[11] Perhaps the memory of the 1973 military coup in Chile and its aftermath was too unpleasant for neoliberals to remember, or the fact that the coup was backed by American corporations along with the US government and its intelligence apparatus. The neoliberal ideas implemented by the Pinochet regime in Chile had, in any case, come from a most important American business school (the University of Chicago School of Business), that would later prove very influential in the US and throughout the world as a beacon of neoliberal thought. Neoclassical economics, and particularly its monetary specialty, was intimately entwined with this ideological movement, as would be shown by various Nobel prizes (most prominently Milton Friedman's) won for theoretical frameworks that joined neoclassical economics with neoliberal dogma.

The most important target of the neoliberal agenda turned out to be government itself, and its historical role as guardian of the public interest and of the societal commons (the resources that belong collectively to society or to the public, and to no one in particular). The underlying objective of the neoliberal agenda was to benefit corporate power first and foremost, by redefining the role of the state and by dismantling restraints to corporate power.[12] This fundamental motive was typically camouflaged with various guises and pretexts, such as the imperative

---

10   Those policies had long been espoused by American conservatives and by the corporate elites; see Kim Phillips-Fein, *Invisible Hands: The Making of the Conservative Movement from the New Deal to Reagan* (New York: Norton, 2009); Alan J. Lichtman, *White Protestant Nation: The Rise of the American Conservative Movement* (New York: Atlantic Monthly Press, 2008).

11   Among those lessons was the application of so-called economic shock (or "shock therapy") policies; see Naomi Klein, *The Shock Doctrine: The Rise of Disaster Capitalism* (New York: Metropolitan Books, 2007). See also the articles in Philip Mirowski and Dieter Plehwe (eds.), *The Road to Mont Pelerin: The Making of the Neoliberal Thought Collective* (Cambridge: Harvard University Press, 2009).

12   An objective that had a major global impact, and was largely achieved under the guise of promoting representative democracy and individual freedom; see, for example, Noam Chomsky, *Profit Over People: Neoliberalism and Global Order* (New York: Seven Stories Press, 1999).

of making governance and the economy more efficient, the notion that the social good would be optimized by "maximizing" the reach of markets and of market transactions into any aspect of human existence, the assumption that wide-ranging property rights, free trade and unhindered capital flows would promote greater individual and political "freedom" (a word used in practically all neoliberal propaganda), and the idea that all forms of government intervention that placed collective interests above those of individual judgment were wrong.

Neoliberal arguments in favor of "free" markets and of market competition masked the fact that the real objective was the advancement of corporate power, first and foremost, in a generic sense. In any market economy, some corporations may drive other corporations out of business, but corporate power always wins. It therefore matters little whether Corporation X or Corporation Y comes out on top—corporate power, generically speaking—wins no matter who the winners or the vanquished are. Oligopolistic markets only make the game more predictable, since the powerful are more likely to accumulate power and to trounce the weaker, or will in any case be more likely to continue their domination. Competitive markets, however, have always held greater thrill for neoliberal ideologues because of their Darwinian dynamic—which can be less predictable than with oligopolistic markets—and because of the belief that corporate power (embodied in whichever corporations happen to "win") emerges stronger, more dynamic, and therefore more capable of overcoming whatever obstacles may be placed on their road.[13] Darwinian natural selection, set in motion through market competition, is thereby assumed to sort out "the best." This perspective gained increasing favor among neoliberals during the past three decades, using the work of many neoclassical economists (usually based in American business schools) to legitimize their arguments. In reality, however, it was not free-market play that neoliberals sought to favor, but corporate power (generically). Markets, in the neoliberal conception, were simply vehicles to preserve and augment corporate power.

---

13 A premise that is implicit in most of the contemporary literature on corporate competition. See, for example, George Stalk Jr., Robert Lachenauer and John Butman, *Hardball: Are You Playing to Play or Playing to Win?* (Boston: Harvard Business School Press, 2004). In a related article, Stalk and Lachenauer put forth five "killer" strategies for corporate executives to follow, thereby providing a general template upon which to base corporate action and decision-making; see George Stalk Jr. and Robert Lachenauer, "Hardball: Five Killer Strategies for Trouncing the Competition," *Harvard Business Review* (April 2004): 62–71. The publication of such recipes by what is arguably the top professional management journal in the world, based in one of the world's most prestigious business schools (and whose alumni are most influential among the world's business graduates), speaks volumes about the acceptance of those aggressive recipes in the corporate world. In many ways, the acceptance and practice of those recipes as corporate strategy provides an indication of the anti-social dimension of corporate power in contemporary society; see, for example, Joel Bakan's *The Corporation: The Pathological Pursuit of Profit and Power* (New York: Free Press, 2004).

The visible mechanisms of the neoliberal agenda involved *privatization* of most every government function that could turn a profit for corporate entities, including the sale of the collective resources of society to corporate power. Whenever such sales became difficult or impossible, the alternative was to lease those resources to corporate interests such that they could turn a profit from their use or management.[14] Privatization also helped reduce government spending, but in the case of the US it allowed government resources to be recycled to expand American global military power (a major objective of the Reagan administration in the 1980s).

A second visible mechanism involved the *deregulation* of most every aspect of governance that restrained corporate power, whether in finance, banking, manufacturing, education, housing, the environment, basic utilities, and even in areas closely related to human health and survival.[15] The deregulation trend would later prove to be important to corporate technocapitalism and to its globalization, particularly in the new sectors related to human life, nutrition and health, such as agro-biotech, genetic engineering, biopharmacology and genomics. Deregulation of finance would also prove to be a boon for technocapitalist corporatism and for high tech corporate power in general, through the rise of venture capital as a major source of investment and through unfettered speculation in technology corporations.

The *withdrawal of the state* from many areas of social and economic provision was a third important mechanism of the neoliberal agenda, particularly when privatization became untenable. Such withdrawal often meant that functions previously under the oversight of public governance would either be abandoned altogether, or would be left to non-governmental groups to look after. This third visible mechanism therefore resulted in greater socioeconomic insecurity for the most vulnerable segments of society, such as the poor, the homeless, the unskilled and the disabled. For the working mass of the population, it diminished the social safety net intended to care for the unemployed during economic downturns (a key

---

14   Privatization often involved the partial or complete corporate takeover of government functions, even when doing so was wasteful to taxpayers, as in the case of the US program of guaranteed government loans to college students. The privatization of that program guaranteed profits to the private lenders (usually banks) that loaned funds to students, at a cost of close to $7 billion per year to taxpayers. See Walter Hamilton and Larry Gordon, "House Oks Student Aid Overhaul," *Los Angeles Times* (March 23, 2010): B1.

15   Among the least noticed in the myriad laws that deregulated the US economy to benefit corporate interests and speculators was the Commodity Futures Modernization Act of 2000. By and large, this deregulatory act may have been the single most important legal force driving the commodities bubble and the bust of 2008; see Thomas Frank, "Drill Now? Try Regulate Now," *Wall Street Journal* (April 7, 2010): A13. In many cases, deregulation granted oversight responsibility to the very corporate interests that regulators had previously overseen, creating conflicts of interest and triggering accidents and abuses. See Russell Gold, "Regulator Ceded Oversight of Rig Safety to Oil Drillers," *Wall Street Journal* (May 7, 2010): A1.

aspect of the social contract in most rich nations). At the same time it also reduced the competence of government to deal with crises and with urgent social problems.

At the global scale, the neoliberal agenda sought to generate "free" trade and "free" flows of capital by taking down trade tariffs, by promoting corporate investment capital (most of all from the richer nations of the planet), by favoring foreign corporate ownership of any domestic resources and businesses (most of all from rich-nation multinational corporations), along with the previously mentioned triplet mechanisms of privatization, deregulation and the withdrawal of government from social provision. To further neoliberalism's "free" trade objective a worldwide body, the World Trade Organization (WTO) was created in 1995, to replace the General Agreement on Tariffs and Trade (GATT), the mechanism that had long been used to reduce trade barriers. Long before the creation of the WTO, other global organizations such as the International Monetary Fund (IMF) and the World Bank, had been prescribing and imposing neoliberal policies on governments through monetary requirements, development project assistance, government loans and wide-ranging economic policy recipes that favored the three mechanisms noted above.[16]

Most important for the emergence of technocapitalism and for its globalization was neoliberalism's promotion of corporate intellectual property rights, and of property rights in general, in every area of human endeavor. Property became as important to neoliberalism as the stone ax was to prehistoric societies. No property right, no matter how insignificant, could be overlooked in the neoliberal quest to legitimize the ownership of resources, most of all by corporate power. At the same time the range and definition of resources to be appropriated, most of all by corporate power, expanded remarkably to include most anything that could generate any profit, be it tangible or intangible. Given the evolution of capitalism toward intangibles, intellectual property came to have primordial importance in the neoliberal agenda.[17]

All of the agenda items mentioned before were propagandistically justified in terms of the promotion of "free" markets, "free" trade, and individual "freedom." Neoliberal social engineering was thus predicated on the notion of promoting freedom and "free choice," even though choice was all too often vacated through corporate hegemony and the elimination of collective resources. Freedom was

---

16   See Richard Peet, *Unholy Trinity: The IMF, World Bank and WTO* (London: Zed Books, 2009).

17   Corporate power's dependence on intellectual property, even in traditional economic sectors and industries (not associated with technocapitalism) has become a major characteristic of the contemporary global economy, leading to an astronomical rise in intellectual property litigation. See Michael Perelman, *Steal this Idea: Intellectual Property and the Corporate Confiscation of Creativity* (New York: Palgrave Macmillan, 2002). The rising importance of corporate intellectual property is also reflected in the growth of financial speculation on patents; see *The Economist*, "Patents as Financial Assets: Trolls Demanding Tolls" (September 12, 2009): 84.

therefore a clever and powerfully appealing concept in which to clothe neoliberal propaganda, and it reverberated throughout the political discourse of the late twentieth and early twenty-first centuries, justifying any policy no matter how misguided or how unjust.

In reality, as we will see later in this book, the application of neoliberal policies throughout the world greatly increased socioeconomic inequalities between haves and have-nots, they dispossessed the poor and the working classes of economic security, of their employment rights and social dignity. Neoliberal policies also redistributed political power and wealth from the vast majority of the population toward the corporate elites, and toward the richer classes of society associated with those elites and with corporate capital.[18] The main vehicle for this global dynamic of redistribution and dispossession was government's monopoly over force and legality, to impose measures that would benefit corporate interests above everything else. Curiously, therefore, the withdrawal of the state that neoliberalism espoused did not apply to its use of government power, to impose the kind of redistribution that benefits corporate power.

In general, the rise of neoliberalism as a global force helped set the conditions for the emergence of technocapitalism and its globalization. The global expansion of corporate power and of related capital flows made it possible to dynamize accumulation (a most vital component of capitalism) on an unprecedented scale. The accumulation of capital, in particular, was greatly affected by the global projection of neoliberalism, as new financial vehicles made it possible to generate venture capital for new technology companies, that later became global powerhouses.[19] This aspect, the dynamization of capital accumulation through financial deregulation and the concoction of new speculative vehicles, was part of a larger phenomenon that started in the early 1980s.

Financialization

Financialization was possibly the most important phenomenon of neoliberalism and of its globalization, marking a shift of capitalism away from production and services toward finance and speculation as prime drivers of economic growth. Financialization was a direct outcome of the visible mechanism of deregulation discussed earlier, and it targeted practically all types of finance.[20] The deregulation that financialization represents opened the floodgates to unfettered, diverse and

---

18 See Harvey, *Brief History*, chapters 1–3.

19 See, for example, James Wallace and Jim Erickson, *Hard Drive: Bill Gates and the Making of the Microsoft Empire* (New York: Wiley, 1992); David Stauffer, *Business the Sun Way: Secrets of a New Economy Megabrand* (Oxford, UK: Capstone, 2002).

20 Financialization is therefore defined as the long-term economic shift from production (in manufacturing and services) to finance as the prime source of economic growth. See John Bellamy Foster, "The Age of Monopoly-Finance Capital," *Monthly Review* (February 2010): 1–13. Early manifestations of the shift toward finance in advanced

very complex financial speculation, creating mountains of debt through a multitude of risky vehicles that would eventually bring the world's financial system to near collapse.[21] The global economic crisis that started in 2007 was one result of financialization, and in many ways it revealed major flaws in the neoliberal ideological agenda that created it.[22]

At its core, financialization was about generating growth, the kind of growth that had been so worrisomely exhausted in the 1970s by stagflation and that threatened the long-term survival of capitalist regimes. Financialization was largely created in the United States in the 1980s through the initial deregulation of banking and finance implemented by the Reagan administration. Later, it was compounded by the deeper dismantling of controls and safeguards, such as the erosion and eventual abrogation of the Glass-Steagall Act in 1999 (a key safeguard created during the Great Depression), by the rise of global mega-banks and hedge funds with enormous stakes in speculative schemes, by the concoction of extremely complex and risky financial vehicles, and by the easy monetary policies of central banks, particularly in the US and other rich nations.[23]

Another core aspect of financialization was the blind faith that markets would ultimately correct any distortions and excesses that ensued. This was a key feature of the kind of market fundamentalism that underpinned the neoliberal agenda and, it might be recalled, was derived from the sort of markets-know-best fallacy that had driven the abrogation of the Bretton Woods Agreement. At its most absurd, this faith in the self-corrective power of markets had driven some neoclassical economists to concoct models that purported to show the supreme rationality of markets, upon which many neoliberals deposited their trust that any crisis would be easily overcome by self-generated market actions. This ridiculous fallacy was

---

capitalist economies were detected by Paul A. Baran and Paul M. Sweezy in their prescient *Monopoly Capital* (New York: Monthly Review Press, 1966).

21   Evidence of financialization's growing importance in the economic panorama is provided by the share of financial sector profits as a percentage of total US corporate profits, which rose from 17 percent in 1960 to 44 percent in 2002, a historically unprecedented trend. See US Council of Economic Advisers, *Economic Report of the President, 2010* (Washington: US Government Printing Office, 2010); John Bellamy Foster and Hannah Holleman, "The Financial Power Elite," *Monthly Review* (May 2010): 1–19. An early (mid-1980s) critique of this phenomenon was Harry Magdoff and Paul M. Sweezy's *Stagnation and the Financial Explosion* (New York: Monthly Review Press, 1987).

22   See Edward S. Herman, *The Roller Coaster Economy: Financial Crisis, Great Recession, and the Public Option* (New York: Sharpe, 2010); Joseph Stiglitz, *Freefall: America, Free Markets and the Sinking of the World Economy* (New York: Norton, 2010).

23   The deregulation of banking and finance in the US started long before the repeal of the Glass-Steagall Act in 1999—a fact illustrated by the waves of bank mergers and consolidations that began in the early 1980s. See Foster and Holleman, "Financial Power Elite"; Joseph E. Stiglitz, "Checking the Banks," *Los Angeles Times* (January 29, 2010): A35, and his *Freefall*; Thomas Frank, "Bring Back Glass-Steagall," *Wall Street Journal* (January 13, 2010): A21.

also behind the justification for the massive waves of deregulation that swept through most every economic sector starting in the early 1980s. Most every nation in the world would sooner or later find itself caught up in this maelstrom of deregulatory fever, prodded or forced to do so by meta-national organizations such as the International Monetary Fund and the World Bank, by the mega-banks with substantial stakes in currency speculation and government debt, and by the global credit-rating agencies that evaluated such debt.

Much of the ideological justification and the policies that supported financialization around the world came from the so-called Washington Consensus, an influential group of policy-makers, politicians, technocrats and academics who sought to direct the fate of nations through neoliberal economic policies. The Washington Consensus was so named because of its grounding in the US and because of its undivided attention to fostering and imposing American-style governance on the rest of world.[24] In many respects, the work of the Washington Consensus represented an agenda for a deeper penetration of American power into practically every aspect of national interest, anywhere in the world. The US, which took up the pioneering role in financialization, was logically the nation upon which to base this global crusade for a new world order, in which corporate power and market fundamentalism would play major roles. American business schools, with their well-developed history of pro-corporate propaganda and their support of market fundamentalism, were fervent supporters of the Consensus, with neoclassical economists becoming the most visible advocates for the globalization of financialization.

An important but usually unmentioned political objective of financialization was to align the interests of corporate power with those of the mass of the population. Politically, such alignment could guarantee the ascendance of the neoliberal agenda and of its associated corporate interests over the long term, thus creating a major safeguard for the sustenance of neoliberal regimes everywhere. Making everyone's economic well-being dependent on corporate performance was the key to such alignment, and the stock (and bond) markets were the vehicle.[25] Trying to turn everyone into a stock market gambler was a difficult proposition, however, which required structural changes in the social contract and in the social

---

24   The US government, the International Monetary Fund and the World Bank were the prime supporters and enablers of the Washington Consensus. See *The Economist*, "A Plague of Finance" (September 29, 2001): 21–5, and the articles in Narcis Serra and Joseph E. Stiglitz (eds.), *The Washington Consensus Reconsidered: Toward a New Global Governance* (New York: Oxford University Press, 2008).

25   Some authors misleadingly referred to this objective as a "democratization of finance", arguing that the public was smart enough to figure out extremely complex financial vehicles that even highly experienced financial specialists could not understand. The best-known mutual fund manager in the late 1980s, for example, exhorted small investors to "stop listening to professionals," adding that "any normal person…can pick stocks just as well, if not better, than the average Wall Street expert"; see Thomas Frank, "Goldman and the Sophisticated Investor," *Wall Street Journal* (May 5, 2010): A19.

benefit systems that had supported working people in most every rich nation since the late 1940s. Pension systems, for example, had to be restructured so that gains in benefits would accrue from stock market bets, as opposed to government-mandated allocations or union agreements.

The restructuring of pension systems that started in the mid-1980s in the US and in other rich nations, to shift responsibility for old-age sustenance from corporations toward their employees, was thus a major feature of the neoliberal agenda. Pension restructuring became a top political priority of corporate power, mainly because pensions were the most important long-term corporate obligation toward employees, which tied up considerable amounts of capital in corporate coffers and reduced profit flows, that could instead go to enrich executives with larger bonuses, golden parachutes and handshakes, and other perks. Financialization was vital to this effort, mainly because of the diverse array of speculative instruments it provided to employee-funded pensions programs, all practically designed to benefit corporate power by providing it with much needed capital.

The shift was largely achieved by forcing an end to conventional pension programs and instead having employees contribute to fund pools that would be invested in the stock and bond markets.[26] Responsibility for losses in those retirement fund pools could thus be shifted to employees, with blame placed on poor personal investment decisions (thus blaming individuals instead of the system) since employees had a choice of sectors or stocks in which to invest their contributions, much as one chooses a gaming mode in a casino. The intensive deregulation of finance that financialization entailed thus created diverse vehicles for stock market speculation, where employees' pension contributions could be invested in a wide range of possibilities.[27]

The grand scheme for alignment of the population's economic and political interests with those of corporate power and with the neoliberal agenda tacitly assumed that the prospect of radical social upheaval would be eliminated, if most

---

26 The creation of the so-called "401k" program in the US was instrumental in this regard (and was later imitated in numerous other nations).

27 New and extremely complex financial instruments, such as collateralized debt obligations and credit default swaps, were among the vast array of new investment possibilities. A trading executive for one of the most important Wall Street investment banks referred to collateralized debt obligations, a common financial instrument, as having"no purpose", an instrument "which is absolutely conceptual"; see Nathaniel Popper, "Goldman Trader in Spotlight," *Los Angeles Times* (April 27, 2010): B1. Such instruments were often designed to fail, because of the risky loan obligations they contained. See Thomas Frank, "Please Tread on Us," *Wall Street Journal* (April 21, 2010): A19, and his "Goldman and the Sophisticated Investor". One highly experienced investor (a top executive of the American investment firm Berkshire Hathaway), referred to the investment banks involved in such sales in the following way: "they were very competitive in maximizing profits in a competitive industry that was permitted to operate like a gambling casino...the whole damn industry lost its moral moorings"; see Scott Patterson and Susan Pulliam, "Buffett is Expected to Fire at Will," *Wall Street Journal* (April 30, 2010): C1.

everyone could be made to depend on stock markets and on corporate performance for their old-age subsistence. Turning everyone into a stock market gambler thus had an ulterior motive: to co-opt the mass of the working population in such a way that public governance which favored corporate power would become widely acceptable. This was a vital ambition of the neoliberal agenda, and financialization was a vehicle to bring it about. After all, the popularization of stock market gambling required diverse speculative vehicles that only financialization could create, by expanding the repertory of gaming possibilities that individuals, groups, pension funds, trusts and most any entity could plunge their money into.[28]

Individual and collective greed, along with the mountains of debt that speculation and unfettered consumerism would create, were important ingredients in this grand scheme of neoliberal social engineering. Keeping the mass of the working population on an economic treadmill of high debt, stock market speculation, greed, and high consumerism became a way to prevent the kind of social awareness that corporate power and neoliberal ideologues detest. Among such awareness was the heightened economic insecurity that those in the treadmill were being plunged into, the increasing inequalities, and the enormous debts that consumers were saddling themselves with.[29]

During the decade of 2000–09, for example, for the first time since the second World War Americans' average net worth (the sum of assets, such as housing equity and property, minus debts) declined by thirteen percent. The population of the US increased by thirty-five million during that period, yet employment increased by only 0.5 percent, while wealth became more concentrated in fewer hands than at any time since 1917.[30] Most American families had two working

---

28   The two main justifications given by apologists of financialization involve its expansion of credit, and the notion that it supposedly spread risk. However, the credit rating agencies that should have provided accurate assessments of risk were often colluding with the clients they rated in order to secure higher fees and their loyalty. Also, the three main credit rating agencies in the US (Fitch, Standard and Poor, and Moody's) compete fiercely with each other for business. See John D. McKinnon and Fawn Johnson, "Credit Raters' Emails Show Concerns," *Wall Street Journal* (April 23, 2010): C3. Regulatory agencies that should have detected this conflict of interest were either so weakened, or so supportive of the prevailing culture of neoliberal finance (and of powerful corporate interests), that they neglected to look into such matters.

29   Hedge funds added to economic insecurity by borrowing vast amounts of money to take over companies, and then loaded the debt onto the acquired companies. The highly indebted companies would then have to lay off employees and reduce benefits in order to cut costs, or file for bankruptcy. See Richard L. Trumka, "It's Time to Restrict Private Equity," *Wall Street Journal* (April 13, 2010): A17.

30   Based on data compiled by the US Department of Commerce and the US Bureau of Economic Analysis; available at www.commerce.gov and www.bea.gov. See also Tim Rutten, "It Was the Worst of Times," *Los Angeles Times* (January 2, 2010): A27; S. Mitra Kalita and Nick Timiraos, "Housing Imperils Recovery: Home Prices Sink to 2002 Levels; Consumer Confidence Falls as Pessimism Grows," *Wall Street Journal* (June 1, 2011): A1.

adults during the decade of 2000–09, yet most had to borrow in order to maintain their standard of living, thereby getting into historically unprecedented amounts of debt through various vehicles, such as home equity loans (one of the products of financial deregulation), credit cards and personal loans. Meanwhile, the total annual compensation of corporate chief executives in the US, which was approximately twenty times that of the average worker during the decade of the 1960s (1960–69), rose to 400 times by 2006, another historically unprecedented benchmark.[31] This panorama of greater inequality and economic insecurity was also accompanied by a series of severe crises that affected the US and the global economy.

Repeated crises since the mid-1980s, such as the junk bond market crash of 1987, the real estate bust of the early 1990s, the derivatives and savings bank crises of the early 1990s, the tech stock crash of 2000, the triplet finance-housing-commodities global crisis that started in 2007, among others, raised serious questions about the global viability of financialization and of the neoliberal agenda.[32] During the 1981–2004 period (two-and-a-half decades), there were a total of 114 sovereign debt crises, almost all affecting poor countries, with severe impacts on their most vulnerable populations, such as the poor, the elderly, children and the working class.[33] In contrast, the total number of sovereign debt crises between 1941 and 1980 (four decades) was 23, revealing a deep contrast between the neoliberal era and the preceding period. Many nations were thus driven into monetary and insolvency crises, with meta-national organizations such as the International Monetary Fund and the World Bank usually demanding that they restructure their economies and to follow the neoliberal path as a condition for aid.[34]

The accelerated cycle of crises has made it apparent that financialization is unsustainable over the long-term. In addition, the unjust inequalities it created by concentrating extraordinary amounts of wealth in the corporate elites (particularly the mega-bank and hedge fund executives) became more noticeable than ever.

---

31 Jim Webb, "American Workers Have a Chance to be Heard,"_Wall Street Journal_ (November 15, 2006): A23.

32 The frequency of significant economic crises accelerated since the late 1970s. See Carmen M. Reinhart and Kenneth S. Rogoff, _This Time is Different: Eight Centuries of Financial Folly_ (Princeton: Princeton University Press, 2009).

33 Based on data compiled by the International Monetary Fund, available at www. imf.org. See also _The Economist_, "Economic Focus; Default Settings" (April 3, 2010): 80.

34 In all sovereign debt crises since the 1970s, the International Monetary Fund demanded cuts in government programs that supported the most vulnerable populations and the working people. In almost all cases where IMF aid was offered, no demands were made to increase taxes for the wealthy, for the corporate elites or for corporate entities. In the case of Greece in 2010, for example, the list of demanded cuts was expanded to include public investment and public sector salaries. Requirements were also imposed to privatize government-owned industries, and to deregulate the labor market and all industries. These impositions were a component of other major IMF bailouts. See Charles Forelle, Nick Skrekas and Bob Davis, "Greece Gets Aid, Promises Austerity," _Wall Street_ Journal (May 3, 2010): A1; Peet, _Unholy Trinity_; and data available at www.imf.org.

Among the mega-banks, for example, the total compensation of chief executives was in some cases 600 times that of the average compensation of their employees. Even during the global crisis that started in 2007, executives from failed financial corporations and banks retired with huge fortunes, adding substantial sums in "performance-based" bonuses to sweeten their departures, despite the fact that the companies they headed went bankrupt, leaving tens of thousands unemployed.[35]

Meanwhile, taxpayer-funded government bailouts of many of those companies revealed who was really in charge of public governance. Corporate power was at the core of many nations' public governance, with undisputed control of government, and in many ways the neoliberal project to align the interests of the political classes with those of corporate power showed itself to have been successful.[36] The global crisis that started in 2007 was estimated to cost approximately $17 trillion dollars over the following three years, in taxpayer-funded bailouts of failed companies, and in subsidies, stimuli and other mechanisms.[37] The prime beneficiaries of those bailouts and subsidies, which were the largest ever in history, were the corporate elites and the richer classes of society tied to corporate capital.[38] The losers were hundreds of millions of working people and poor around the world, who lost their jobs or their subsistence, and the masses of taxpayers who had to pay for

---

35 See, for example, Lucian Bebchuk, "Congress Gets Punitive on Executive Pay: We Want Compensation Tied to Performance," *Wall Street Journal* (February 16, 2009), available at http://online.wsj.com/article/SB123483031127995587.html (accessed on March 30, 2010). In many cases, corporate executives manipulated operations in order to benefit their stock options. This practice has apparently been so widespread that a well-known columnist at the US's top business newspaper even provided advice to investors, to enable them to detect it; see Jason Zweig, "How the Little Guy Can Prey on Executive Pay," *Wall Street Journal* (May 1, 2010): B7.

36 Corporate influence over governance was greatly aided by the "revolving door" syndrome, whereby top corporate executives join the government and serve in key regulatory positions for a limited time, in agencies charged with regulating the very sector and companies that they presided over, and to which they will return once their government service ends. See Thomas Frank, "The Gulf Spill and the Revolving Door," *Wall Street Journal* (May 12, 2010): A17; Tom McGinty, "Revolving Door at the SEC: Staffer One Day, Opponent the Next," *Wall Street Journal* (April 5, 2010): C1.

37 See, for example, *The Economist*, "The Gods Strike Back" (February 13, 2010): 3–5 (Special Report on Financial Risk). Among other indicators of the crisis, the write-downs by the world's largest banks were estimated to be about $4 trillion between 2007 and 2010, and the stock market value destroyed was placed at about $2.3 trillion between October 2007 and March, 2009; see Michael Corkery, "Like Watergate, on a Shoestring: Panel Will Try to Explain Global Financial Crisis on an $8 Million Budget," *Wall Street Journal* (Pairl 2, 2010): C3.

38 Analyses of *Forbes* magazine's "Forbes 400" data, which comprise the wealthiest individuals in the US (and can therefore be considered an indicator of the American capitalist elite) have provided some evidence on the link between financialization and the wealth of the corporate elites and richer classes in US society. See Foster and Holleman, "Financial Power Elite," pp. 9–11.

the corporate welfare programs implemented by politicians bound to corporate interests.

Financialization was nonetheless important for the emergence of technocapitalism, and for its globalization. Most of all, financialization dynamized capital accumulation, even if in highly speculative and risky ways. Capital accumulation, the most distinctive form of accumulation sustaining capitalism since its earliest times, as we will see in the following chapter, was thereby expanded greatly, more than at any other time in the course of the twentieth century. Financialization and its highly speculative vehicles generated much venture capital to start up new technology companies. It also provided much speculative investment capital to expand existing technology corporations. Through these vehicles, financialization was a boon to technocapitalism and to its global spread.

The new dynamism of capital accumulation introduced by financialization did not come without a serious downside, as evidenced by the technology stock market crash of 2000. In a matter of months the NASDAQ, the most important global market for technology companies (which comprises thousands of companies from all technology sectors) lost four-fifths of its value, thus wiping out millions of investors and thousands of firms, not only in technology but also in related activities. Ten years after the 2000 crash, the NASDAQ had barely recovered one quarter of the value it lost. Several decades might pass before the NASDAQ's highest level in 2000 is once again attained, thus dashing hopes for those who expected a quick upswing and the recovery of their capital. Fantasies and ambitions of great riches to come from unfettered speculation in new technology companies were thus destroyed for millions of individual speculators, pension funds, mutual funds, mega-banks, hedge funds and assorted other entities who committed their capital to technology businesses.

The frequent crises experienced through financialization, and in particular the near collapse of the global financial system in 2008–09, showed how unsustainable this phenomenon was as a vehicle for stimulating growth.[39] The growth that financialization generated was not only ephemeral but also deeply flawed, because of the high risk and the mountains of debt it was accompanied by. We might, in retrospect, see the emergence and reign of financialization as an aberration of the neoliberal era, of its fantasies and of its flawed ideological precepts, were it not for the social and economic harm it brought to the poor and the masses of working people around the world.

Growth Dilemma

The unsustainability of financialization brings up an important question about the generation of growth in contemporary capitalist regimes. If financialization is not a sustainable means for generating growth, is there another vehicle that

---

39   See John Bellamy Foster and Harry Magdoff, *The Great Financial Crisis* (New York: Monthly Review Press, 2009).

can do so?[40] This question is of vital importance, all the more so when we recall the fundamental fears that were raised whenever stagnation set in throughout capitalism's long and crisis-prone history. Without growth, generally speaking (in profits, employment and economic product, for example), corporate capitalism cannot be sustained over the long term. Growth is as vital to capitalism as water is to fish.

The 1970s, the most recent period of fundamental fear for the future of capitalism, were the cradle for financialization and neoliberalism. Previously, the 1930s saw the emergence of Keynesianism and of populist government intervention as a new era. During each of those crisis periods, corporate capitalism safeguarded its power by finding new ways to refloat a failing economic system. Reinventions of capitalism thereby occurred during each of those crises, with corporate power co-opting the new mechanisms that provided a new lease on life to capitalism, whether through weapons and war (as in the late 1930s and the 1940s), or through deregulation and the corporatization of public governance, as in the 1980s.[41]

Reforming financialization by introducing greater regulation over speculation, the mega-banks, and the myriad financial vehicles created during the past thirty years is likely to lead to stagnation, the very condition that the corporate elites and richer classes have long feared. Yet, re-regulation of the financial sector seems unavoidable, if another major global crisis is to be avoided. A new and more severe crisis might entail the collapse of the world's financial system, with central banks' role as lenders of last resort becoming ineffective, deficits and debts climbing to unprecedented levels, and governments becoming insolvent. That scenario would be much worse than stagnation for the corporate elites and the richer classes, if a prolonged global depression takes hold and jeopardizes their hold on power. For the poor and working classes, a global depression would involve greater misery and a search for alternatives to capitalist regimes. A new global crisis therefore poses great risk to the power of corporate elites, and of the richer classes associated with corporate capital.

The unsustainability of financialization brings up the urgent need for the corporate elites and the richer classes to find alternatives to sustain capitalism. This is also a major preoccupation for neoliberals and for those with vested interests in the sustenance of capitalist regimes everywhere. Clearly, conventional

---

40   Efforts to deal with the economic crisis that started in 2007 have largely attempted to return to financialization as the vehicle for growth. For a discussion of the potential consequences of a return to financialization, and the dilemmas it poses to capitalist regimes, see Foster, "Age of Monopoly-Finance Capital", and Foster and Holleman, "Financial Power Elite," p. 17.

41   Wars were particularly profitable for corporate power throughout the history of industrial capitalism, also serving as catalysts to reconstruct failing economic systems. See Eric Hobsbawm, *The Age of Extremes: The Short Twentieth Century, 1914–1991* (London: Michael Joseph, 1994), and his *Industry and Empire: From 1750 to the Present Day* (London: Penguin, 1999).

manufacturing industries are not a viable growth option for rich nations, for reasons that are now rather obvious. The deindustrialization of the United States and of most other rich nations over a period of fifty years, for example, with much manufacturing industry being liquidated or moving offshore to lower wage nations, makes it practically impossible to re-create what was lost. Neither heavy industry nor most consumer industries therefore seem viable to be re-created in the US and in most other rich nations. To make the US viable for conventional manufacturing would require a long-term drop in labor costs and the standard of living to the level of many poor nations, with a high risk of social upheaval that would imperil corporate power and its elites.

Beyond manufacturing, conventional services do not provide a viable alternative for growth in rich nations either. The saturation of possibilities throughout the low and middle income spectrum make it unlikely that this economic sector can generate much growth, all the more so when population growth is limited (as it is in most rich nations). Moreover, conventional services usually employ a lowly skilled labor force and pay minimal wages, even for high-risk occupations.[42] Many services that serve the richer classes also pay very low wages, provide no employment security, and all too often draw their employment from the undocumented immigrant labor pool, not only in the US but also in most other rich nations. Most government services now also mimic private sector services in these characteristics, and have been considerably downsized or outsourced to private companies. The prospects for conventional services to generate substantial long-term growth in contemporary capitalist regimes therefore seem quite limited. The dynamism of the so-called "post-industrial" services sector that seemed so promising in the 1950s and 1960s is therefore a historical relic, as low wages, widespread economic insecurity and debt constrain growth in rich nations.

From the standpoint of the corporate elites and the richer classes, the answer to the longer term sustainability of capitalism may thus lie with technocapitalism and with the new sectors it is spawning. Biotechnology and its various fields, such as genomics, genetic engineering and agro-biotech, the emerging sectors of nanotechnology, bioinformatics, biopharmacology and biomimetics may, among others, hold the only possibility of providing capitalism with a new lease on life. Although it is not well known what their full industrial potential might eventually be (as sources of manufactured products or of new types of services), their promise to generate skilled and better paid employment, and to revolutionize existing fields, such as medicine, computing, pharmacology, natural resource exploitation, energy, health care and nutrition, for example, seems high. From the perspective of corporatism, and for its ever more pressing quest for profit and power, the promise of the new sectors being spawned by technocapitalism may hold the

---

42 For example, airline pilots and mechanics, who are highly skilled and require years of experience to maintain their employment, are seeing declining incomes and living standards in the US—a trend that also applies to many other service occupations. See Scott McCartney, "The Parking Lot where Pilots Sleep," *Wall Street Journal* (April 15, 2010): D1.

best (or perhaps the only) promise for substantial long-term growth. It should not surprise, therefore, that practically every economic or corporate think-tank, most speculative capital funds, innumerable foundations that delve in economic issues, and the vast majority of business schools around the world are keenly interested in these new sectors.

Technocapitalism, however, depends on new modes of accumulation and on a new ethos. The need for new accumulation modes, as we will see later in this book, is partly due to the failure of the capital accumulation process (of which financialization was the most recent example) that is at the core of capitalism. The new ethos that technocapitalism imposes means that new accumulation modes based on experimentalism—that is, experimentalist research, carried out for the sole purpose of advancing corporate power and profit—rule over everything else. As we will see in the following chapters, those new modes of accumulation have serious flaws that affect corporate power, public governance, and the global spread of technocapitalism.

Technocapitalism, its ethos, and the new reality it imposes seem filled with major problems and dilemmas for humanity, and for the corporate apparatus that sustains this evolution of capitalism. For humanity, most every important aspect of existence, including work, our social relations, life and nature, stand to be transformed by the new fields spawned by technocapitalism. For corporate power, the high risk and uncertainty of research, as we will see later in this book, require the creation of new global organizational frameworks to secure the creative resources that corporatism must exploit. The risk that accompanies technocapitalism is not the same kind of risk that financialization generates—that is, the collapse of financial systems, the accumulation of mountains of debt, or the insolvency of governments—but it is a risk that will likely have major effects on society.

Experimentalist World

More than any other feature, experimentalism represents the ethos of technocapitalism. Experimentalism is at the core of technocapitalist corporatism—experimentalism for the sake of profit and power above everything else. And, to have any chance of success, experimentalism must have no bounds. It must encompass everything, anything, that corporate strategy deems worthy of pursuing—human existence, life, work, nature, the planet or even the cosmos—whenever they happen to be of use to corporate power.

Perhaps it is not too difficult to see why experimentalism and neoliberal ideology are consonant with each other. Experimentalism seeks and requires unbridled corporate power. Deregulation, the corporatization of most any human activity, of governance, and the withdrawal of the state from social action, are very important for technocapitalist corporate power to experiment, roam and exploit new domains that were previously out of reach. Those new domains are now attainable through technology and science and through the manipulation of life, nature and human existence, in ways that were unknown to prior capitalist eras.

Experimentalism's boundless quest for corporate profit and power is exercised through research. *Research must therefore generate profit and eventually power if it is to be of any value to the technocapitalist corporation. Research that only generates knowledge for its own sake, or for the pure and simple joy of learning and discovery, is therefore practically worthless to technocapitalist corporate power.* Experimentalist research is thus not primarily concerned with solving technological or scientific problems per se—its main and primary concern is profit. *Profit* is the real problem to be solved, and any profits obtained must preferably lead to greater corporate power—economic, political, social, or in any domain that corporate power considers to be strategically important.

The ethos and scope of experimentalism, which are deeply grounded in technology and science, help differentiate technocapitalism from prior versions of capitalism. For industrial capitalism, factory production and the labor process were defining elements. They were part of what may be referred to as *productionism*— the ethos and driving cultural element of industrial capitalism. It was largely grounded in tangible resources, such as raw materials, labor and capital, upon which factory routines depended. Productionism encompassed myriad features that are deeply associated with industrial culture and with factory labor processes, from the piece rate system to the repetitive assembly routines of mass production, to the automation of work processes and the deskilling of labor.[43] The corporate culture of productionism spread around the world starting in the early part of the nineteenth century, taking down cultural barriers, social constraints and regulatory regimes that stood in the way of profit, exploitation and power. In its global reach, it imposed a model of accumulation, exploitation and corporate power that differed greatly from that of mercantile capitalism, its predecessor.[44]

---

43 Deskilling of labor through the design of new technologies that made work processes less intelligent, more repetitive and more fragmented, and at the same time made it easier for management to control the worker performing the task, was a feature of production under industrial capitalism throughout the twentieth century. Technology was thus enlisted to serve the interests of corporate power. Its design was therefore not autonomous of corporate power nor was it wholly functional (in the sense that the efficiency it introduced was not detached from the priorities of corporate power). See Harry Braverman, *Labor and Monopoly Capital: The Degradation of Work in the Twentieth Century* (New York: Monthly Review Press, 1974). Automation took this trend to the extreme, by ridding many production processes of labor altogether, or by reducing labor substantially over time. See David F. Noble, *Forces of Production: A Social History of Industrial Automation* (New York: Knopf, 1984).

44 See Michel Beaud, *A History of Capitalism, 1500–2000*, transl. T. Dickman and A. Lefebvre (New York: Monthly Review Press, 2001). It must be noted, however, that the effectiveness of this model seems to have been more intense whenever it was accompanied by empire-building; see Eric Hobsbawm, *Industry and Empire: From 1750 to the Present Day* (London: Penguin, 1999).

Mercantile capitalism, in turn, was characterized by commodity exchange. *Mercantilism* was the driving ethos of this era of capitalism, which depended on extraction through agriculture, mining and other nature-bound activities. Tangible resources were also very much at the core of mercantilism, in the form of commodities, capital and labor. Mercantilism spread globally largely through imperialism, through the exploitation of labor in places where valuable commodities could be found and extracted, and in many cases through slavery. Slave labor, or at least the intensive exploitation of labor in nature-bound activities, along with the accumulation of capital through exchange (as opposed to production) were defining elements of mercantilism.[45]

In contrast with productionism and mercantilism, experimentalism depends on *intangibles*, and most of all on research creativity—the most precious resource of technocapitalism.[46] Those intangibles, as we will see later in this book, are at the core of the new accumulation modes associated with technocapitalism. Those intangibles (and most of all creativity) also define the global projection of technocapitalism and of its corporate apparatus. It is partly because of the character and qualitative nature of those intangibles, that corporate experimentalism acquires a boundless projection that is intrinsically global, and that respects little in the way of cultural barriers, social restraints, human impediments, or the need for regulatory regimes. This fundamental aspect of the ethos that experimentalism imposes makes it highly consonant with neoliberal dogma.

In many respects, therefore, experimentalism has to turn the world into its laboratory in order to be viable. Global society, all of humanity, life and nature therefore potentially stand to become guinea pigs of experimentalism and of the technocapitalist corporate apparatus.[47] The whole world, in a sense, becomes the corporate laboratory of technocapitalism, as the insatiable quest for profit and

---

45   A most interesting discussion of the nexus between agriculture and the emergence of mercantile capitalism (and its peculiar form of accumulation), placed in the context of the seventeenth and eighteenth centuries, can be found in Karl Marx's *Capital: A Critique of Political Economy*, vol. I (New York: International Publishers, 1967), Part VIII, "The So-Called Primitive Accumulation," pp. 713–74.

46   For an extensive discussion of this aspect, see the chapter "Experimentalism" in Luis Suarez-Villa, *Technocapitalism: A Critical Perspective on Technological Innovation and Corporatism* (Philadelphia: Temple University Press, 2009).

47   Interrelationships between society and the earth's ecology become more noticeable, as the negative impacts of corporate capitalism on nature (and nature's feedback effects on human existence) are felt more quickly and more intensely, given the technological and scientific grounding of the emerging technocapitalist era. An interesting and in many respects unique outlook on this emerging condition is provided by Richard Levins, a prominent ecologist and biologist, founder of the human ecology program at Harvard's School of Public Health. See Richard Levins and Richard Lewontin, *The Dialectical Biologist* (Cambridge: Harvard University Press, 1985) and their *Biology Under the Influence: Dialectical Essays on Ecology, Agriculture, and Health* (New York: Monthly Review Press, 2007).

power spares nothing that can serve those corporate priorities.[48] No aspect left out of prior eras of capitalism is likely to be left alone, so long as there is a potential to extract greater corporate profit and power.

This new reality of domination that corporate experimentalism imposes is now becoming apparent around the world, as technocapitalism advances its quest to secure the intangibles it needs. It is globalizing faster than those imposed by prior eras of capitalism, aided by the worldwide reach of neoliberal policies and by advances in communication. *It is in many ways a new global order that rearranges priorities to suit corporate power in an all-encompassing way—more so than prior eras of capitalism could accomplish because of its deep grounding in technology and science, and because of its potential to affect most every aspect of human existence, of life and nature.* Experimentalism therefore also involves the "design" of a new world in which corporate power is uppermost in its control over society. Neither productionism nor mercantilism ever had the capacity to transform human existence and the planet to the extent that experimentalism can, nor to subordinate human existence to corporate interests in such a comprehensive, boundless way.

Features

Three features underpin this emerging global reality of experimentalism. These features will be revisited at various points later in this book, since they are fundamental components of technocapitalism and of its corporatist ethos. Nonetheless, considering them briefly at this time should help our understanding of experimentalism's ethos and its importance for technocapitalism. The *first* feature involves experimentalism's need to *systematize* research on a global scale, to serve the boundless corporate quest for profit and power. This means that research must be pursued continuously for the sake of corporate profit and power. Continuity here refers to the vital need for corporate research to generate an endless stream of new inventions and innovations—the sort that can only be achieved through the systematization of research programs.[49] Because the technocapitalist corporation lives or dies by research, and by the appropriation of the results of research, systematization thereby becomes a fundamental necessity.

How research is systematized also becomes a prime aspect of corporate strategy, and its importance for corporate survival cannot be overestimated. This means that corporate power actively (and strategically) sets research agendas,

---

48   And it is increasingly becoming clear that nature is a major target of that global corporate crusade for greater profit and power. See John Bellamy Foster, "A New Stage in Capitalism's War on the Planet," *Monthly Review* (September 2007): 53–4.

49   Internally, within the technocapitalist corporate organization, the *systematized research regime* becomes a fundamental vehicle to achieve this outcome; see Suarez-Villa, *Technocapitalism*, "Experimentalist Research Organizations" chapter, for a consideration of these internal aspects of technocapitalist corporate organizations.

and that it strives to control and manipulate the course and scope of research programs, along with their outcomes, and whatever results can be appropriated in order to extract value. Without systematization, research simply becomes too uncertain and risky, with timelines that are difficult to establish, and most of all with the troubling prospect of no results (or of no results that can be appropriated). In the context of technocapitalism and of its corporate apparatus, however, systematization must have a global scope, since the intangible resources needed—most of all creativity—must be drawn from diverse sources. The global reach thereby provides the boundless—or boundaryless—element that technocapitalist corporatism so vitally needs in order to tap, control and exploit the diverse resources that are vital to its effort to systematize research.

The *second* feature involves experimentalism's need for new forms of corporate organization. Such organizations must necessarily revolve around research and its systematization as the foremost internal concern of corporate power. To the technocapitalist corporation, research is therefore as important as production was to the industrial capitalist corporation. It must be noted, however, that the qualitative, uncertain and risky nature of research and of it most precious resource—creativity—sets the technocapitalist corporation apart from the organizational modes of all prior capitalist eras, as we will see later in this book. The organizations that embody the experimentalist ethos are therefore not only deeply grounded in technological research, but must also exploit a vital intangible, creativity, whose qualitative character makes it practically impossible to program, unlike the factory production routines of industrial capitalism.

The new corporate organizations that experimentalism fosters are global in scope and reach. They are global because invention and innovation are global, because technological knowledge is no longer confined within national boundaries, and most of all because the talent and creativity they seek must now be tapped globally. This global need and scope makes these new organizations highly consonant with the neoliberal objective of dismantling boundaries and barriers to serve the needs of corporate power. All the more so, when one considers that ideas and intangibles are the driving force of invention and innovation. The fact that they do not have a tangible presence and that they can diffuse around the world rapidly, makes them ideally suited to the neoliberal call for a boundaryless world where corporate power reigns supreme.

A *third* feature of experimentalism is its vital need for *social mediation* in order to exploit creativity. Social mediation means that society at large—culture, educational systems, social class structures and social relations, for example—influences greatly the quality of creativity, its accessibility, and the areas of knowledge to which it is related. This means that creativity cannot be generated or reproduced internally by corporate power, through its control of the corporate domain. As we will see later in this book, the socially mediated nature of creativity imposes major dilemmas on technocapitalist corporate power, mainly because of its curtailed control over its most vital resource, and because of its need to influence the external societal forces that reproduce creativity.

Experimentalism's need for social mediation is also global in scope and reach, mainly because the areas of knowledge in which technological creativity is grounded are now global and transcend boundaries. Social mediation in a globalized context cannot be compartmentalized or ascribed to one society, but is now often the product of diverse cultures, social relations, educational experiences, communications and exchange. More and more, the reproduction or regeneration of creativity is a global enterprise, where diverse sources of knowledge and experience must be tapped, where multidisciplinary talent from different parts of the globe must be used, and where the application of creativity in research contexts occurs in diverse locales and corporate contexts. As we will see later, social mediation is behind some of the more important phenomena of our time, such as the global brain drain flows that nurture corporate experimentalism in its quest for greater profit and power. This kind of social mediation that reproduces creativity is therefore also increasingly global in scope and reach—it is an unfolding phenomenon that is related to the previously discussed spread of neoliberal precepts and policies. In many ways, the obliteration of boundaries and restraints that neoliberalism has promoted and executed during past three decades has made it possible for social mediation to be globalized.

Globalization and Domination

The globalization of technocapitalism, of its experimentalist ethos, and of the new form of corporate power it embodies attempt to regenerate the relations of power of capitalism. Those relations of power embed multi-faceted aspects of domination—domination of corporate power over society and over its governance, domination of the corporate elites and the richer classes over other component classes of society, domination of the supporting ideology of governance over alternative visions of society, and domination over the means and sources of accumulation. None of these facets of domination are new. In various forms and guises, they have been part of capitalism since its earliest days—corporate forms, the supporting ideology, the approach to governance and the modes of accumulation may have changed due to the dynamic and malleable nature of capitalism, but the fundamental framework of domination remains. The globalization of technocapitalism regenerates these facets of domination by expanding the reach and scope of conquest, and by providing more ways to tap the resources needed by corporate power.

Three premises underlie the global relations of power and domination that technocapitalism imposes. The *first premise* establishes that corporations are more than vehicles for economic action—they are sources of power and domination over society. In the context of technocapitalism, corporate power depends on the commodification and exploitation of creativity through research, on the appropriation of any results of research, and on the extraction of profit that commercial exchange may provide. One general but fundamental process common to all prior versions of capitalism—commodification—takes up a global scope in the context of technocapitalist corporatism, mainly because this is a process that corporate power can control internally, as we will see later in this book.

Commodification also takes up a global scope because it is *the* vehicle to exploit creativity—the most precious resource of technocapitalism—and because it is also the means to appropriate the results of creativity. As a vehicle for corporate exploitation, commodification provides the framework through which corporate power systematizes research, sets and manipulates research programs, and develops strategies to generate new inventions and innovations as frequently as possible. The failure of commodification therefore threatens the survival of corporate power in a very fundamental way. Since the technocapitalist corporation lives or dies by its research, and by its appropriation of research results, the potential failure of commodification is an ever present danger given the high risk and uncertainty of research. This fundamental aspect of technocapitalist corporatism is the source of dilemmas and pathologies for corporate power, an aspect that will be explored later in this work.

The *second premise* underlying the global relations of power and domination that technocapitalism imposes involves *both* the corporate *commodification* of creativity *and* its dependence on the *reproduction* of this most precious resource. Without reproduction, commodification cannot occur, without commodification there can be no appropriation of the results of creativity (as intellectual property, for example), and without appropriation profit cannot be extracted—the effectiveness of this chain process is crucial to the survival of the technocapitalist corporation. It is a chain process that is quite complex, that is subject to a high degree of risk and uncertainty, and that involves multidisciplinary talents and capabilities.

The reproduction of creativity, however, depends on external social mediation and is therefore—unlike commodification—outside the control of corporate power. The split between commodification and reproduction is a distinctive feature of technocapitalism that sets it apart from prior capitalist eras. It is a split that is worldwide in scope, primarily because social mediation, which is vital for reproducing creativity, is now global. The split between commodification and reproduction also sets technocapitalism apart from previous capitalist eras, since it removes a fundamental process from the control of corporate power. Commodification and reproduction were both largely under the control of corporate power under industrial capitalism and mercantile capitalism, mainly because their most important resources were tangible, quantifiable and subject to in-house programs of control and deployment.[50] The technocapitalist corporation, however, has no such control over the reproduction of creativity, and finds itself riddled with greater uncertainty and risk than its industrial and mercantile predecessors. As we will see later in this book, the split between commodification and reproduction that is so characteristic of technocapitalism is also the source of major dilemmas and social pathologies for corporate power.

---

50   See Braverman, *Labor and Monopoly Capital*; Eric Hobsbawm, *Labouring Men: Studies in the History of Labour* (London: Weidenfeld and Nicolson, 1964).

The *third premise* underlying the relations of power and domination involves corporate control over public governance and over society at large. Dialectically, this is partly an outcome of the loss of control over reproduction noted earlier, which sets up the corporate drive to redress it by gaining greater control over society instead. In many respects, this means that the technocapitalist corporation cannot be considered to be an isolated entity from society, contrary to what some neoliberal ideologues and neoclassical economists have long proclaimed or implied. In their view, corporations can do the most benefit to society only when they simply maximize profits and shareholder value, above any other consideration—in other words, when they only look after their own self-interest. The context of technocapitalism and of its corporate power, however, negates this longstanding notion, mainly because the urgent need to reproduce that most precious resource—creativity—requires the mediation of society at large and of myriad cultural and social influences, which the technocapitalist corporation cannot avoid.

Corporate manipulation of public governance and society attempts to turn most any governmental or societal function to benefit corporate interests, in a generic sense.[51] In the context of technocapitalism, this panorama of corporate manipulation and co-optation acquires new and troubling dimensions, mainly because of the technocapitalist corporation's deep grounding in technology and science, which provides it with the capacity to change many aspects of human existence, of life and nature in irreversible ways. Moreover, the global scope of corporate power means that such manipulation now cuts across boundaries and transcends most any culture or regulatory regime. Corporate manipulation of governance and society is therefore not a phenomenon specific to a given nation or to some nations—it is a global phenomenon, a problem made all the more difficult by the fact that many corporations already have more power, resources and influence than most national governments. Because of the vital importance of the new sectors that technocapitalism is spawning, technocapitalist corporations are bound to gain greater global power than their industrial predecessors.

Component Phenomena

The three premises discussed above underlie the component global phenomena of technocapitalism that will be considered in this book. One of those phenomena is *accumulation*, historically one of the most important processes of capitalism. Capital accumulation, in particular, has been at the core of capitalism's emergence and development since its earliest days. At the onset of the industrial era in the late eighteenth century, for example, capital accumulation was vitally important

---

51   Even when the intent is to benefit a specific corporate entity, precedents are set that benefit other corporate actors down the line. See, for example, Ted Nace, *Gangs of America: The Rise of Corporate Power and the Disabling of Democracy* (San Francisco: Berrett-Koehler, 2005).

for the deployment of resources to finance the factories, the labor power and the production hardware they needed. Capital accumulation was nonetheless at the core of the deepest crises of industrial and mercantile capitalism, leading to cycles of economic depression and deep recession that were often associated with wars, and with widespread misery for the laboring classes and for the most vulnerable elements of society. Capital accumulation is therefore a flawed process prone to crises, the most recent of which involved financialization as noted earlier in this chapter—such crises are therefore as much a part of our time as they were in centuries past.

In the context of technocapitalism, new modes of accumulation emerge that are directly associated with the ethos and resource needs of this new era. The new modes involve the accumulation of knowledge, which is a fundamental support for the reproduction of creativity, and the accumulation of technological infrastructure, which is also important for reproducing this most important resource. These new modes of accumulation depend greatly on societal mediation, as we will see in the following chapter, yet they are also intrinsically tied to corporate power. Technocapitalist corporate power cannot survive without them, because they are fundamentally important for commodifying creativity, in addition to the reproduction of this most precious resource as noted earlier. These new accumulation modes are nonetheless flawed, in different ways from the longstanding capital accumulation mode, but flawed nonetheless. The societal pathologies they contribute are a symptom of those flaws, and most of all they are linked to technocapitalist corporate power and to its global projection.

A second component phenomenon of technocapitalism that will be addressed in this book is its global dependence on *intangible commodities*, of which creativity is by far the most precious one. Unlike the commodities of prior capitalist eras, intangibles such as creativity are primarily qualitative in character and performance, and are therefore very difficult if not impossible to program, quantify or control. Tangible commodities, which were the most important resources of industrial and mercantile capitalism, on the other hand, could be controlled and quantified physically simply because they were tangible. Those tangible commodities of prior eras could therefore be commodified and reproduced internally (in-house) by corporate power. As noted earlier, however, this framework of control breaks down in the context of technocapitalism, mainly because reproduction must occur externally through societal mediation, which is largely out of the control of corporate power.

The third component phenomenon of technocapitalism's globalization is the emergence of a new culture of corporate power—a *new corporatism*—that is deeply associated with technocapitalism and with its roots in technology and science. The new corporatism is accompanied by new forms of corporate organization that are largely oriented toward exploiting intangibles, and that try to deal with the fundamental split between reproduction and commodification noted before, as well as the resulting loss of control over reproduction. The loss of control over reproduction means that corporate control can only be retained over commodification, which is largely an internal (in-house) function in the context of technocapitalism.

Such control, exercised through the new corporate organizations, is essential for corporate power to manage the high uncertainty and risk associated with research, and to appropriate (as intellectual property) any results derived from research. The intangibility of the most precious resources exploited by technocapitalism is therefore directly associated with new corporate organizations where research is of primordial importance, in contrast with the organizations typical of industrial and mercantile capitalism, where production reigned supreme. As we will see later in this book, the new organizations associated with technocapitalism are part of a new global order of corporate power that collapses boundaries and restraints in its quest for intangibles.

The scope of the intangible commodities associated with technocapitalism is therefore global, in the sense that no single nation or group of nations can be considered an exclusive source. This situation contrasts with the first century of the industrial era, when the know-how to set up large factories and to marshall the needed tangible resources was circumscribed to a small group of nations. Large industrial corporations oriented toward factory production and the exploitation of labor were therefore highly concentrated in the rich—and most of all in the empire-building—nations of the time. In contrast, today the globalization of technological know-how, the massification of technological education even in many relatively poor nations, the rapid diffusion of knowledge, and advances in communication allow the intangible commodities that the technocapitalist corporation requires, to emerge out of multiple sources around the world. This multiple sourcing of intangibles introduces complexity to the globalization of technocapitalism, but to corporate power it provides many possibilities for tapping those vital resources.

Although rich nations—mainly the US, western Europe and Japan—have considerable depth in generating the intangibles required by the new sectors of technocapitalism, there are nonetheless many other nations around the world that can generate them, even though they may lack the corporate infrastructure associated with technocapitalism. This capacity to generate intangibles increasingly encompasses research creativity—the most precious intangible of technocapitalism. This means that large scale brain drain flows, stoked by technocapitalist corporations are now a global reality as we will see later in this book. At the same time, as a counterpart to the brain drain flows, many technocapitalist corporations from rich nations are either subcontracting or setting up research operations in poor nations, as a way to evade regulatory oversight in their home countries, achieve lower costs or gain direct access to creative talent.[52] The outsourcing of research operations by technocapitalist corporations

---

52   See Elizabeth Svoboda, "Sidestepping the FDA: According to One Small Biotech, the Best Way to Launch a Stem-Cell Revolution is To Do It Overseas," *Fast Company* (December 2009): 60–63; Shirley S. Wang, "Most Clinical Trials Done Abroad," *Wall Street Journal* (February 19, 2009): D3. Beyond any evasion of regulation, it must be noted that

is an ongoing development which, although selective and different from industrial outsourcing, is becoming more noticeable.

The fourth component global phenomenon of technocapitalism to be considered in this book involves *corporate influence over public governance* and over society at large. Far from being a splintered process, the corporate co-optation of the means of governance and over the state itself is now a full-blown global phenomenon. The spread of neoliberal dogma around the world during the past three decades, supported by meta-national organizations such as the International Monetary Fund (IMF), the World Bank and the World Trade organization (WTO), and by powerful influence groups such as the Washington Consensus have made *corporatocracy* a global reality. Pro-corporate global media networks (usually controlled by large corporations), the outreach of business school training into most every human endeavor, and the spread of consumerism helped cement the notion that what is good for corporate power is good for society. As a result, corporatocracy— public governance to serve corporate interests above everything else—has largely replaced other forms of governance in many parts of the world.[53]

At no other time did this global reality—public governance of/by/for corporate power—become more clear than during the global economic crisis that started in the United States in 2007, as governments around the world bailed out, subsidized and otherwise buttressed corporate power at public expense. And also at the cost of very high and unsustainable public debt, while corporate elites continued to compensate themselves with billions of dollars in salaries, performance bonuses, golden parachutes, stock options and highly inflated perks. The public, anesthetized by three decades of neoliberal propaganda touting the glory and virtues of "free" corporate enterprise, could do little more than watch or be fearful, as politicians co-opted by corporate power poured in trillions of dollars in a matter of months, to buttress failing corporate behemoths.[54] This pathetic legacy of neoliberalism has in effect redistributed public resources, power and wealth from the public— and most of all from the poor and the working classes—toward corporate power,

---

the quality of research personnel in many developing nations is an important factor, and can be as important as lower research costs; see, for example, Jerry Thursby and Marie Thursby, "Where is the New Science in Corporate R&D?," *Science* 314(December 8, 2006): 1547–8.

53   See Noreena Hertz, *The Silent Takeover: Global Capitalism and the Death of Democracy* (London: Heinemann, 2001). According to Hertz, more than half of the world's 100 largest economies are corporations (measured through various economic indicators shared by, or compatible to, both corporate entities and nations).

54   Co-optation (and in some cases intimidation) of politicians is expanding to include pressure groups (also referred to as "advocacy" groups) that systematically concoct strategies to either support or destabilize political campaigns using diverse means, such as television advertisements in a politicians' home district, visitations of a politicians' home district office by pressure groups to voice their opinions, or researching individual details in politicians' lives to expose any unwelcome ideological attitudes. See Edwin J. Feulner and Michael A. Needham, "New Fangs for the Conservative 'Beast'", *Wall Street Journal* (April 12, 2010): A19.

the corporate elites, and the richer classes associated with corporate capital. The dispossession of economic rights and economic security of the mass of the population during the past three decades, accompanied by a massive accumulation of consumer debt, has been part of this redistribution dynamic.

For technocapitalism and most of all for its corporate apparatus, corporate influence over public governance, and particularly regulation, is of vital importance. Being deeply grounded in technology and science, with the capability to impact most every aspect of human existence, of life and nature, induces technocapitalist corporate power to influence governance so as to collapse (or at least neutralize) regulatory barriers that can block the quest for greater profit and power. How else could, say, a corporation with a highly profitable genetically engineered seed that irreversibly eliminates the ecology associated with an entire agricultural crop—with unknown long-term effects—be able to market its seed?[55] How else but through a manipulation of regulation and governance, could such a corporation undertake global propaganda campaigns to tout its engineered seed as the ultimate savior of humanity, claiming it will stamp out crop diseases, food shortages and hunger, while muzzling, defaming or otherwise damaging those who question the ecological and health viability of its seed?

The fifth component global phenomenon of technocapitalism's globalization involves *neo-imperialism*—not the neo-imperialism of the twentieth century but a new kind that is deeply grounded in technology and science, through new weapons and strategies, and most of all through the emergence of a techno-military-corporate complex that effectively replaces the military-industrial complex of the last century. Technocapitalist corporate power is at the core of this kind of neo-imperialism, given its capacity to generate new weapons for military conquest. Through technocapitalist corporatism, the dirty work of fighting wars may be largely lifted from humans at some point in the twenty-first century, making aggression, military conquest and regime change more acceptable politically to those who perpetrate them, when intelligent (and unmanned) war machines and engineered humanoid soldiers do most of the killing.[56] Moreover, this kind of neo-imperialism

---

55   See Marie-Monique Robin's documentary, "The World According to Monsanto" (Ottawa: National Film Board of Canada, 2008). More than 70 percent of all field corn and more than 80 percent of all cotton and soybeans harvested in the US have at least one patented Monsanto gene; see Roger Parloff, "Seeds of Discord," *Fortune* (May 24, 2010): 94–106.

56   Although objectionable on ethical and moral grounds, new instruments for killing must be placed in the long-term ethical and moral context of warfare. Weapons and their usage have a long history of bypassing moral and ethical concerns whenever their effectiveness can grant victory to those who use them. Such weapons may become more acceptable to politicians and military strategists when accompanied by long-term warfare, such as the planned 50- to 80-year "Long War" strategic plan developed by the Pentagon; see Tom Hayden, "War Never-Ending: U.S. Proponents of the Long War Foresee a Global Battle Against Insurgents Lasting 50 to 80 Years," *Los Angeles Times* (March 28, 2010): A31. For a discussion of likely warfare scenarios that might incorporate the

may be greatly targeted at regime change to impose corporatocracies—governance for/by/of corporate power—around the world under the guise of democratization, when in fact the real objective is to establish corporate hegemony over society.[57]

This emerging panorama of neo-imperial conquest is accompanied by deepening inequalities between rich and poor nations, between social classes within and across borders, and most all between the conquerors and the conquered. Those inequalities are becoming a necessity in order to allow corporate power to tap the intangibles it needs through brain drain flows from poor nations to their rich-nation home bases, and through other intangible and tangible resource flows. Such brain drain flows today provide a lot of the creative talent needed by technocapitalist corporations, especially in the case of the United States, where a deficient educational system fails to provide enough native-born talent for the new sectors of technocapitalism. The brain drain flows occur not only at the level of highly skilled (and already educated) specialists, but now also involve massive flows of university students recruited from abroad to pursue degrees in technology and science fields in rich nations—most of all in the US—who will eventually be recruited by their technocapitalist corporations. The costs of their prior education, health care and other support for those students and highly skilled specialists will have been provided and paid for by their nations of origin, out of their scarce resources, while the ultimate beneficiaries are the technocapitalist corporations based in the richest nations of the planet.

Needless to say, the nations of origin—which are usually poor or at least not rich—of those flows are never compensated for their losses by the rich nations and their corporations. In some cases, talent recruited through the brain drain flows may return later to their nations of origin to establish operations for their corporate employers (typically based in rich nations), in order to colonize national markets or to tap the brain drain flows more effectively. Moreover, the nations of origin of the brain drain flows often have substantial foreign debts, contracted with financial

---

kinds of weapons that technocapitalist corporations can create, see Philip Bobbitt, *Terror and Consent: The Wars for the Twenty-First Century* (New York: Knopf, 2008); Andrew F. Krepinevich, *Seven Deadly Scenarios: A Military Futurist Explores Warfare in the 21st Century* (New York: Bantam Dell, 2009).

57   The increasing importance of new technologies—the kind that technocapitalist corporations can create—for intelligence cannot be overestimated. See Siobhan Gorman, "Technology is Central to CIA's Strategic Plan," *Wall Street Journal* (April 27, 2010): A7. Intelligence, military aggression and corporate power are becoming more entwined. Courses on "expeditionary economics" that train American military personnel on a wide array of business functions, from setting up local chambers of commerce to securing corporate supply chains, to identifying "entrepreneurial" elements in a conquered locale, have been developed for the Pentagon by the Kauffman Foundation (an American organization that promotes entrepreneurship and corporate interests). See Jeff Chu, "Joint Venture: Admiral Mike Mullen Says the Sea Was His Business; Now, as America's Top Military Officer, He's Reshaping Strategy for a World in Which Economics and Security are Intertwined," *Fast Company* (May 2010): 73–9.

institutions from the rich nations that receive the flows. This kind of subsidy from the nations of origin to the rich nations that benefit from the brain drain flows is, of course, never taken into account whenever demands for debt repayment are made. And, all too often, debt repayment demands have in the past been accompanied by pressures for neoliberal reform that subject the nations of origin to even greater brain drain outflows. This self-perpetuating form of inequality, which is global in scope and reach, is likely to be an important component of the kind of neo-imperialism that we will see in the twenty-first century.

The kind of military conquest and regime change that the techno-military-corporate complex promotes may therefore not merely involve imposing new governance to favor corporate power above everything else. It may also likely involve the draining of vital intangible resources from the conquered nations to benefit rich nations and their corporations. This sort of resource drain is not unlike the ones executed by imperial powers throughout human history, capitalist or pre-capitalist, even though the kinds of resources being drained from the conquered are quite different from those of prior times.

We may therefore witness the perpetuation of imperial conquest, no doubt in a different form from those of past eras, perpetrated by a techno-military-corporate complex grounded in technocapitalist corporatism. It may be also a form of imperial conquest that is likely to be more effective than those of past imperial ventures, mainly because of its grounding in technology and science, and because of the complex new weapons that are being devised—which may potentially render the conquered more helpless than their predecessors. Corporate power, the corporate elites, and the richer classes associated with corporate capital, can be expected to pursue this kind of neo-imperial strategy whenever they can get away with it. It will increase their profit and power, and most of all the cost of this new kind of imperial enterprise is likely to be borne by the conquered, and by the poor and working segments of society everywhere.

Conclusion

The globalization of technocapitalism is a complex phenomenon that is largely grounded in the corporate quest to extract higher profit, to wield greater power over society, and to collapse boundaries and restraints. This corporate quest, which is deeply grounded in technology and science, in the exploitation of creativity and in the manipulation of research, is part of a larger historical panorama. It is a historical panorama that was greatly influenced by the crises of capitalism, by ideological reactions to those crises, and by the urgent need to refloat corporate capitalism on the basis of a new, more rapacious, and more intrusive quest for profit and power. *The globalization of technocapitalism is therefore part of the longstanding evolution of capitalism, and of its all-encompassing search for new frontiers of profit, accumulation and growth.*

The slow growth, stagnation and crises of capitalism from the late 1940s to the late 1970s fomented the rise of neoliberalism three decades ago. Neoliberal ideology, driven by deregulation, the privatization of government functions and market fundamentalism, favored corporate power above everything else, taking down barriers and restraints as it swept around the world. One of the effects of this new global reality was the emergence of financialization as a vehicle to stimulate growth and capital accumulation—a flawed process that accelerated crises and led to the near collapse of the global financial system. It is within this historical panorama that the emergence of technocapitalism and of its globalization is taking place.

Neoliberalism was not the sole factor driving the search for a new global capitalist regime, and neither was financialization, but they were important for the emergence of technocapitalism and of its corporate apparatus. As a potential source of long-term growth, with its deep grounding in technology and science, technocapitalism kindled hopes for a new era that might renew capitalism's long-term viability. Such hopes were based on neoliberalism's capacity to help this new form of capitalism through its global reach, its collapsing of restraints to corporate power, its opening up of new markets, and its influence over public governance.

The evolution of capitalism that technocapitalism represents is accompanied by a new ethos that is all-encompassing and global. It is an experimentalist ethos that underpins technocapitalist corporatism, which has counterparts in the productionist ethos of industrial capitalism and in the mercantilist ethos that characterized mercantile capitalism. The ethos of technocapitalism places experimentalism at the core of corporate power, much as production was at the core of industrial corporate power, undertaken through factory regimes and labor processes. And, much as the ethos of past capitalist eras was accompanied by social pathologies and by frameworks of domination, so the new ethos of technocapitalism introduces pathological constructs of global domination that are likely to be hallmarks of the twenty-first century.

The following chapters will consider the new global reality that technocapitalism imposes and its accompanying phenomena. It is a reality that is deeply entwined with a new form of corporate power and with its authoritarian control over technology and science—making it central to its global quest for greater profit and power. In this quest, technocapitalist corporatism leaves no stone unturned, taking over any process that can further its objectives while intruding into most every aspect of human existence, of life and nature. Accumulation, for example, a key process of capitalism since its earliest days that will be dealt with in the following chapter, is configured to benefit corporate power above everything else. New accumulation modes associated with the emergence of technocapitalism therefore become part of the realm of corporate power, negating their larger societal dimension and the vast accumulation of public resources that created them.

Fast Accumulation

Accumulation processes have been at the heart of capitalism since its earliest days. They played a major role in every stage of capitalism, making it possible to tap resources that were turned into commodities. Accumulation made it feasible for capitalism to obtain value and profit from commodities, providing the means to exploit and exchange them. It allowed industrial capitalism and its corporations to spread around the globe, appropriating and commodifying resources while imposing new relations of power.

For technocapitalism to emerge, new and more dynamic forms of accumulation became essential. These accumulation processes will be referred to as *fast accumulation* in this book. The term fast accumulation will denote their distinctive character, to differentiate them from the already well-known forms of accumulation associated with previous stages of capitalism. As we will see in this chapter, fast accumulation underpins the character of technocapitalism and its corporatist ethos, making it possible to spread its influence and pathologies around the world.

Fast accumulation is therefore a distinctive feature of this new version of capitalism. Only through fast accumulation can the fundamental resources of technocapitalism be tapped and commodified. Through them, corporate power appropriates the *intangible* resources that are a hallmark of this new stage of capitalism. Fast accumulation thus makes it possible for the technocapitalist corporation to commodify the most valuable resource of this new era, *creativity*. Attaining power and profit through this elusive social and human quality around the globe is its most important objective.

Fast accumulation is therefore essential for the globalization of technocapitalism and its corporate interests. Much as the manufacturing corporations of industrial capitalism appropriated the tangible resources upon which production depended, so the corporations of technocapitalism appropriate the intangible resources needed to obtain power and profit. As industrial capitalism extended its reach around the globe during the nineteenth and twentieth centuries, so technocapitalism seems poised to leave its mark (and pathologies) in every corner of the globe, no matter how remote or unprepared a society might be for its onslaught.

This new, more clever and rapacious version of capitalism knows few bounds in its quest for power and profit. Its deep roots in technology and science, its global scope, and its exploitation of research creativity through corporate power, make any contestation of its ways and pathologies a difficult proposition. More aggressive and far-sighted than any previous version of capitalism, technocapitalism seeks to re-engineer humanity and nature itself, for its own ends. The pathological effects of this new era are already becoming apparent, in the destruction of nature and the demeaning of many aspects of human existence on a worldwide scale. Fast accumulation is making this possible as it compounds the resources that sustain this new version of capitalism and its globalization.

This chapter will provide an overview of the phenomenon of fast accumulation, and its importance for the incipient globalization of technocapitalism. We are at an early stage of this new era, and many features are still unknown or cannot be clearly profiled. This chapter should therefore be viewed as an initial attempt to grasp the meaning of fast accumulation, its modes of support for the new era, and the pathologies with which it is associated. We have barely begun to move along the road which technocapitalism and its corporate agents are laying out, and upon which the twenty-first century will traverse.

Modes

Fast accumulation encompasses traditional modes of capitalist accumulation *and* new modes that are intrinsic to technocapitalism and its emerging global reach. The new modes help differentiate technocapitalism from previous eras. Thus, they cannot be found with the same intensity or importance in any previous stage of capitalism. Most important, the new modes of accumulation are vital for the reproduction and commodification of the fundamental resources of the new era.

New Modes

The new modes provide a platform for the reproduction and commodification of creativity on a global scale. Creativity, the most important resource of the technocapitalist era, is the main target of accumulation. The contribution of the new modes to the reproduction of creativity, an inherently social phenomenon at the core of the technocapitalist dynamic, is vital. Without the new modes, the reproduction of creativity would be practically impossible to achieve, on the global scale and intensity required by this new phase of capitalism.

The new modes of accumulation also make it possible to commodify creativity, at a pace and scale unknown in any prior stage of capitalism.[1] Such commodification is at the core of all extraction of value in the technocapitalist

---

1   Although parallels might be conceived with the commodification of certain resources in prior stages of capitalism, the commodification of an intangible is a particular feature of technocapitalism. Nonetheless, intangibility does not exempt a commodity from the Marxian considerations of Use-Value and Exchange-Value. See Chapter 1, Section 1 ("The Two Factors of a Commodity: Use Value and Value," pp. 35–40), and (same chapter) Section 3 ("The Form of Value or Exchange Value," pp. 47–83), in Karl Marx, *Capital: A Critique of Political Economy*, Vol. I: The Process of Capitalist Production, ed. by F. Engels [New York: International Publishers, 1967; orig. published in 1867 (Hamburg: Verlag von Otto Meissner)].

dynamic. It is also the main support of corporate power and its globalization in this emerging stage of capitalism. The new modes of accumulation therefore help spawn new forms of corporatism, along with their pathologies, deploying them on a global scale.[2]

The importance of the new modes for the globalization of technocapitalism cannot be underestimated. They have allowed much technological knowledge to be accumulated in rich nations, creating the conditions for a vast technological platform to emerge. This platform has spawned a vast and very diverse array of inventions and innovations that are diffusing globally. Those inventions and innovations have been very important for the new sectors that are symbolic of technocapitalism. New forms of corporate organization, that attempt to commodify technological creativity in ever faster and more effective ways, are emerging. The new modes of accumulation have also expanded the global reach of corporate power, allowing it to impact previously untouched areas of human existence and nature itself.[3]

There are two new modes of accumulation linked to the emergence of technocapitalism. The *accumulation of tacit knowledge* is of greatest importance for this new phase of capitalism. Tacit here refers to new or unwritten knowledge, that can support the reproduction of creativity. Tacit knowledge is the composite of unwritten (or unstandardized) ideas, experience, insights, norms, procedures, relations, and informal ways of doing that support technological creativity. Such knowledge is often culturally grounded, in a broad sense, and is built up over a long period of time. Tacit knowledge is also inherently social, in the sense that it is cultivated and imparted through social interactions and relations. Social norms, customs and specific histories influence its accumulation.

The most important forms of tacit knowledge are found in any activity that involves research creativity. Tacit knowledge in the form of insights, ideas, and experience derived through experimentation have, for example, been very important in biotechnology research. Decoding genetic data and understanding its significance through the marriage of laboratory experimentation with computer science has been a tacit, knowledge-intensive activity from the start. A new field, bioinformatics, has been born through the accumulation of tacit knowledge derived from the interaction of these research activities. No educational program existed

---

2   The experimentalist corporation (and its systematized research regime) is the prime example of technocapitalist business. See the chapter "Experimentalist Organizations" in Luis Suarez-Villa, *Technocapitalism: A Critical Perspective on Technological Innovation and Corporatism* (Philadelphia: Temple University Press, 2009).

3   A matter which can be readily observed in the genetic manipulation of numerous plants and crops by multinational agribusiness. See, for example, Daniel Charles, *Lords of the Harvest: Biotech, Big Money, and the Future of Food* (Cambridge, MA: Perseus, 2002); Clive James, *Global* Status *of Commercialized Biotech/GM Crops* (Ithaca, NY: ISAAA SEAsiaCenter, 2006), and the articles in Susan Gordon (ed.), *Critical Perspectives on Genetically Modified Crops and Food* (New York: Rosen, 2006).

from the start, to train researchers in this new field. Rather, the field emerged tacitly through experimental collaboration, and the social interaction of interdisciplinary talents in research.

Similarly, software research based on Open Source platforms has thrived on the accumulation of tacit knowledge. Such accumulation of knowledge is typically collective, involving thousands of individual researchers around the world, who share their experimental insights with everyone else.[4] Underlying its non-proprietary and collectively-shared character, tacit knowledge derived through Open Source software research is inherently social. It is cultivated through social interactions where certain norms, such as the collective, free and open sharing of all results, underlie relations.

In the Open Source model of research, the accumulation of tacit knowledge works hand in hand with the reproduction of creativity. The interactions involved in the open sharing of new knowledge regenerate creativity as new ideas or insights induce others to test, combine or extend the work of any members of the network. This is probably the best example of how a global research network can be harnessed to accumulate tacit knowledge and reproduce creativity. The Open Source software research network is also an example of how the accumulation of tacit knowledge and the reproduction of creativity can occur outside the domain of corporatism, on a global scale. The results of Open Source platforms can, however, be used by corporate organizations to boost corporate power and profit, because they are freely available to anyone. Nonetheless, the open, non-proprietary character of Open Source work, and the network's self-organizing nature, means that such networks can exist largely outside the control of corporatism, even though their work might ultimately be used by corporate entities.

Whether it occurs under or outside the reach of corporatism, the accumulation of tacit knowledge has been a major force in the emergence of technocapitalism, and in its incipient globalization. The most precious resource of this form of capitalism, creativity, cannot be reproduced without new tacit knowledge. A lot therefore rides on the accumulation of this form of knowledge, and its connection to creativity makes it a most important element for the sustenance of technocapitalism.

A second new mode, the *accumulation of codified knowledge*, involves conventional, standardized forms of knowledge. Educational programs, training routines, patents, other forms of intellectual property, and formal procedures are part of this global accumulation dynamic. The accumulation of codified knowledge supports the reproduction of creativity in ways that are more established or formalized than those found through tacit knowledge. In that regard, codified knowledge is less well connected to new knowledge and the regeneration of creativity than tacit knowledge. This has to do with the fact that codified knowledge is far more accessible than tacit knowledge, all the more so with the global reach of the Internet and the Web.

---

4   See Johan Söderberg, *Hacking Capitalism: The Free and Open Source Software Movement* (New York: Routledge, 2007).

The accumulation of codified knowledge therefore tends to be of a different social character than that of tacit knowledge. For one, it is less culturally grounded, since the diffusion of codified knowledge can more easily transcend specific cultures and fields. For example, established knowledge in an area of physics can often be transferred to an engineering specialty without much interaction between engineers and physicists. Social interaction for research or technical adjustments in such cases is bound to be very limited, if know-how about the transfer process is widely available. The social character of this accumulation mode therefore makes it easier for it to operate on a global scale.

Codified knowledge can often be built up over shorter time horizons than tacit knowledge, since the requisite rules and knowledge platforms are likely to be widely available, and are global in scope and scale. Thus, the question of how fast such knowledge will be accessed can be left up to the interested parties to decide. In contrast, the time horizon for acquiring tacit knowledge is subject to the uncertainties of trial and error, and to the social dynamics of research teams, which include the ability to work together, sustain trust, or generate constructive reciprocity. Dealing with the unknown, and with the social relations of those who explore the unknown, tend to introduce a great deal of uncertainty in the time frame for accumulating tacit knowledge.

Social relations nonetheless influence the learning and spread of codified knowledge, since education is first and foremost a social process. Learning, whether through socialization in a classroom, through cyberspace or virtual communities, involves social interaction. However, social relations are likely to be less crucial for accessing codified knowledge, since there is less uncertainty about the means and methods needed to acquire such knowledge. The avenues for acquiring codified knowledge, in other words, are well trod.

The accumulation of codified knowledge has been most dynamic since the middle of the twentieth century. The massification of higher education in rich nations which started at that time created a vast educational and training platform with substantial long term effects.[5] That vast platform supported the rapid growth of technological skills to an extent never before experienced in human history. This phenomenon was largely responsible, in turn, for exponential increases in invention patent applications and awards since the middle of the twentieth century.[6]

The explosion of intellectual property claims and rights, particularly those related to technology, was therefore a byproduct of the massification phenomenon. The importance that such claims have acquired in our time can be seen in an

5 See Roger L. Geiger, *Research and Relevant Knowledge: American Research Universities since World War II* (New York: Oxford University Press, 1993); Hugh D. Graham and Nancy Diamond, *The Rise of American Research Universities: Elites and Challengers in the Postwar Era* (Baltimore: Johns Hopkins University Press, 1997).

6 Luis Suarez-Villa, "Invention, Inventive Learning, and Innovative Capacity," *Behavioral Science* 35(1990): 290–310.

unprecedented amount of intellectual property theft and litigation.[7] Corporate litigation on intellectual property is now more common than ever and is in some cases affecting international relations, setting the stage for major international disputes that can affect trade, investment, and legal cooperation. It is not inconceivable that during the twenty-first century wars over intellectual property might occur, much as the lust for raw materials triggered wars in the eighteenth and nineteenth centuries.

The rapid accumulation of codified knowledge since the mid-twentieth century, made ever more dynamic by the global reach of the Internet and the Web (and by prior advances in computing), has also made it possible for corporatism to make inroads into higher education. For-profit e-diploma programs are proliferating, turning what once was a domain of learning and individual self-realization into a global "business."[8] At the same time, universities around the world (both private and public) are imitating and internalizing corporate culture.[9] Academic administrators see themselves as "executives," hoping to match their salaries with those of their corporate counterparts, students are seen as "customers," faculty as either "assets" or "salespersons," publications as "tools" to attract grant money and contracts, physical facilities as "service production" hardware, and institutional names as "brands." This transformation is often accompanied by the censorship of dissent (self-imposed or not) against the power of academic "executives," who increasingly mimic the mindsets and procedures of their corporate counterparts.

No longer apart from the commercialization of everyday life, the accumulation of codified knowledge is turning into an appendage of corporatism. Learning and codified knowledge are therefore subject to marketing strategies, not to mention bottom-line "return on investment" criteria that involve corporate donations, contracts that can compromise academic integrity, school rankings as prime indicators of "value", and the widespread placement of money above academic interests. At no previous time in human history was learning so subservient to corporate performance criteria, or to the global objectives of corporatism.

The emergence of the corporatist university is a phenomenon that can be best understood in the context of technocapitalism and the growing global hegemony of corporate power and profit, that this new form of capitalism promotes. Whether in cyberspace or in brick-and-mortar facilities, educational organizations are

---

7   See Pat Choate, *Hot Property: The Stealing of Ideas in an Age of Globalization* (New York: Knopf, 2005); Michael Perelman, *Steal this Idea: Intellectual Property and the Corporate Confiscation of Creativity* (New York: Palgrave, 2002).

8   Such degree programs are considered to provide "training" (as opposed to education, broadly defined). See, for example, David F. Noble, *Digital Diploma Mills: The Automation of Higher Education* (New York: Monthly Review Press, 2002).

9   See Jennifer Washburn, *University, Inc.: The Corporate Corruption of American Higher Education* (New York: Basic Books, 2005), and the articles in Benjamin Johnson, Patrick Kavanagh and Kevin Mattson (eds.), *Steal this University: The Rise of the Corporate University and the Academic Labor Movement* (New York: Routledge, 2003).

internalizing the traits and pathologies of corporatism. Institutions traditionally charged with accumulating codified knowledge thus become handmaidens of corporate power. How far the corporate takeover of codified knowledge can reach is difficult to predict, but there should be no doubt that a major transformation of the character of higher education is underway.[10]

In sum, the two new modes linked to the emergence of technocapitalism, the accumulation of tacit knowledge and of codified knowledge, have distinctive characteristics that set them apart from the more traditional forms of capitalist accumulation. *Intangibility* is their most distinctive feature, one which they share with the most precious resource of the new era: creativity. A second characteristic is their *qualitative* nature. The new accumulation modes resist quantification, particularly in the case of tacit knowledge accumulation, given its elusive, qualitative character and the challenges it poses to any attempts to establish comparative measures.

The third distinctive feature is their inherently *social* character. The accumulation of tacit knowledge, in particular, can only occur through active social relations, grounded in trust, reciprocity and specific cultural norms. Such qualities are often particular to a field of expertise and to specific histories, particularly in research settings that are oriented toward invention and innovation. Social relations are also very important for the accumulation of codified knowledge, as any learning process will reveal. However, the fact that codified knowledge is standardized makes it less dependent on active social relations to acquire. These characteristics also make it more global in scope and scale, and allow it to diffuse rapidly. These features of the new accumulation modes will become more salient as the traditional modes of capitalist accumulation are taken into account.

Conventional Modes

The conventional modes of capitalist accumulation involve capital and infrastructure. The *accumulation of capital* has been the defining feature of market capitalism since its emergence. In his seminal analysis of capitalism, Karl Marx built a foundation for critical analyses of the role of capital in society.[11]

---

10 A major contradiction is the conflict between universities' role as social institutions (and as motors of progressive social change), and their co-optation by corporate power and money. See Roger L. Geiger, *Knowledge and Money: Research Universities and the Paradox of the Marketplace* (Stanford: Stanford University Press, 2004); Washburn, *University, Inc.*

11 See Part VII, "The Accumulation of Capital," chapters XXIII-XXV, and Part II, "The Transformation of Money into Capital," chapters IV-VI, in Marx, *Capital*, Vol. I. The analyses of Vol. I (parts VII and II) were followed up in Vol. II: The Process of Circulation of Capital, in Part I, "The Metamorphoses of Capital and their Circuits," chapters I-VI, and Part II, "The Turnover of Capital," chapters VII-XVII [Karl Marx, *Capital*, Vol. II, ed. by F. Engels (New York: International Publishers, 1972; orig. published in 1893 (Hamburg: Verlag von Otto Meissner)].

By the middle of the nineteenth century, when Marx addressed the character and pathologies of industrial capitalism, capital accumulation was recognized as the predominant dynamic of economic life.

The main characteristics of the accumulation of capital that Marx analyzed in the mid-nineteenth century are still very much with us. However, the scope, the global reach, and the speed of capital accumulation have changed substantially since then. The accumulation of capital is more dynamic today than it was in the nineteenth or twentieth centuries, having achieved a global reach that intrudes on practically all human activities.

Technocapitalism requires considerable amounts of capital, given the high expenses and complexity of state-of-the-art research. Activities emblematic of this new form of capitalism, such as biotechnology, genomics, bioinformatics, nanotechnology or biopharmacology, are supported by large capital infusions. The massive capital needed to sustain their research is usually available only through corporate power, or through the financial apparatus that serves corporate power. However, more complex capital-raising and accumulation schemes have emerged as finance and speculation take over the global economy.

The term *financialization* has been used to refer to a significant shift of capitalism away from production and services toward finance.[12] This phenomenon, which became visible and increasingly global in the 1990s, is grounded in financial speculation through myriad new instruments and schemes. High liquidity created by many central banks' monetary policies supported it.[13] Financial deregulation, along with the Internet and the Web, aided this phenomenon considerably by making it possible to execute transactions instantaneously across the globe. Nations and activities that were previously out of reach of international finance were thus brought into the global speculative apparatus. The Internet and the Web also depersonalized financial transactions greatly, by eliminating the sort of face-to-face contact that once accompanied negotiation and agreement.

Financialization has become a major force behind the spreading hegemony of corporatism around the globe. It is closely related to globalization in myriad ways: through the expansion of corporate power, the spread of market fundamentalism, and the dominance of neoliberal recipes for most every area of the economy and public governance, for example. Financialization comprises an array of complex, "fast" capital-raising and accumulating schemes that have spread across the globe. Those schemes typically involve new "instruments," such as credit derivatives, structured investment vehicles, default swaps, hedge fund financing, futures and options betting. The schemes themselves are quite diverse, and can occur in the

---

12   The term *financialization* can be traced to Kevin Phillips' *Boiling Point* (New York: Random House, 1993) and his *Arrogant Capital* (New York: Little, Brown, 1994). See also Giovanni Arrighi, *The Long Twentieth Century* (New York: Verso, 1994).

13   See John Bellamy Foster, "The Financialization of Capital," *Monthly Review* 59 (April 2007): 1–12, and the articles in Gerald Epstein (ed.), *Financialization and the World Economy* (Northampton, MA: Elgar, 2005).

form of corporate buy-outs, take-overs, debt, mergers, or carry-trade speculation involving currencies and financial instruments, for example.[14]

A major effect of financialization has been to dynamize capital accumulation. A more dynamic capital accumulation has also introduced greater risk into global finance. The "instruments" that accompany financialization are so complex that they can become impossible to value or trade when economic conditions change. Vast amounts of corporate debt have been "structured" through those "instruments" in order to finance corporate buy-outs and other power schemes. Because they involve very large quantities of capital, amounting to many trillions of dollars, the "instruments" can precipitate economic crises requiring massive bail-outs by central banks.[15]

Despite the high risk, speculative character and complexity of its "instruments," financialization has made much capital available to corporate power. Among the beneficiaries of the overflow of finance capital have been the activities that are symbolic of technocapitalism. The lure of inventions and innovations in new sectors, that might someday be turned into profitable products, has been powerful. Patents and other forms of intellectual property held by technocapitalist companies have attracted large amounts of capital, even when returns seem far-fetched. Financialization, driven by rampant financial speculation and higher monetary liquidity on a global scale, also made more capital available than could be invested in production or service activities. Investment of this surplus capital in risky research activities thus became a reality, with the sectors emblematic of technocapitalism becoming targets for this surplus capital.

It is well known, for example, that a majority of biotechnology companies have never made any profit, yet enormous amounts of capital have been invested in this sector. Similarly, the nascent nanotechnology sector has attracted substantial amounts of capital, despite the unlikely prospect of returns over short- or medium-term horizons. Initial stock listings of Internet-related technology companies attracted enormous amounts of capital during the tech stock market boom in the late 1990s, despite the fact that most had neither realistic business plans nor any prospect of profit. Despite the tech stock market bust of the early 2000s, much capital continued to flow to the surviving, but often profitless, companies started during the boom years. This reality of much capital searching for relatively few investment possibilities is a hallmark of "fast" capital accumulation.

The *accumulation of infrastructure* comprises all the physical facilities that support the accumulation of tacit and codified knowledge, and of capital. Infrastructure is often referred to as "physical capital" to differentiate it from monetary capital. It is, however, a distinctive accumulation mode. Because of its very costly nature, and the difficulty of extracting short-term returns, most

---

14   See Epstein, *Financialization*.

15   The global notional value of credit derivatives was estimated to be approximately 26 trillion dollars in the first half of 2006. See Foster, "Financialization," p. 7; Doug Henwood, *After the New Economy* (New York: New Press, 2005).

infrastructure are built with public funding. This feature sets this mode apart from the accumulation of capital.

Infrastructure accumulation has a direct link to the accumulation of codified knowledge. It is difficult to imagine that any society could accumulate much codified knowledge without a substantial, long-term accumulation of educational infrastructure, for example. This mode is also vital for the accumulation of tacit knowledge, since such knowledge must ultimately rely on available infrastructure for it to be communicated or learned, and for creativity to be reproduced. The stronger the infrastructure support it receives through ease of access and speed, the more dynamic can the accumulation of tacit knowledge become.

Most infrastructure is built and sustained with public funding. Infrastructure spending takes up a substantial proportion of government budgets around the world. Between 80 and 90 percent of all US state and local government capital expenditures, for example, have historically been allocated for construction.[16] Public funding for educational facilities has traditionally been one of the two largest categories of public infrastructure construction—the other being road construction.[17] About four-fifths of all US educational infrastructure construction was financed with public funds in the twentieth century, and similar or higher allocations have typically occurred in other rich nations. The corporate research infrastructure often also receives much public funding, in the form of grants, contracts and tax rebates. Society at large therefore pays for most infrastructure.

The hegemony of corporatism, however, turns the accumulation of public infrastructure into an appendage of corporate power. Research and educational facilities, not to mention communications and most every other kind of infrastructure, end up benefiting corporate power first and foremost. What sets much physical infrastructure apart from other forms of investment is that corporate capital often does not find it profitable enough to finance it. Corporatism therefore benefits greatly from public infrastructure while society shoulders most of its cost. This asymmetrical relationship is sustained through innumerable schemes for co-optation of public governance by corporate power, to appropriate and control the benefits of infrastructure accumulation, and to chart the course of infrastructure spending.

Corporate appropriation and control schemes revolve around two salient features of infrastructure. One of them involves the fact that most infrastructure has a fixed

---

16   See American Public Works Association, *History of Public Works in the United States, 1776–1976* (Washington: U.S. Government Printing Office, 1976); U.S. Bureau of the Census, *Construction Reports: Value of New Construction Put in Place in the United States, 1964 to 1980* (Washington: U.S. Government Printing Office, 1981); U.S. Department of Commerce, *Construction Review* (Washington: U.S. Government Printing Office, various years).

17   See Luis Suarez-Villa and Syed Hasnath, "The Effect of Infrastructure on Invention: Innovative Capacity and the Dynamics of Public Construction Investment," *Technological Forecasting and Social Change* 44(1993): 333–58; American Public Works Association, *History*.

location, and is therefore tied to locales. The immobility of infrastructure places public authorities at a disadvantage in the games of power deployed by corporatism. Corporate power today is largely footloose, global, and prone to pitting authorities in one locale against those in others, in order to extract advantages. Through its mobility and global reach, corporate power thus often coopts public governance to provide infrastructure that suits corporate interests. Tax rebates, providing subsidies in the form of lower rates, building accessory facilities with public funds, and restricting access to competitors are a few examples of what this co-optation game involves.

A second feature involves the very large capital spending required by much infrastructure construction. Those large expenditures often have to be made at one time, or over a short period of time. At the same time, very long-term horizons are required to recover the expenditures, if they can be recovered at all. The large amounts of capital and the pressure to recover the expenditures also place public authorities at a disadvantage in the face of corporate power. The schemes deployed by corporatism typically involve profiting from attempts to recover some of the public expenditures—imposing corporate control, after infrastructure is built (with public funds), is the usual means.

The most important scheme of corporate control over this accumulation mode involves privatization.[18] Privatization of public infrastructure, the mantra of global corporate power and neoliberal schemes, is typically advocated as a way to increase efficiency and recover some of the construction costs. Gains in efficiency are, however, offset by restricting public access, particularly to the most disadvantaged populations.[19] Privatization also often turns facilities built by and for the public domain into private monopolies. No longer accountable to society as public authorities would be, monopolistic corporate power tends to care little about any considerations that stand in the way of profit. This deplorable situation is compounded by the co-optation or outright corruption of public officials as a means of overcoming obstacles to corporate profitability.[20] This pattern of co-optation and corruption has been massively replicated around the world since

18 Privatization, broadly defined, may involve either outright ownership or operational control (leased or contracted). The Build-Operate-Transfer approach to infrastructure privatization, in particular, helped craft many schemes throughout the world on a neoliberal frame. See United Nations Industrial Development Organization, *Guidelines for Infrastructure Development through Build-Operate-Transfer (BOT) Projects* (Vienna: UNIDO, 1996), and Sidney M. Levy, *Build, Operate, Transfer: Paving the Way for Tomorrow's Infrastructure* (New York: Wiley, 1996).

19 See the articles in Vicente Navarro *(ed.), Neoliberalism, Globalization and Inequalities: Consequences for Health and Quality of Life* (Amityville, NY: Baywood, 2007); Nik Heynen (ed.), *Neoliberal Environments: False Promises and Unnatural Consequences* (New York: Routledge, 2007).

20 Among the most vivid examples were Central and Eastern Europe's experience with the privatization of public resources. See Andrew Schwartz, *The Politics of Greed: How Privatization Structured Politics in Central and Eastern Europe* (Lanham, MD: Rowman & Littlefield, 2006).

the 1980s, when neoliberal policies started spreading, and has become a tacitly accepted part of governance in many nations.

The prospect of privatizing public infrastructure is also attractive to many public officials, particularly when they try to justify large public outlays. The often false claim that public moneys spent on construction will be "recovered" through privatization has been part of many public construction campaigns. From research labs to classrooms, to stadiums, communication facilities and toll roads, the misleading notion that it is alright to spend substantial funds on public facilities so long as they are later privatized has taken hold in the minds of many public officials. Propaganda campaigns, often financed by the corporate interests that will appropriate, operate, or benefit from the facilities have become commonplace.[21]

As financialization has made much capital available for accumulation, so privatization has supported the rapid accumulation of public infrastructure. Privatization and corporatism are therefore at the root of the "fast" accumulation of infrastructure. Corporate control of facilities, directly or indirectly tied to technocapitalism, have been part of this dynamic. Privatization has therefore seeped into most every aspect of public construction, and even when public facilities are not privatized their construction is usually undertaken by corporate entities. Also, like financialization, privatization comes in numerous forms and guises. Corporate control of administration, operational contracts, leases, and outright ownership are a few examples of the possibilities. In all such cases, the hegemony of corporatism ensures that corporate power will benefit from the use of public infrastructure, regardless of how it is financed or operated.

Global Imperative

The necessity of fast accumulation springs from several factors, all of which are closely related to the nature of technocapitalism and its globalization. The urgent corporate need for scarce and costly *intangible* resources is by far the most important factor. Those intangible resources comprise creativity, experience, and all related forms of knowledge, and they are as important to technocapitalism today as factories and labor processes were to industrial capitalism.

The new accumulation modes considered previously impinge greatly on those resources. It would be practically impossible for the new sectors and corporations that are symbolic of technocapitalism to emerge without them. Those corporate frameworks depend greatly on intangibles on a global scale, the magnitude of which only the fast accumulation modes can provide. Without them, the new sectors of technocapitalism would be little more than craft-like endeavors.

---

21 Privatization of public facilities has also been promoted by supranational organizations, on a systemic basis; see Daniele Calabrese, *Strategic Communication for Privatization, Public-Private Partnerships and Private Participation in Infrastructure Projects* (Washington: World Bank, 2008).

Parallels can be found with the emergence of the factory system in the nineteenth century and the accumulation of capital, as distinctive features of industrial capitalism. The emergence of capital accumulation in that era, dynamized by the deployment of stock markets, made it possible for large-scale factories to emerge. Thus, the factory-based production platform of industrial capitalism, its corporate underpinnings, its relations of power, its globalization and its pathologies were fundamentally based on an accumulation mode that provided a scarce resource.[22] The accumulation of capital also supported the exploitation of raw materials and labor, without which the factory system could not be sustained. Such exploitation increasingly took up a global scope as industrial capitalism spread.

For the emerging technocapitalist era, the accumulation modes for tacit and codified knowledge play the role that capital accumulation performed for nineteenth and twentieth century industrial capitalism. The accumulation of those intangibles, and its global scope, is to the systematized research regimes of technocapitalism what capital accumulation was to factory production. As, for example, steel production was supported by capital accumulation, so biotechnology, nanotechnology, bioinformatics, and other sectors emblematic of technocapitalism are sustained today by the new modes of fast accumulation and their global scope.

Those new modes also support older, more traditional sectors that are increasingly dependent on research. In the automotive industry, for example, research has become more important than ever. It has taken on a multi-dimensional character, from industrial design and styling, to diverse power systems, to crash-and-safety experimental programs, among others. All those research dimensions, which often happen in different places around the world, are each of them quite challenging and expensive, and must be coordinated and integrated rapidly. In contrast with previous times, they usually occur simultaneously. It should not surprise, therefore, that almost 85 percent of the value of new automotive vehicles is made up by intangibles, and that those intangibles now have a worldwide scope.[23]

Corporate power and profit are therefore more closely entwined with research, in all its many forms and guises. For the technocapitalist sectors and corporations, intangibles often make up all of the value of their products or services. Take, for example, the case of genetic decoding companies. Serial genetic decoding of organisms, and the patenting of genetic features, is often their only source of corporate power and profit. Once patents are obtained, they are made available for licensing to others, such as pharmaceutical or agribusiness companies. The only

---

22   See Joan Robinson, *The Accumulation of Capital* (London: Macmillan, 1956); Marx, *Capital* Vol. I, Part VII, "The Accumulation of Capital," pp. 564–647.

23   This refers to the rising importance of intangibles' share of the value of products, rather than any absolute decrease in tangible materials. See Oliviero Bernardi and Riccardo Galli, "Dematerialization: Long-term Trends in the Intensity of Use of Materials and Energy," *Futures* 25(1993): 431–48; and Pim den Hertog, Rob Bilderbeek and Sven Maltha, "Intangibles: The Soft Side of Innovation," *Futures* 29(1997): 33–45.

source of profit is the licensing revenue obtained from the users of the patents, or the royalties derived from any new products or service they might create.

A second factor underlying the need for fast accumulation is the very high *risk* of failure faced by most every technocapitalist corporate research regime. The high risk requires a rapid accumulation of intangibles, of high quality and at great expense, and on a global scale, to have any chance of success. Drawing from the global pool of accumulated intangibles whenever needed, often in great magnitude and in diverse ways, is essential. High failure rates are often a reality. In some areas of biotechnology research, for example, it is common for only one compound to succeed out of 8,000 new ones.[24] Experimental and clinical trials thus take a high toll on what a complex, expensive and long-in-gestation set of intangibles turn out. The fact that so few succeed is a poignant reminder to corporate power that having the best-quality intangibles, the most talented researchers, and the best hardware money can buy does not guarantee success.

Compounding the high risk of research is the fact that the vast majority of patents obtained are never put to any use. A very small percentage of all patent awards in the new sectors of technocapitalism are ever used for any economic or social purpose, and there is no guarantee that they will ever be profitable. This means that for the relatively few new inventions that are profitable there is great urgency to obtain high returns. This consideration makes the fast and global accumulation of intangibles all the more pressing and necessary.

Adding to the risk is the fact that most of the experimental hardware used in the sectors spawned by technocapitalism are very expensive. Custom-made equipment is usually employed. Sometimes, the hardware may be so specific and unusual that it has to be designed or built in-house. Selling such equipment after experimental programs are completed is usually impossible, since there is no market for them. Thus, the hardware costs can only be recovered through the inventions they might generate, if those happen to be profitable.

Risk is therefore a central feature of fast accumulation. It induces corporate power to depend greatly on the fast accumulation modes, to try to reduce the risk and uncertainty of research. As the high risk of research also affects investment, the urgency of augmenting and tapping fast accumulation is passed on to most other dimensions of corporate power. Undertaking speculative buy-outs of technocapitalist corporations, manipulating their stock prices, or concocting joint ventures, alliances, and other schemes ride on the perception of how well corporate power can tap into the fast accumulation dynamic.

Risky research, expensive hardware, and the fast accumulation imperative also make technocapitalist invention and innovation inherently corporate. The days when self-sufficient individuals, tinkering on their own initiative, could undertake invention are past. The high risk, the diverse and expensive intangibles needed, their global character, the multidisciplinary nature of research, the costly hardware, not

---

24   See Ernst and Young, *Beyond Borders: The Global Biotechnology Report* (Palo Alto, CA: Ernst and Young, 2002).

to mention high capital investment, make individual (self-supported) invention all but impossible to undertake. Experimentation as a craft-like, individual endeavor therefore becomes practically impossible in an era when corporate finance must sustain invention and innovation.

The third factor behind the fast accumulation imperative is the *competitive* strategies deployed by corporate power. This goes beyond the sectors of technocapitalism to encompass the broader corporate ecology on a worldwide scale. However, in the sectors spawned by technocapitalism competition takes up more aggressive undertones, as inventions and innovations mature rapidly or are quickly displaced by new rivals. Rapid maturity or competitive displacement make it more difficult to recover research costs, not to mention achieving profitability. Tapping the resources made available by fast accumulation is fundamental for corporate power to have any chance of establishing control over market niches, no matter how temporary that control may turn out to be.

The rapid maturity of global product cycles for new technologies is a fact of life for corporate power. Product cycles that used to take years to mature now get to that stage in a matter of months. A reflection of these "fast" product cycles is the reduction in lead times between the introduction of a new invention as a product, and the entry of rival ones. Those lead-time reductions make it more difficult to recover research costs, which are usually the largest cost segment in the sectors spawned by technocapitalism.

Patent protection also often means little when rival products enter the market or product cycles mature rapidly. Even when pilfering is suspected, the difficulty of establishing malfeasance, the high cost of legal action, and the long time required for resolution (if that should occur) are strong deterrents to pursuing redress. Also, in today's corporate ecology, rivals with deeper pockets and greater political influence are more likely to get away with infringing others' patents, particularly when the pilfering is subtle, as often happens with reverse engineering or the theft of unpublished ideas.

Where oligopolies or monopolies occur, the need to tap the resources provided through fast accumulation is also important. Global companies with monopolistic power often engage in self-obsolescence, to safeguard their market niches from incursions by companies in other sectors. This is evident, for example, in computer software, where Microsoft innovates continuously, replacing its desktop and laptop operating systems regularly, despite the fact that it has had a virtual monopoly in that area.[25] Windows 95 was thus replaced by the 98 version, the latter by 2000 (XP), and that one by Vista. In duopolistic or oligopolistic situations, such as the server software market, Microsoft systematically innovated on its product despite the fact that it had one significant rival. The latter, being the Linux Open Source

---

25 A characteristic feature of Microsoft from its earliest days; see, for example, James Wallace and Jim Erickson, *Hard Drive: Bill Gates and the Making of the Microsoft Empire* (New York: Wiley, 1992).

kernel, was not profit-driven and had no predatory market strategies. Yet, all the same, Microsoft felt compelled to invent and innovate continuously.

Rapid invention and innovation can also be found in the case of Internet search engines, which have an oligopolistic market that is usually global in scope and scale. Despite having practically taken over the search engine market, Google, for example, systematically innovates on its services. As it provides newer and more versatile ways to search, it makes its own algorithms obsolescent. Striving to become the library of the world, by digitizing every item published in history, Google will also likely have to revamp its entire framework.[26] In a time when systematic invention and innovation are the norm, monopolists and oligopolists can no longer feel safe. They might have felt that way under industrial capitalism. Now, given the increasing speed of change in technologies and market conditions, and their global scope, that is no longer possible. Tapping into the global resources made available through fast accumulation, to invent and innovate continuously, is today the most important way to control market niches.

Global Effects and Pathologies

Fast accumulation has several important consequences. The global importance of those effects is predicated by their capacity to trigger other phenomena which are themselves causes of serious social dysfunctions. It is therefore impossible to think of fast accumulation as a self-contained dynamic, isolated from the larger social and economic context of technocapitalism, or from its worldwide scope.

By far the most important consequence, which is also cause (in a dialectical sense), is the *global corporatization of invention and innovation*. Technological invention and innovation have become part of the deeper structure of corporate power. In the context of technocapitalism and of its globalization, corporate power depends greatly on those two functions, both of which are an outcome of creativity. In the technocapitalist mold, corporate power thus lives or dies based on its capacity to profit from that most elusive human quality.

Creativity and its outcomes, invention and innovation, make intellectual property a matter of fundamental importance to corporate power. As we shall see later, this characteristic is also a source of pathology in technocapitalist society. Acquiring, managing, and deploying intellectual property on a global scale become a major task for corporate strategy. The aggressive corporate preoccupation with appropriating any and all forms of intellectual property, through which profit and power might be obtained, is a major feature of

---

26   This can be considered part of a strategy to monopolize the search engine market. See Jean Jenneney, *Google and the Myth of Universal Knowledge: A View from Europe*, transl. T.L. Fagan (Chicago: University of Chicago Press, 2007).

technocapitalist corporate culture. The aggressive drive to secure any and all forms of intellectual property means that most any source of tacit knowledge becomes a target for appropriation, wherever it may happen to be.

Most prominently, universities, which are major sources of tacit knowledge and vast repositories of codified knowledge, are a target of global corporate influence. Corporate interest in universities, often mythically portrayed as philanthropic (or tax deduction-driven), is also a treasure hunt for knowledge that can be turned into intellectual property. University research, in particular, is the prime target of corporate influence. Feeding new ideas to corporate R&D (Research and Development) requires the kind of state-of-the-art research findings that many universities can provide. It should not surprise, therefore, that co-optation of universities, their research capabilities, and their governance has become a prime interest of corporate power.[27]

Joint ventures with universities, where corporations fund and set institutional research agendas (directly or indirectly), are of increasing interest to corporate power. Although university and corporate research have often been considered at odds with one another, because of the former's ethical need to be open and immediately publishable (as opposed to the secrecy and proprietary character of the latter), universities' pressing need for funding has made corporate lock-ins unavoidable.[28] A good example of this unequal marriage can be found in the proliferation of university "research parks," for which technology corporations are assiduously recruited. Those "parks" serve as conduits to market research results that further corporate profit and power, while allowing universities to claim some royalties (or maybe profits, if any happen to be made). More broadly, they are a tool for corporate power to extend its global influence into the major repositories of tacit and codified knowledge that universities are today.

The influence of corporate power on universities through these and other arrangements is more palpable than ever, and can be found in various guises. Imitations of corporate governance, for example, are increasingly common in the management of many universities. The most affected are American private universities, but the trappings and pathologies of corporate governance are also spreading throughout public universities. A rationalization of university culture as fragmented entities has been part of this phenomenon. As a result, intellectual creativity ends up becoming a commodity and university recognition becomes synonymous with the kind of product rankings that companies obtain through market surveys.[29] Among the pathological effects of this corporatization

---

27 See Ibrahim Warde, "For Sale: U.S. Academic Integrity," *Le Monde Diplomatique* (March 2001): www.MondeDiplo.com; Alan P. Rudy, *Universities in the Age of Corporate Science: The UC Berkeley-Novartis Controversy* (Philadelphia: Temple University Press, 2007).

28 See Washburn, *University, Inc.*

29 Providing rankings of universities and their programs has become a profitable business for some media companies. When the president of an elite American college, for

of universities is the rise of authoritarian governance, evident in the spread of command-and-control management, the suppression of controversial ideas inimical to corporatism, and the granting of "advisory" power (formally or not) to corporate donors over the hiring of administrators and faculty.[30]

Another symptom of this pathological effect is that university administrators see themselves more as corporate "executives" who rule over faculty, rather than as members of an academic community that requires shared governance and debate to thrive intellectually. As a result, faculty in universities are increasingly seen as salaried workers, or "jobbers," subject to the interests of a hierarchy of university executives that ranges from those at the highest level to deans and department heads. Evidence of this pathology is also evident in the rising number of temporary lecturers and professors, part of a large and growing contingent of surplus academics who have little prospect of finding permanent employment.[31] The question of whether tenure for faculty is needed at all is now in the minds of many academic executives. If the surplus army of well-qualified academics is becoming so large and deep that revolving-door hiring can occur, why bother to tenure? Eliminating tenure would save considerable amounts spent on pensions, health care, and other benefits. This mindset is very much in line with corporate practices of the day, and it is a mindset that is becoming worldwide in scope and reach.

At the same time, the growing disparities between corporate executive compensation and employee salaries are becoming a reality in universities. Not happy with only the thought of acting or imagining themselves to be like corporate executives, university administrators are raising their compensation and perks, at a pace geared to put universities in line with the great disparities that reign in the corporate world.[32] Some top administrators in private universities are already being

---

example, decided not to submit data to one of the main providers of such rankings (*U.S. News and World Report*), the magazine decided to estimate the college's ranking in a largely arbitrary way. See Naomi Schaefer Riley, "College Rankings Rancor: Should College Presidents Withhold Data from U.S. News?," *Wall Street Journal* (March 30, 2007): W13.

30   See Bernard Wysocki Jr., "Ivory Power: Once Collegial, Research Schools Now Mean Business," *Wall Street Journal* (May 4, 2006): A1; Charles Ornstein, "Firing of UCSF Dean a Climax to Years of Disputes Over Finances," *Los Angeles Times* (December 16, 2007): B1. Tenure decisions are also being affected by corporate influence; see Michael Hiltzik, "Biotech Deal Still Clouds Tenure," *Los Angeles Times* (July 7, 2005): C1.

31   This is an alarming trend in American higher education, which (among various consequences) portends a loss of academic freedoms. See Rick Wolff, "The Decline of Public Higher Education," *Monthly Review* (February 16, 2007): www.monthlyreview. org/mrzine/. Declining conditions in American academic employment contrast with rising compensation and perks for administrators. See Marc Bousquet, *How the University Works: Higher Education and the Low-Wage Nation* (New York: New York University Press, 2008).

32   Between 1995 and 2005, the median of presidential salaries at single-campus universities in the US rose 29 percent, while salaries of full-time faculty salaries increased 9 percent. Aiding the rising disparities is the practice of hiring executive search firms when

compared to hedge fund executives, arranging deals, perks and compensation for themselves that resemble those of financial speculators.[33]

Large corporations that consider universities too unwieldy for their interests are also setting up their own narrowly-focused, in-house degree programs and mini-campuses.[34] Their curricula involve *training* more than education, in any intellectual sense. Those programs allow corporate power to issue academic-sounding credentials to their own or to prospective employees. The training provided is typically for MBA-like diplomas that cater to specific corporate needs of the moment, using the corporate name to try to elicit worldwide recognition for the "credentials." The corporate names involved are, naturally, well-known ones belonging to global behemoths. Such diplomas are tacitly meant to convey the notion that individuals who hold them may be "safe" or, in other words, not influenced by the kind of questioning or dissent that can be found in conventional universities, with their diversity of ideas and viewpoints.[35]

The corporatization of invention and innovation, and corporations' growing interest in education, are related to the urgent need to *speed up* invention and innovation. "Fast" invention and innovation, concomitants of fast accumulation, involve sustaining a rapid and continuous stream of new inventions and innovations, that can be turned into new products or services. Those streams of new inventions and innovations can only be sustained by tapping the global repositories of knowledge and creativity, and in the context of technocapitalism, fast invention and innovation thereby become a major part of corporate strategy.[36]

Fast invention and innovation are very important strategically, as means to reduce risk. Research is inherently risky, perhaps the most risky activity

---

presidential posts become vacant. See Larry Gordon and Rebecca Trounson, "Audit of UC Pay Revives Debate," *Los Angeles Times* (April 29, 2006): B1; John Hechinger, "More College Presidents Get Million-Plus," *Wall Street Journal* (November 2, 2009): A4.

33 John Hechinger and Rebecca Buckman, "The Golden Touch of Stanford's President: How John Hennessy's Silicon Valley Connections Reap Millions for the University—and Himself," *Wall Street Journal* (February 24, 2007): A1.

34 In 1993, the number of "corporate universities" (those owned or setup by corporations to provide in-house training) in the US was approximately 400. By the mid-2000s, their numbers were estimated to be upwards of 3,000. The best-known corporate university is possibly the McDonald's Corporation's "Hamburger University" (based in Chicago). Among the more notorious are the business-seminar "universities," such as "Trump University," operated by the American real estate developer Donald Trump. See David Lazarus, "Trump Name Sells Old Game," *Los Angeles Times* (December 12, 2007): C1, and his "Trump's a Grump About Column On His 'Priceless' Tips," *Los Angeles Times* (December 16, 2007): C1.

35 It may be partly for this reason that some corporations seek to influence earlier (pre-college) stages of the educational chain, in order to create opportunities to pre-select or train potential employees. See Anne Marie Chaker, "Teacher's Aide: High Schools Add Classes Scripted by Corporations," *Wall Street Journal* (March 6, 2008): A1.

36 See "Systematized Research Regimes" in Suarez-Villa, *Technocapitalism*.

in existence, in terms of potential profit or market value. The more basic or potentially path-breaking research is, the higher its risk profile. This is one of the ineludible characteristics of technological research in the new era of technocapitalism. Even with relatively routine development work (the "D" in R&D), which may involve minor innovations or "tweakings" of existing technology, the risk of failure is usually significant. Corporate power thus tries to reduce and control this inherent risk by speeding up the stream of inventions and innovations in the R&D "pipeline."

Research risk refers to not only high failure rates (as occurs in many areas of biotechnology, for example), but also the high cost of experimental hardware and the diversity of talents needed. In addition to these endogenous factors, global competitive pressures also pose risk, even under oligopolistic conditions. The actual market protection provided by patents is more limited than ever, as fast invention and innovation uncover ways to side-step existing patents. Patent-protected technologies and products are therefore made obsolescent more rapidly, as rival products that work better or cost less (or both) invade global market niches. This means that the time window available to recover research costs, or even turn a profit, has become shorter, adding to the pressure to come up with profitable results.[37]

The risk involved often prompts corporate power to resort to new managerial schemes, that can sustain research and provide "pipelines" of new inventions and innovations. As we shall see later, fast invention and innovation requires new corporate organizational arrangements that can systematize research.[38] Such systematization is key to commodifying creativity in the technocapitalist corporation.

The stress to sustain fast invention and innovation has introduced a serious pathology, which reflects both the declining social accountability of corporate power and the aggressive character of corporate strategy. Intellectual property theft on a global scale is a major pathology unleashed by the technocapitalist ethos. This new pathology was not as substantial or pervasive during previous stages of capitalism, but it is characteristic of technocapitalism, as the pressure to appropriate creativity increases. Fast invention and innovation place demands on corporate power which can sometimes only be fulfilled through pilfering. Far from being lapses in the corporate psyche, the high and rising incidence of

---

37   The time lag between the market introduction of a new product and the first entry of a competitor has shortened considerably over the years. A study of 46 major product innovations showed the lag was approximately 33 years at the beginning of the twentieth century, declining to three years by the period 1967–86. See Rajshee Agarwal and Michael Gort, "First-Mover Advantage and the Speed of Competitive Entry, 1887–1986," *Journal of Law and Economics* 44(2001): 161–77.

38   For an extensive discussion of those organizational forms see the chapter "Experimentalist Organizations" in Suarez-Villa, *Technocapitalism*.

this pathology, and its worldwide presence, indicates that it has become part of corporate strategy.[39]

Corporate intellectual property theft is thus becoming a pathology of the "fast" culture of technocapitalism. Far from being an isolated problem, corporate intellectual property theft is important in an environment where "winning" is everything, regardless of how it is accomplished, and where being "second-best" usually garners substantially fewer rewards, if anything.[40] When "winners" extract profit and power vastly greater than those who follow, the prospect of being a follower is not attractive to corporate power, or to shareholders. All the more so, given the high risks and cost of research, and the all-too-real possibility that those costs may not be recovered when a new product is marketed.

Corporate espionage, typically done covertly, has also achieved a place in the corporate strategic arsenal of hardball strategies. It is sometimes done through hired third-parties, such as private investigators, through inside informants working for rival companies, or through computer hackers.[41] This cloak-and-dagger business is now global, and often employs former government intelligence operatives who apply their skills to the more profitable area of corporate intelligence. How far this espionage game has advanced can be seen in the ranks of intelligence contractors now available for hire, most of whom profess to work "legally" (though not ethically) in extracting valuable data from any company targeted by a rival, anywhere around the world. If recent trends are any indication, this sort of intelligence-gathering is becoming a prime component of corporate strategy, as the value of secrets rises and hardball tactics gain more favor in the corporate mindset.

Conclusion

The dynamics of fast accumulation have made it possible for a new version of capitalism to emerge. Technocapitalism, unlike its predecessors, depends largely on *intangibles*, which only new modes of accumulation can provide. Those new

---

39 See Choate, *Hot Property*; Perelman, *Steal this Idea*. The proliferation of "hardball" corporate strategies, and their legitimation through the work of well-known management "gurus" is also a symptom of this pathology. See, for example, George Stalk Jr., Robert Lachenauer and John Butman, *Hardball: Are You Playing to Play or Playing to Win?* (Boston: Harvard Business School Press, 2004).

40 Corporations often use their power to buy up their lesser rivals, in order to increase their market presence or preempt any challenge from the "second-best" tier of companies in their field. See Ben Worthen, "Cash-Rich Oracle Scoops Up Bargains in Recession Spree," *Wall Street Journal* (February 17, 2009): A1.

41 See Hedieh Nasheri, *Economic Espionage and Industrial Spying* (Cambridge: Cambridge University Press, 2005); Choate, *Hot Property*. Use of hacking to steal corporate secrets has also become commonplace; see Ben Worthen, "Lessons Learned: A Hacking Spree Demonstrates How Not to Become a Victim," *Wall Street Journal* (December 11, 2007): R4.

modes are at the core of the technocapitalist dynamic, directly affecting its capacity to commodify vital resources and provide new means of hegemony to corporate power.

Among the fast accumulation modes, two are distinctively associated with the emergence of technocapitalism and its globalization. *The accumulation of tacit knowledge, on the one hand, and the accumulation of codified knowledge on the other, fundamentally sustain the most important resource of the technocapitalist era: creativity.* Those two new modes, combined with "dynamized" traditional modes of capitalist accumulation (capital and physical infrastructure) are major supports for the globalization of this new version of capitalism.

The two new accumulation modes, in particular, occur primarily in rich nations today. In this regard, the globalization of technocapitalism is fraught with undertones of domination and hegemony. Only nations with the resources to sustain a vast and deep apparatus of scientific and technological research, including state-of-the-art academic institutions, can hope to support the new accumulative modes. Corporate power is the main beneficiary of those resources, and of the results of fast accumulation, as it seeks to expand its influence around the world. Research-intensive corporations are thus at the receiving end of this new capitalist phenomenon and they, more than any other entity, are responsible for articulating it on a global scale.

A major outcome of fast accumulation is the rising global hegemony of corporate power. Not the traditional form of corporate power known under industrial capitalism, but a more clever, rapacious, and intrusive form of corporate power based on the exploitation of technology and science. This new kind of corporatism seeks to appropriate and exploit the intangible resources provided through fast accumulation, wherever they may be found. Its quest for greater power and profit therefore draws it to the sources of knowledge that are at the core of fast accumulation. Universities and most every type of intellectual property thus become targets for appropriation. It should not surprise, therefore, that pathologies and effects largely unknown in previous stages of capitalism become commonplace in this new era. No form of creativity, knowledge, or intellectual property that can be turned into power and profit can be considered safe from corporate appropriation, as technocapitalism expands its global reach.

Much as no source of creativity, knowledge or intellectual property is safe from appropriation, neither can any part of the globe be considered out of the reach of corporate power, or of its pathologies. Corporate intellectual property theft, already at levels unseen in any previous version of capitalism, is spreading as corporate technocapitalism extends its reach around the globe. Corporate espionage, often done in the mold of intelligence agency cloak-and-dagger operations, is becoming more common. Such "operations" now also involve hacking of computer systems, by means that are either untraceable or practically impossible to evade. Pilfering through espionage and diverse "hardball" schemes, along with traditional practices, such as reverse engineering, have also become an integral part of global corporate strategy.

The implications of fast accumulation, coupled with the advance of technocapitalism and its new forms of corporate power, pose major problems for humanity. The resources made available through fast accumulation, placed at the service of technocapitalist corporate power, portend a renewal of imperial conquest of markets, cultures, societies, and nature itself. Neo-imperial conquest through technocapitalist corporate power may become more effective than military action, or may be used to enhance the latter, whenever the appropriation of resources becomes a priority. We have barely begun to see the profile of a new era where imperial domination may come not from the power of missiles or guns, but from laboratories where life, attitudes and mindsets are engineered.

Intangible Global Commodities

Turning resources into commodities has been a major characteristic of capitalism throughout its history. Commodifying tangible resources, such as capital and raw materials, allowed industrial capitalism to systematize production and appropriate their product. Technocapitalism, in contrast, depends on intangible resources which are elusive, qualitative, and require much social intervention to be replenished.

Social relations and culture are inextricably linked with the intangible resources of technocapitalism. The search for those resources has acquired a global scope which transcends boundaries, cultures and governance. Globalization thereby acquires new horizons, which are greatly influenced by corporate power and its control over technology and research. This global quest to tap, commodify, and appropriate intangible resources makes corporate technocapitalism more intrusive than any previous corporate form. No aspect of society, life, or nature that can provide commodifiable intangibles is likely to be overlooked.

The sectors where corporate technocapitalism has taken hold, and where the commodification of intangibles is most noticeable and urgent, will be symbolic of the twenty-first century. Biotechnology is one of those sectors. Genomics, proteomics and bioinformatics, for example, are making it possible to "design" most any kind of organism. The "industrialization" of biotech may produce genetically-targeted replacement organs serially, for humans, animals or plants. Certain animals are already being genetically engineered to be "living factories" and produce proteins and hormones on a large scale, to be used in biomedications. Biopharmacology seems bound to transform pharmaceuticals and medical care, by providing genetically targeted medications and therapies.

Nanotechnology is another emerging sector where commodifiable intangibles are essential. Its convergence with biotech may generate a nano-biomedicine that can radically transform medical diagnostics. Nanotech's convergence with computer hardware may replace silicon chips with nanochips that have vastly increased power and are so small they can be implanted in most any gadget or organism. Its interphase with telecommunications and software may produce extremely small gadgets that can transmit or receive from anywhere to anywhere, and be very difficult to detect. Biorobotics is another sector that depends greatly on commodifiable intangibles, and may engineer devices and organisms that imitate animal or human functions to, for example, explore the ocean floor, mine, do warfare, or engage in pervasive surveillance.

The globalization of these sectors might seem farfetched, but it is already underway. Commodifiable intangibles are the common denominator that bind them together, and that make them valuable for corporations to appropriate. The commodifiable intangibles upon which they depend for research are creating a massive "brain drain" of talent that benefits the rich nations where technocapitalism is taking hold. Those rich nations thus become beneficiaries of the educational and social investments made by many less well-off nations, often at great sacrifice to their peoples. Rich nations that are the home of these emerging sectors therefore benefit from the fast accumulation dynamics discussed in the previous chapter.

Important features of intangible commodities that are the lifeblood of technocapitalism will be explored in this chapter. The commodification and reproduction of creativity, two major phenomena of technocapitalism, will take up much attention. Their relationship with notions of value will be explored broadly, taking into account corporatism's role and its power over research. A final component will then consider the relationship between these crucial elements of technocapitalism and globalization. The techno-divide between rich and poor nations, and the contradictions that are generated by the commodification of intangibles, will be considered in that component.

Creativity and Knowledge

Creativity is by far the most important resource of technocapitalism. Its intangible character makes it a *social* resource. Today, it is also a global resource. This means that the exercise of creativity is greatly influenced by the social context through which it is exercised, and by the global spread of technocapitalism. The social context typically encompasses social relations, such as those established with professional communities, with individuals who have similar interests, or with society at large. The social context also encompasses global relations of power that deeply influence how, by whom, when and where creativity is exercised.

Creativity can be defined as the ability to come up with new ideas, processes, tools, formulas, methods, or services. The ability to exercise creativity is both personally and socially driven. In the exercise of creativity, the personal (or individual) cannot exist without the social. Its exercise therefore has a strong social dimension. In the global context of technocapitalism, the results of exercising creativity are usually new inventions and innovations, and research units are the organizational settings where such exercise occurs. Those settings are typically corporate, and they operate under the calculus of profit and control over the research process. Those research settings are also increasingly global in scope and reach, as we will see later in this book.

The exercise of creativity typically involves the ability to absorb existing knowledge and to transform it into new inventions and innovations. This means that knowledge, both tacit and codified, is intimately related to the exercise of creativity. It is a result, an essential ingredient, and a prerequisite for the exercise of creativity. Because of their intangibility, creativity and knowledge are inherently social, in the sense that both are cultivated, supported, transmitted and embedded in social contexts, and are advanced through social relations.[1] Through the worldwide spread of technocapitalism, those social relations are increasingly global.

Beyond knowledge, imagination (another intangible quality) also influences the exercise of creativity. The exercise of creativity typically involves the combination of imagination *with* knowledge.[2] The mere absorption of knowledge, although an essential prerequisite, cannot generate a significant exercise of creativity unless imagination is also present. Imaginative thoughts (combined with a strong base of knowledge, tacit or codified) are the platform from which creative searches are usually launched. Those creative searches, more than at any previous time in history, are global and are strongly supported by new communications technologies that emerged during the last two decades.

Experience, which also rests on knowledge, is another important ingredient in the exercise of creativity. In many respects, experience is itself knowledge, and it may seem unnecessary to consider it separately from that larger rubric.[3] Nonetheless, codified knowledge can exist without experience, as often happens with students or with recent graduates of training programs in many fields. The exercise of creativity thus rests on qualities (knowledge, imagination, experience) which require considerable persistence, effort and time to build up. Those qualities are antithetical to the "fast" schemes that are commonly found in capitalism's contemporary global culture, with its short-term horizons and "quickly-get" programs. At the individual level, these qualities seldom accumulate fast, and must be cultivated, looked after, nurtured, and examined critically, with enormous persistence and a steady resolve to advance them over the long term.

Socio-Dimensional Features

There are four socio-dimensional features that influence greatly how, when and where creativity is deployed. One of them is the previously mentioned *social context* and the relations it supports. The social context enables and stimulates those who exercise creativity to come up with and implement new ideas, to think

---

1   Social influences have long been recognized as a major motivator of technological and scientific creativity; see Richard C. Levins and Richard Lewontin, *The Dialectical Biologist* (Cambridge: Harvard University Press, 1985), Part 3; Michael Schiff and Richard C. Lewontin, *Education and Class: The Irrelevance of IQ Genetic Studies* (New York: Oxford University Press, 1986).

2   Imagination has often been stressed in histories of scientific creativity; see Gerald J. Holton, *The Scientific Imagination: Case Studies* (Cambridge: Cambridge University Press, 1978).

3   Harry Braverman's *Labor and Monopoly Capital: The Degradation of Work in the Twentieth Century* (New York: Monthly Review Press, 1998 edition; chapters 6, 8, 15, 16, 17) showed how experience and knowledge were practically inseparable in the formation of skills. The social dimension of experience was also an important aspect of Herbert Marcuse's *One-Dimensional Man* (Boston: Beacon, 1964), where their manipulation at the service of corporate capitalism led to widespread social alienation.

differently from the norm, and to break with existing conventions and precepts. To the extent that the social context supports the subversion of the status quo, it can become a revolutionary medium.

The social context's role in supporting technological change has all too often been neglected in favor of functionalist explanations. Accounts of "paradigm shifts" that significantly changed technology or science have all too often emphasized such interpretations. They have tended to explain change in terms of isolated factors, such as specific experimental approaches, serendipitous discoveries, intensive tinkering, or individual genius, to the neglect or exclusion of the social context and its relations.[4] Functionalist explanations have also woefully neglected the global dimensions of technology and science, the relations of power and domination that occur, and the resulting social injustices. In the functionalist interpretations society, the social context, and its social relations are thus regarded as exogenous elements, if they are considered at all. An unfortunate effect of this mindset has been the impression that technology or science are *separate* from society.[5] Or, that inventors and innovators operate in a reality that is removed from the social and the global, exercising their creativity without a social dimension, or exercising it where the latter is mostly irrelevant.

Another socio-dimensional component is the *social relations* and their influence on the exercise of creativity. Social relations are embedded in the social context and are inseparable from it, in a broad sense. They are essential for diffusing tacit knowledge, insights, and ideas that can be improved through interactions. The latter, when they occur with a professional community, also affect individual social status within the community. Such professional communities are embedded in the larger global panorama of technocapitalism and of its urgent need to use and appropriate creativity, and their effect on social status is therefore broader and deeper. Status positions affect individuals in multiple ways through, for example, self-perception of their role in society, their social esteem, and their understanding of reciprocity and trust toward others in the community.[6]

Tacit knowledge, in particular, is greatly affected by social relations. Tacit knowledge, as defined in the previous chapter, involves new (or unwritten) ideas

---

4 Historical accounts of individual inventors and scientists have often been most neglectful in this regard. Constructivists such as Kuhn tried to move away from that tendency by taking social influences into account, though in a rather limited way; see Thomas Kuhn, *The Structure of Scientific Revolutions* (Chicago: University of Chicago Press, 1962), chapters 11 and 12. Kuhn's work nonetheless neglected the role of social class and of class-, gender- and race-based relations of power in his account of how social relations can influence paradigm shifts.

5 Andrew Feenberg's *Critical Theory of Technology* (New York: Oxford University Press, 1991) criticizes the functionalist notion (often promoted by contemporary neoliberals) of technology as governed by "laws" that are largely unaffected by social action.

6 Status positions are inextricably related to social class, particularly in roles where knowledge is important; see Stephen A. Resnick and Richard D. Wolff, *Knowledge and Class* (Chicago: University of Chicago Press, 1987), Chapter 3.

that have not been codified, or have not become part of any formal (established) procedures. Such knowledge can be understood as the combination of insights, ideas, or procedures that support creativity, which remain outside any established standard. Tacit knowledge, and the ideas it generates, is often viewed as unorthodox, unconventional, or eclectic. In this sense, tacit knowledge can be subversive and revolutionary, to the extent that it helps overturn oppressive realities and established ideas.

Social relations are also important for overcoming the social alienation that accompanies global capitalism and its depersonalization of social, national and cultural identity. In the context of research creativity, alienation manifests itself through the fragmentation and disengagement of the creative process from its authors.[7] The results of creativity are thus assembled as research "products" that exist independently from the creative process, from those who exercised their creativity, and sometimes even from the originally intended purpose. Alienation often also involves transferring control (in the form of ownership) of the results of creativity to a corporate entity that is functionally and intellectually removed from the creative process. In the context of technocapitalism, such transfer of control is increasingly global, transcending borders, cultures and social identities. This takeover (or tacit expropriation) of the results of creativity from those who exercise it is part and parcel of the functional fragmentation of research, that is commonly found in global corporate organizations.

Social relations can take up an emancipative role against alienation. One way in which they can do so, for example, is by helping researchers understand the rights they have over their creativity. Another way is to help empower those who exercise creativity by creating alternative arrangements to the control exercised by corporate power over their creativity. An example of this possibility can take the form of Open Source-type relations, where individual participants collaborate and share their creative efforts to come up with results that cannot be appropriated by corporate power.[8] Making those results public and allowing them to diffuse globally can effectively break the proprietary control over research creativity that is part and parcel of technocapitalist corporate power.

A third socio-dimensional feature can be described as the *inexhaustibility* of creativity. This is a social property of creativity that is intimately entwined with creativity's intangibility. This feature relies on social relations for support and renewal, and it contrasts greatly with the case of tangible resources. Tangible resources are typically devalued and exhausted whenever they are used, resulting in lower or disappearing value. In the case of creativity, however, its benefit

---

7 This is analogous to Marcuse's understanding of social alienation (related to "one-dimensionality") in the larger context of capitalism and its corporate structures; see Marcuse, *One-Dimensional Man*.

8 Software design has been a major beneficiary of this relational mode. See Johan Söderberg, *Hacking Capitalism: The Free and Open Software Movement* (New York: Routledge, 2007).

tends to increase whenever it is deployed. The more creativity is exercised, the more benefit it is likely to generate. Praxis and experience in the exercise of creativity lead to potentially greater benefit and value. Praxis and experience are thus intimately tied to the social context, to its relations, and to benefit or value. Experience, in particular, often stimulates the further exercise of creativity, as any tacit knowledge gained makes it possible to deploy creativity more effectively. In the context of technocapitalism, such deployment is now increasingly global, as both corporate power and non-corporate social networks cut across boundaries and cultures.

The fourth socio-dimensional feature can be considered a composite that includes experimentation, along with the closely related uncertainty and risk. This socio-dimensional combine is found in most any exercise of creativity, and all the more so in research in the sectors that are symbolic of technocapitalism. Experimentalism is, more than ever, a social endeavor and it is also more international than ever. Technological research today requires much teamwork and interaction with professional communities around the world, even when it occurs within the confines of the corporate domain. This makes it impossible for experimentation to remain isolated, even when the research activities are secretive, mainly because the knowledge required tends to be quite diverse and can only be accessed through wide-ranging external social networks that are increasingly global.

Experimentation in the technocapitalist context requires openness to new ideas and critiques, but only the social context and its relations can provide those in abundance. The social context of professional communities is, for example, a major source of new ideas and critiques. Those are typically provided through various vehicles, such as conferences, reviews of research, publications, socio-political interest groups and lobbying, among others, that now tend to have an international (if not a global) scope. Such social influences are often important supports of persistence, an indispensable trait in the exercise of research creativity. Criticism provided through those increasingly global relations often also opens avenues to collaboration that cross-fertilizes ideas, or that starts networks which empower individuals (and groups) independently from the corporate domain.[9]

Commodification

Commodifying creativity is the key to corporate power and profit in the era of technocapitalism. Although it increasingly has global ramifications, it is a process that is nonetheless under the control of corporate power and occurs within the

---

9   In Open Source networks, for example, collaboration and network-based relations have been an important support for individual and collective skill development. See Söderberg, *Hacking Capitalism*; Samir Chopra and Scott D. Dexter, *Decoding Liberation: The Promise of Free and Open Source Software* (New York: Routledge, 2007).

corporate domain. Commodification is defined here as the process through which results of creativity are turned into commodities, such that they can be commercialized and surplus value can be extracted. This definition follows the historical Marxian formulation of commodification, initially applied to the context of industrial capitalism and to its reliance on production and factory labor processes.[10] In the technocapitalist dynamic, however, research rather than production, and the exercise of creativity rather than the application of factory labor, are defining features.

Commodification therefore has a fundamental role in the capitalist dynamic of the twenty-first century. It is as much a part of technocapitalism as it was part of the apparatus of industrial capitalism. The main objective of commodification, to commercialize the results of creativity such that surplus value can be obtained, therefore adjusts to the new reality imposed by technocapitalism and its global corporate underpinnings. This modified definition of commodification does *not* exclude the historical one, which involved the products of factory labor (and of labor in services).[11] Both the historical and the new definition of commodification offered here are compatible with one another, but they pertain to different historical realities, and are part of capitalism's long process of transformation.

The long transformation of capitalism from factory-based production to research-oriented, creativity-exploiting regimes therefore poses some changes to our understanding of commodification. Corporate power is behind both the historical reality and the technocapitalist definition, providing a common link between the two.[12] Global expansion was also part of industrial capitalism and of its relations of domination. In many respects, therefore, commodification under technocapitalism shares much the same traits with commodification under industrial capitalism, even though the main resources and historical realities are different.

For any process of commodification, obtaining *market value* is a fundamental objective. On market value or, in other words, the possibility of exchanging the results of creativity for commercial gain, rides the hope of survival for corporate technocapitalism. Market value is also the fundamental prerequisite for attaining *surplus value*. Surplus value refers to the difference between the total cost for the technocapitalist corporation of supporting research and all its ancillary functions,

---

10   As with so many other aspects, Marx's pioneering critical analyses of capitalism provided the groundwork upon which many studies of commodification were subsequently developed. His earliest insights on commodification as a concept can be found in Karl Marx, *Grundrisse: Foundations of the Critique of Political Economy* (New York: Penguin, 1973), pp. 140–53 (based on Notebooks I and II, dating from 1857–58).

11   The original definition dealt with capital as a resource. See Marx, *Grundrisse*, pp. 113–238.

12   Although corporate power itself evolved along with industrial capitalism. See Eric Hobsbawm, *The Age of Capital, 1848–1875* (New York: New American Library, 1979); Richard Barnet, *Global Reach: The Power of the Multinational Corporations* (New York: Simon and Schuster, 1974); David F. Noble, *Forces of Production: A Social History of Industrial Automation* (New York: Knopf, 1984).

and the market value obtained from commercializing the results of creativity.[13] Surplus value is often equated with profit, although it need not necessarily be so, since profit can be obtained through vehicles other than market value.[14] Obtaining market value and, most of all, surplus value are therefore the desired end results of commodification. No corporate entity can survive long without obtaining surplus value for the results of creativity, an objective that is at the core of every technocapitalist enterprise.

In the technocapitalist context, commodification depends on *experimentation*. Corporate power tries to reduce risk and uncertainty by *systematizing* experimentation as much as possible. Systematization typically involves standardization or, in other words, establishing patterns (or templates) for approaching projects and research programs, if not the very exercise of creativity.[15] Standardization also involves codifying new (tacit) knowledge obtained through the exercise of creativity, within the specific corporate domain that appropriates the results of creativity. Such appropriation typically entails restricting access to the newly codified knowledge, meaning that the corporate entity has appropriated the results for its own ends.

Systematizing research and the exercise of creativity has produced new kinds of corporate organizations.[16] Those organizations are quite different from the ones spawned by industrial capitalism, as they are highly focused on research and are increasingly global in scope and reach. Within those organizations, research units provide the settings where creativity is exercised and where its results are appropriated by corporate power. Those new organizations are thus functionally responsible for structuring and implementing creative processes according to the research agendas set by corporate power. Corporate power is therefore ultimately in control of research, and of the internal apparatus that appropriates the results of creativity even though it must depend on external social (and global) influences to access creativity. As we will see in the following chapter, those organizations are introducing practices and pathologies that influence the global reach of technocapitalism and the corporate quest for talent.

Functional Features

Commodification comprises three major functions. The first one can be referred to as *fragmentation*, and involves a splitting up of the exercise of creativity into various components. This function brings creative processes under greater

---

13   This definition is consonant with Marx's, as noted in his *Grundrisse*, pp. 376–98.

14   Although surplus value might equal profits in many situations, this need not necessarily be so; see Marx, *Grundrisse*, pp. 381–86.

15   Standardization can contribute to the "one-dimensional" character of human activities; see Marcuse, *One-Dimensional Man*, Chapter 1.

16   See the Chapter "Experimentalist Organizations" in Luis Suarez-Villa, *Technocapitalism: A Critical Perspective on Technological Innovation and Corporatism* (Philadelphia: Temple University Press, 2009).

oversight by corporate management. Each of the components might be managed separately, to determine how well they comply with the overall research agendas set by management, and to make it easier to evaluate commercial potential of any inventions and innovations quickly. With the spread of corporate research activities around the world, the rising use of research outsourcing, and the complexity of most research projects, fragmentation has become more difficult to operationalize.

Why is fragmentation necessary? A major purpose of fragmentation is to try to make the exercise of creativity as predictable as possible. This means reducing the uncertainty that accompanies experimentation, which is a major source of anxiety for corporate power. Another important and related objective of fragmentation is to reduce the risk of failure as much as possible. Fragmenting the exercise of creativity can help reduce uncertainty and risk by making it possible for corporate power to monitor those who exercise creativity more closely. Such monitoring can include, for example, watching or stopping activities that stray from the research agendas set by corporate power, or restricting the autonomy of researchers to make decisions on their own.

Control is therefore at the heart of fragmentation. Greater corporate control over those who exercise creativity all too often becomes part of the attempt to reduce risk and uncertainty in the mindset of corporate power. Improving timeliness in advancing the research agendas set by corporate power is another motive for fragmentation, particularly when deadlines are short and external competition is fierce. Timeliness is often perceived to reduce uncertainty and the risk of failure, and it can help corporate power examine results quickly, to determine their possibilities for commercialization.

This apparatus of control also involves standardizing research activities as much as possible within the corporate domain. Standardization and fragmentation are therefore entwined, to the extent that they help corporate power gain some control over the exercise of creativity. Standardization typically introduces analytical benchmarks for the activities it affects. Analyzing the exercise of creativity in terms of its findings (as in the case of new inventions that can obtain patents) is an important aspect of corporate control and can help reduce uncertainty. Such analysis usually helps determine commercial potential, cost and timeliness, and therefore turns into a vehicle to enhance corporate control over creative processes.

A major effect of fragmentation is to turn creativity and knowledge into disembodied inventory items.[17] Those vital resources of technocapitalism thus

---

17 Fragmentation may therefore contribute to narrow, uni-dimensional approaches which demean creative processes and those who exercise creativity. The results are usually consonant with Marcuse's views on technological rationality in the larger corporate-capitalist context. See Marcuse, *One-Dimensional Man*, Chapter 6 ("From Negative to Positive Thinking: Technological Rationality and the Logic of Domination"). Fragmentation also has parallels in the factory system and labor processes of industrial capitalism. See, for example, Braverman, *Labor and Monopoly Capital* (chapters, 4, 5 and 10); Noble, *Forces of Production*, Part 2.

become little more than stocked items in the corporate arsenal, to be used at the command of corporate power whenever it suits its agendas. Turning out a continuous stream of new inventions and innovations that can be commercialized in a timely way, with certainty and little risk of failure, is the main priority. The continuity and speed of this stream of inventions and innovations is critically important for corporate entities in the sectors symbolic of technocapitalism, and most of all in medical biotechnology and biopharmacology. Extremely high failure rates, often in the order of 8,000:1 compounds, and very lengthy trial periods (lasting as long as 5–10 years) require a fast and abundant stream of new inventions and innovations (in the form of new compounds) to reduce the odds of failure.[18] Beyond this daunting challenge is the risk of marketing failure, made all the more likely by the global scope of marketing, when new products are preempted by new rivals or by harmful side effects.

The second function of commodification can be referred to as *disengagement*. This function involves the detachment of the results of creativity from the fragmented parts of a creative process *and* from those who exercise creativity. The results of the exercise of creativity are thereby assembled as corporate property, to be turned into corporate "products" or "services." Disengagement therefore involves the corporate appropriation of the results of creativity, such that they can be used for any objective that corporate power deems appropriate, anywhere in the world.

Disengagement also involves the alienation of those who exercise creativity from its results. Loss of control by those who exercise creativity is an outcome of this function. The loss of control can take various forms. One of the most common is to sign over the property rights for an invention (in, say, the form of a patent award) to the corporate entity that employs the individuals to whom the rights were awarded. This is now a global phenomenon, institutionalized and made legal through intellectual property regimes that are embedded in national legal frameworks. This handover of intellectual control is now so common that it is routinely included in hiring agreements in most research-oriented corporations everywhere.[19] Such agreements are legally binding and their violation can subject those who breach them to demotions, and to loss of employment, income or career.

Another example of loss of control can be found in the corporate misappropriation or theft of the results of creativity from employees. This occurs more often with ideas or concepts which do not fit the conventional intellectual property frameworks (such as patents, copyrights or trademarks). Corporations

---

18   See Ernst and Young LLP, *Beyond Borders: Global Biotechnology Report* (Palo Alto, CA: Ernst and Young LLP, 2006), and their *Convergence: The Biotechnology Industry Report* (Palo Alto, CA: Ernst and Young LLP, 2000).

19   The signing away of control (and intellectual property rights) can be considered a tacit confiscation of employees' ideas. See Michael Perelman, *Steal this Idea: Intellectual Property Rights and the Corporate Confiscation of Creativity* (New York: Palgrave Macmillan, 2004).

typically claim the right to appropriate employees' ideas, arguing they are covered by corporate intellectual property regimes, or that the ideas were conceived through employment in the corporate context and would not have occurred otherwise.[20] Much of the misuse or theft may also be surreptitious, difficult to trace, and impossible to challenge legally for lack of hard evidence or because of the high cost of litigation. Corporations have a vast arsenal of means at their disposal to prevent such contestation, including coercive measures, such as threatening the loss of employment or career. In general, the more valuable the idea, the more likely it is that coercion will be used to prevent contestation. Coercive tactics to prevent contestation of corporate intellectual appropriation have also acquired a global scope with the spread of technocapitalist corporatism, as we will see later in this book.

Why is disengagement necessary? The main objective of this function is the appropriation of the results of creativity by corporate power. Such appropriation is fundamentally necessary for a corporate entity to be able to commercialize and obtain market value from the results of creativity. Property, disengagement, and the alienation of those who exercise creativity are therefore intimately linked with one another in the process of commodification. At no previous time in the history of capitalism have intellectual intangibles acquired so much importance for commodification as they do today. At no previous time in history did they acquire the global scope and importance that they now have.

The third function of commodification involves *exchange* of the results of creativity. Market exchange is the usual target, although the results of creativity may in some cases be exchanged for resources other than money or capital, through non-market means. Generating market (or exchange) value is the prime purpose of exchange, and it is also a major objective of commodification. The generation of exchange or market value has also acquired a global scope in the context of technocapitalism, as corporations seek any and all possibilities to sell products or services, based on the inventions and innovations that they appropriate.

Market (or exchange) value is the key to obtaining surplus value. The latter, defined previously as the difference between the market (or exchange) value obtained from commercializing the results of creativity, *and* the cost of supporting all activities related to exercising creativity (such as research), if of vital importance to corporate survival. Without surplus value there can be no corporate power, and no corporate entity can hope to survive without it. Long-term deficits of surplus value (or profit) are therefore the bane of corporatism.

Such deficits often come about through the marketing problems that affect new inventions and innovations. Among the most common is the upstaging (or preemption) of a new product by an also-new rival. The rival product, if more effective or less costly, can foreclose the possibility of obtaining market value (and, ultimately, surplus value) by the upstaged one. It should not surprise,

---

20 See Perelman, *Steal this Idea*; Pat Choate, *Hot Property: The Stealing of Ideas in an Age of Globalization* (New York: Knopf, 2005).

therefore, that corporations tend to invest a great deal of time in preventing rival products from flooding markets targeted by their new products, as we will see later in this book. The reduction of lead time, between the entry of a new product and the arrival of competitors, therefore seems to be an important cause of the market failure of many new inventions and innovations. Such failures are increasingly global in scope and scale, given the collapse of trade barriers and other obstacles to exchange.

Historical evidence has so far shown that such lead-time reductions, between the introduction of new products and rival ones, have been continuous and substantial in many sectors and industries.[21] In sectors with very substantial research costs, such as those symbolic of technocapitalism (biotechnology, nanotechnology, biopharmacology, for example), the reduction of those lead-times is critical, since research costs (often in the hundreds of millions of dollars) may never be recovered. Not to mention, of course, any preemption of the possibility of obtaining surplus value, noted earlier. Thus, the exchange function can compound the risk and uncertainty inherent in commodification (including the risks introduced by the previously discussed fragmentation and disengagement functions). The technocapitalist corporation, it seems fair to say, is therefore plagued by great risk and uncertainty throughout the process of commodification, and such risks tend to be magnified by global phenomena that are larger than the power of any single corporate actor.

Through the exchange function, the results of the exercise of creativity fully become a commodity. The results of the exercise of creativity are sold by the corporate entity that appropriated them. Corporate appropriation thus becomes a prerequisite for exchange, and both exchange and appropriation are now increasingly global. As discussed previously, corporate appropriation involves the alienation of those who exercised creativity from the results of such exercise. In this way, purchasers of the results of creativity typically have no connection with those who exercised their creativity, in order to provide an invention or innovation.

Exchange is therefore typically devoid of recognition for those who exercised their creativity. Recognition, if it occurs, will likely be vested on the corporate entity that appropriated the results of their creativity, and that sold them as a product or service. The corporate appropriator is also the beneficiary of any surplus value, using it to appropriate more results of creativity in turn, and to accelerate commodification whenever possible.[22] Corporate power is therefore in command of commodification from start to finish, appropriating the results of creativity and receiving whatever global surplus value a new invention or innovation may accrue.

---

21   See Rajshee Agarwal and Michael Gort, "First-Mover Advantage and the Speed of Competitive Entry, 1887–1986," *Journal of Law and Economics* 44(2001): 161–77.

22   Sharing surplus value with employees has been avoided most of the time. See Choate, *Hot Property*; J. Rodman Steele, *Is this My Reward?: An Employee's Struggle for Fairness in the Corporate Exploitation of His Inventions* (West Palm Beach, FL: Pencraft, 1986); *Science*, "Letters: The Problem with Patents," (April 15, 2005): 353.

Reproduction on a Global Scale

In contrast with commodification, the reproduction of creativity is primarily a *social* function rather than a corporate one. This means that reproduction must be mediated and sustained by the social context, by its social relations, and by its networks. The reproduction of creativity is increasingly a global process of technocapitalism, given the worldwide spread of communication networks, the long (and global) reach of corporate power, and the previously discussed character of fast accumulation. Reproducing creativity is essential if commodification is to occur. The latter cannot occur without the former. Reproduction and commodification are therefore inextricably tied to one another, despite the fact that one depends on (and is sustained by) the social context, while the other depends on (and is controlled by) corporate power.

Conceptual Perspective

Reproduction is defined in this book as a recurrent and socially-grounded process that regenerates the potential to exercise creativity. Reproduction is mainly a qualitative process which is inherently social, and therefore mostly outside the control of corporate power. Its qualitative character defies quantification, and it is therefore very difficult (if not impossible) to measure in a precise way. Reproduction is made complex by the intangibility of creativity and its multidimensional nature, which must draw upon knowledge, experience and stimuli from many fields, and by its increasingly global dimension.

Reproduction provides access to social support, stimuli and ideas that help regenerate the potential for creativity. Such influences can nurture, for example, the possibility of thinking differently, of persevering with experimentation, and of learning to cope with uncertainty and risk, all of which are important for the exercise of creativity. They are also often closely related to tacit (or uncodified) knowledge, particularly when such knowledge is embedded in customs that have not been formally defined or taught.

The definition of reproduction used in this book follows the historical conceptualization in Marxian political economy and critical analysis. The historical formulation involved the reproduction of capital as a major component of industrial capitalism.[23] It was subsequently applied to other resources by various scholars over the years.[24] Under industrial capitalism, reproduction involved

---

23 Capital's reproduction was a major concern in Marx's original critique of capitalism. See Karl Marx, *Capital: A Critique of Political Economy*, Vol. I: The Process of Capitalist Production, ed. by F. Engels [New York: International Publishers, 1967; orig. published in 1867 (Hamburg: Verlag von Otto Meissner)], Chapter 23 and Part VII.

24 See Louis Althusser, *Sur* la *Reproduction* (Paris: Presses Universitaires de France, 1985); Henri Lefebvre, *The Survival of Capitalism: Reproduction of the Relations of Production*, transl. by F. Bryant (London: Allison and Busby, 1976).

tangible resources (initially capital), which could be easily quantified or measured. Reproduction could thus be sustained and controlled largely within the corporate context of industrial capitalism, because of the tangible character of resources, the possibility of quantifying them, and the nature of factory production.[25] This situation stands in deep contrast with the character of reproduction under technocapitalism.

In the technocapitalist context, *intangibility* poses a major challenge, requiring adjustments to the historical formulation of reproduction. Intangibility, a major feature of the main resource of technocapitalism—creativity—makes the re-conceptualization of reproduction more abstract. This is partly a result of the difficulty of quantifying creativity. As noted earlier, creativity is a *qualitative* resource, first and foremost. It is often practically impossible to quantify, and when this can be attempted it often turns out incomplete. Its multidimensional character therefore makes creativity elusive and difficult to grasp completely, in both specific and general ways—as we will see in subsequent chapters, globalization magnifies this characteristic and enhances the value of this vital resource.

In the context of technocapitalism, reproduction is influenced by the new "fast" accumulation modes discussed in the previous chapter, and by their increasingly global dimension. Most of all, the accumulation of tacit knowledge, which draws from many sources around the world, influences the quality of reproduction. The social context also influences reproduction by providing *legitimacy* to those who exercise creativity. This can involve, for example, support from a professional community, from influential groups, and from society at large. Such support increasingly acquires a global dimension as international networks of researchers proliferate, with participation and visibility increasing legitimacy. *Trust* is an important result of social legitimacy, and is vital for establishing credibility between individuals and groups involved in exercising creativity. Legitimacy and trust are also important for establishing social agendas that seek to redress injustice and promote democratic action. The effectiveness of those agendas has usually been influenced through the legitimacy and trust that only social relations can provide. Corporate power, in contrast, is increasingly unable to elicit such trust, as its pathologies and its manipulation of research for self-serving ends become more noticeable.[26]

---

25   See Braverman, *Labor and Monopoly Capital*; Noble, *Forces of Production*; Eric Hobsbawm, *Labouring Men: Studies in the History of Labour* (London: Weidenfeld and Nicolson, 1964).

26   Particularly in the life sciences. See Jerome P. Kassirer, *On the Take: How Medicine's Complicity with Big Business Can Endanger Your Health* (New York: Oxford University Press, 2004); Marcia Angell, *The Truth About the Drug Companies: How They Deceive Us and What to Do About It* (New York: Random House, 2004); Sheldon Krimsky, *Science in the Public Interest: Has the Lure of Profits Corrupted Biomedical Research?* (Lanham, MD: Rowman and Littlefield, 2003).

The worldwide manipulation of technology and science by corporate power is becoming most noticeable in the field of biotechnology. For example, the cloning of animals to be used as protein-producing, living "factories" to massively generate products for biopharmaceutical companies, the genetic engineering of human body parts from cloned embryo cells to produce replacements in vast quantities, or the corporate marketing of human ova or sperm with desirable physical characteristics, raise many troubling questions.[27] These troubling aspects now spill across national borders and continents, as corporate intellectual property regimes colonize legal systems, and as corporate power increasingly influences societal governance around the world.

Another feature of the global social context and its support for reproduction is the role of *networks*. Social relations typically involve networks that transcend national boundaries and now also language and cultures, where access to interactions, stimuli and support for the regeneration of creativity occurs.[28] Those social relations are increasingly outside the reach of corporate power, or at any rate outside the corporate context, and they are now global in scope and reach. Corporate settings are unable to provide internally the richness, diversity, and quality of stimuli needed to regenerate creativity, or the global dimension that such quality, diversity and richness increasingly require. The broader social context and its global, network-based relations is therefore the vital vehicle for the reproduction of creativity.

Global networks also help provide a platform of relations upon which trust is established and sustained. One of the best contemporary examples of how global networks help reproduce creativity can be found in Open Source-type networks, all of which operate outside the reach of corporate power. In software design, for example, the Linux Open Source network provides a vehicle to reproduce creativity, linking up thousands of volunteer specialists around the world.[29] Its approach is non-proprietary and rests on collaboration and the sharing of all results with everyone, in or outside the network. Such global networks have also been established in other fields, to provide encyclopaedic data and information, for example, or to link researchers targeting specific illnesses, among many others.[30]

---

27 A commodification of life itself is therefore underway. See Finn Bowring, *Science, Seeds and Cyborgs: Biotechnology and the Appropriation of Life* (London: Verso, 2003). The interface between neoliberal policies, political philosophy, genetic manipulation, and corporate interests is an aspect that deserves closer attention; see Antoinette Rouvroy, *Human Genes and Neoliberal Governance: A Foucaldian Critique* (London: Routledge-Cavendish, 2008).

28 See the chapter "Networks as Mediators" in Suarez-Villa, *Technocapitalism*, for insights on networks and their role in the reproduction of creativity.

29 See Söderberg, *Hacking Capitalism*.

30 The most frequently consulted encyclopedia in the world, *Wikipedia* (available online at wikipedia.org), is an example of that network. See Pierre Gourdain, *La Révolution Wikipedia: Les Encyclopédies, Vont-elles Mourir?* (Paris: Mille et Une Nuits, 2007); Andrew Lih, *The Wikipedia Revolution: How a Bunch of Nobodies Created the World's*

Reproduction versus Commodification

There is a fundamental antithesis between reproduction and commodification. This antithesis is grounded in their different contexts of influence, and in the relations of power that affect those contexts. Those relations of power are increasingly global in the context of technocapitalism, because of the worldwide reach and scope of corporate power *and* of the networks that support the reproduction of creativity. Reproduction is an inherently *social* function, embedded in social contexts, whereas commodification is a *corporate* function, subject to the designs of corporate power and embedded in the corporate domain. Reproduction belongs to no one but society, the social context, its relations, and its networks. This is conditioned by creativity's *intangible* nature, its qualitative character and its need for social interactions. Reproduction cannot therefore be appropriated in any real sense, nor can it be effectively or exclusively controlled by any corporate entity.

Commodification, on the other hand, is about corporate *appropriation*. Appropriation of the results of exercising creativity, in whichever form those might be, whether as (intangible) ideas, formulas, methods or processes, or as (tangible) tools, organisms, mechanisms or resources, for example. Such appropriation is fundamental for securing market value, and it is increasingly global as corporate intellectual property regimes colonize legal systems around the world. Corporate appropriation of the results of creativity is prerequisite for commercializing the results of creativity, which typically occur in the form of an invention or innovation, and involve corporate marketing strategies that are global in scope and reach.

The apparatus of technocapitalism vitally depends on those two functions, reproduction and commodification, antithetical as they are, and on the exercise of creativity which they so greatly influence. Technocapitalism is as dependent on them to sustain research, as industrial capitalism was on the reproduction of capital and the commodification of labor to sustain production.[31] Industrial capitalism, however, lacked the contextual split noted above since both commodification and reproduction were largely under corporate control. That contextual split is a major source of pathology for technocapitalism and for its globalization, as we will see later in this book.

Greatest Encyclopedia (New York: Hyperion, 2009). The success of Open Source in this area has attracted similar efforts in other fields. See Axel Bruns, *Blogs, Wikipedia, Second Life, and Beyond: From Production to Produsage* (New York: Peter Lang, 2008); *The Economist Technology Quarterly*, "An Open-Source Shot in the Arm?" (June 12, 2004): 17–19.

31   Although reproduction and commodification under industrial capitalism involved a different modal context (production), a different control and organizational apparatus (the factory system), and very different processes (labor processes, which were typically repetitive, requiring limited skills, and very little or no creativity). See Braverman, *Labor and Monopoly Capital*; Noble, *Forces of Production*; Hobsbawm, *Labouring Men*; Lefebvre, *Survival of Capitalism*.

The antithesis between reproduction and commodification is grounded in several major functional contradictions. Most of those contradictions now have a global scope, because of the worldwide flows of knowledge and talents involved, and because of the global projection of corporate power. One contradiction involves talents and knowledge that *resist* commodification, because they cannot be codified enough, or because their qualitative character prevents them from being turned into a corporate product or service. Such talents and knowledge are often essential for reproduction, because of the stimuli, insights or experience they provide to the regeneration of creativity. In the corporate domain, those talents and knowledge tend to be suppressed or demeaned. Examples of them abound in various fields, most of all in the arts and their intersection with fields of technology.[32] Radical criticism involving deconstruction of new ideas and processes is one of those talents. While it is a talent vital to regenerate creativity, in the corporate context such criticism typically becomes inimical to the designs of corporate power, or to its authoritarian control over research.

The undermining of public trust in the sources of creativity and knowledge is another effect of the antithesis between reproduction and commodification. Corporatism's authoritarian control over research is the main driver of this phenomenon, and it manifests itself in many different ways whenever research is carried out in the corporate domain. The occasional manipulation of research results by placing funding pressures on researchers, or through the co-optation of professional practitioners, for example, has deepened this problem, particularly in biotech, the life sciences, and medical practice.[33] This phenomenon may be largely responsible for an unprecedented questioning of research results, pharmaceutical propaganda and medical claims, which is now increasingly global and undermines the social responsibility of corporate power. Autonomy from corporate power, which is essential for sustaining public trust, has thus been diminished as independent evaluation panels and regulatory agencies become more subject to political pressures that favor corporate interests.[34] The collapse of governmental and regulatory autonomy from corporate power is also a global phenomenon, as we will see later in this book.

---

32 Deconstructivism may provide a good example. See Jacques Derrida, *Limited Inc.* (Evanston, IL: Northwestern University Press, 1988), and his *Ethics, Institutions, and the Right to Philosophy*, transl. and ed. by P. Trifonas (Lanham, MD: Rowman and Littlefield, 2002).

33 See Kassirer, *On the Take*; Angell, *Truth About Drug Companies*.

34 In the U.S. Environmental Protection Agency, for example, more than half of all scientists responding to a very large survey reported political interference in their work, most of it associated with corporate interests (directly or indirectly). See Union of Concerned Scientists, *Interference at the EPA: Science and Politics at the U.S. Environmental Protection Agency* (Washington: Union of Concerned Scientists, April 2008); Judy Pasternak, "Hundreds of EPA Scientists Report Political Interference: The Survey Reveals a Widespread Problem, Advocacy Group Says," *Los Angeles Times* (April 24, 2008): A10.

The functional split between reproduction and commodification also spawns *secrecy* regarding the exercise of creativity and its results. Such secrecy safeguards the corporate appropriation of the results of creativity, and the ever present corporate anxiety to obtain surplus value wherever its products are marketed. Secrecy is part and parcel of contemporary corporate strategy, aimed at preventing competitors from gaining knowledge that may confer them an advantage.[35] From a social perspective, however, such secrecy is antithetical to technological progress and to the open diffusion of knowledge.[36] Maintaining research secrecy also poses formidable challenges to corporate power, because of the global scope of research knowledge and of the reproduction of creativity.

The corporate imperative to maintain secrecy and appropriate the results of creativity also spawns much litigation. Such litigation typically targets what corporate power appropriates, and it usually involves actual or alleged infringements of patents, copyrights, or the theft of ideas and designs through diverse predatory schemes—such as reverse engineering, research espionage, or the targeted hiring of competitors' researchers. Litigation transfers considerable amounts of money to attorneys, which could be used instead for socially beneficial endeavors, such as supporting those who exercise creativity, their compensation, health care and other benefits, or for reinvesting in research and productive activities. The astronomical, global rise of intellectual property litigation in recent years is a symptom of how important corporate appropriation of the results of creativity has become for the advancement of technocapitalism and its corporate agents, and it is also symptomatic of the overwhelming importance that creativity and knowledge have acquired in this new form of capitalism.[37]

Value

Value is an important aspect of any commodity. Achieving value is an objective of any attempt to commodify a resource. Reproduction is also influenced by value, since it is often part of the motivation to regenerate creativity. To corporate power, achieving value through the exercise of creativity is a fundamental imperative,

---

35   Secrecy has become embedded in corporate strategy as a means to surprise and pre-empt competitors. See Joel Bakan, *The Corporation: The Pathological Pursuit of Profit and Power* (New York: Free Press, 2004). Business school how-to texts on corporate strategy increasingly emphasize secrecy (and secret machinations) as one of the ways to destroy or damage competitors; see George Stalk Jr., Robert Lachenauer and John Butman, *Hardball: Are You Playing to Play or Playing to Win?* (Boston: Harvard Business School Press, 2004).

36   A point emphasized by critics of corporate capitalism; see Michael Perelman, "The Political Economy of Intellectual Property," *Monthly Review* (January 2003): 29–37, and his *Steal this Idea*.

37   See Bakan, *The Corporation*; Choate, *Hot Property*.

given its importance for corporate survival. In the context of technocapitalism, achieving such value also becomes a global endeavor, requiring manipulation and control that extends far beyond the boundaries of the corporate domain.

A major priority of corporate power in commodifying creativity is to obtain *market value*. Market value can only be derived through commercialization, a process that is now largely global in scope and scale. For commercialization to occur, the results of the exercise of creativity must be appropriated by a corporate entity. Market value may be determined outside the control of corporate power, when substantial market competition exists, or it may not, as in the case of monopolized contexts. Whether corporate power manipulates markets or not, the fundamental reality is that market value has to be obtained through commercialization.

Exchange value may be considered an alternative to market value, in cases where the results of creativity are commercialized outside conventional market contexts. This occurs, for example, when the results of creativity are traded through barter or some other form of exchange.[38] Commercialization through non-market vehicles is therefore possible, although it often requires trust and tends to be more difficult to arrange than market exchange. Both market and non-market commercialization involve exchange, in a general sense, and the differences between them mostly refer to the vehicles through which they occur. Both forms of commercialization are increasingly global and reflect the spread of exchange networks for corporate innovations.

Surplus value refers to the difference between the benefit (monetary or not) obtained from market (or exchange) value minus the total cost of commodifying and appropriating the results of creativity (including all ancillary costs). Surplus value can therefore serve as an indicator of profit.[39] The latter, however, is subject to different technical interpretations depending on the sector or activity in question. For example, in some contexts (sectoral or national) the definition of profit may include depreciations, tax credits, investment credits and facility construction deductions, among various items.[40] Although surplus value might be considered synonymous with profit, it therefore need not necessarily be so. For practical purposes, however, in this book the terms surplus value and profit have been taken (and will be considered) to be generally equivalent to one another. This

---

38 Such forms of exchange were more common in pre-capitalist times, although they are still practiced in many parts of the world. See Immanuel Wallerstein, *Historical Capitalism* (London: Verso, 1995), and his *The Second Era of Great Expansion of the Capitalist World-Economy, 1730–1840s* (San Diego: Academic Press, 1989).

39 The relationship between surplus value and profit is by no means straightforward, however, in Marx's discussion of the topic. See Marx, *Grundrisse*, Section 3: "Capital as Fructiferous Transformation of Surplus Value into Profit," pp. 745–78.

40 And, any definition of profit must also take speculation into account (as a source of profit), as in the case of financialization. See Lawrence E. Mitchell, *The Speculation Economy: How Finance Triumphed Over Industry* (San Francisco: Berrett-Koehler, 2007); Eric J. Weiner, *What Goes Up: The Uncensored History of Modern Wall Street as Told by the Bankers, CEOs, and Scoundrels Who Made it Happen* (New York: Little, Brown, 2005).

simplification becomes necessary in order to find a common denominator that can be applied globally, to all sectors associated with technocapitalism and to those that are not so associated.

In Marxian political economy the generation of surplus value, its deployment, and its effect on growth (broadly defined) was historically related to the reproduction of capital.[41] Surplus value and reproduction therefore have a conceptual link that cannot be ignored in this discussion. Marxian political economy approached this link through a dual typology that differentiated between simple and expanded reproduction.[42] This dichotomy was later expanded to include a third possibility: contracted reproduction.[43] Simple reproduction involved spending surplus value entirely on consumption or speculation, with no effect on growth in production—a difficult prospect that would be unsustainable in the long run, even though it might create employment and generate economic growth in the short term. Expanded reproduction referred to the reinvestment of surplus value in production, resulting in growth, depending on the quantum reinvested. Contracted reproduction involved a loss of surplus value, such that production declined—a very worrisome prospect that would be accompanied by unemployment and income losses (and possibly deflation). This typology relied greatly on the quantification of surplus value and of production, both of which were quite feasible in the context of industrial capitalism given the tangible (and measurable) character of the main resources utilized.

The emergence of technocapitalism requires a modification of this typology. Research, or the exercise of creativity, replace production in the typology, reflecting the character of this new form of capitalism. Thus, the reinvestment of surplus value in research, that expands the exercise of creativity, is assumed to correspond with the historical notion of expanded reproduction. A redefinition of simple reproduction, in turn, involves the deployment of surplus value toward consumption (or speculation) entirely, thus having no incremental effects on research or the exercise of creativity. The loss of surplus value and any consequent cutbacks in research would therefore correspond to contracted reproduction in the historical definition.

These reinterpretations do not preempt the historical definition, in the sense that surplus value is directly linked to growth, whether under technocapitalism

---

41   Marx, *Grundrisse*, "Theories of Surplus Value," pp. 549–602. These are the notes, originally drafted in 1857–58, which served as the basis of the discussion on surplus value in Marx, *Capital*, Vol. I, parts III, IV and V (on absolute and relative surplus value).

42   See Vol. I of Marx's *Capital*, Chapter 23 ("Simple Reproduction") and in greater detail in Volume II, Chapter 20 ("Simple Reproduction") and Chapter 21 ("Accumulation and Reproduction on an Extended Scale"). Note that the term "extended" was used to refer to expanded reproduction.

43   This third possibility was derived from Ernest Mandel's analysis of long-wave phenomena, and the prolonged cyclical downturns that are often part of the dynamics of capitalism. See Ernest Mandel, *Long Waves of Capitalist Development: A Marxist Interpretation* (Cambridge: Cambridge University Press, 1980).

or industrial capitalism. However, the adjusted interpretation seeks to recognize that research and the exercise of creativity are major concerns in the context of technocapitalism. Capitalism becomes more complex as it evolves, and this is reflected in every stage of its long trajectory.[44] Production, although important, is not the mainstay of technocapitalism. The technocapitalist corporation clearly emphasizes research over production, as we will see later in this book.

The usefulness (or utility) that may be derived from using any results of creativity can also be understood to represent value. Defined as *use value*, it is largely independent of exchange or market value, and of surplus value.[45] Many results of the exercise of creativity are beneficial beyond (or above) whatever market or exchange value they might generate. In many cases, the results of creativity were not commercialized and therefore had no market or exchange value at all. Examples of this condition can be found in the health sciences. Vaccines which were never commercialized saved numerous lives.[46] Those and many other medications were often prepared and distributed by public health agencies in various nations, at no cost to recipients. Such medications had no market or exchange value to speak of, despite their obvious utility (or use value) to those who needed them.

Obsolescence often does not preclude deriving use value from most technologies. Many of them have continued to provide use value decades after they were superseded by newer or more efficient alternatives. Examples can be found in many household appliances, which are often kept in service despite their technical obsolescence. The use value of an older technology may therefore offset the performance improvements provided by a newer one, especially when the cost of replacement is substantial.[47] At an individual or group level, obtaining

---

44 See Wallerstein, *Historical Capitalism*, and his *Second Era*; Eric Hobsbawm, *The Age of Extremes: The Short Twentieth Century, 1914–1991* (London: Michael Joseph, 1994), and his *Age of Capital*. The pathologies capitalism generates as it evolves, not only in society and public governance but on nature as well, also take on greater complexity. See Richard Levins, "Living the 11th Thesis," *Monthly Review* (January 2008): 29–37; Richard Levins and Richard Lewontin, *Biology Under the Influence: Dialectical Essays on Ecology, Agriculture, and Health* (New York: Monthly Review Press, 2007).

45 Although there is an underlying antithesis between use value and market value, based on the relations of production and on need. See Karl Marx, *The Poverty of Philosophy* [New York: International Publishers, 1963 (orig. published in French, 1847)], Chapter I.1: "The Antithesis of Value and Exchange Value, pp. 25–34 (involving his response to Proudhon's "The Philosophy of Poverty").

46 See Arthur Allen's *Vaccine: The Controversial Story of Medicine's Greatest Lifesaver* (New York: Norton, 2007); William H. Foege, *House on Fire: The Fight to Eradicate Smallpox* (Berkeley: University of California Press, 2011). Many vaccines that saved millions of lives or prevented illnesses were not commercialized because doing so would have prevented large numbers of people from having them.

47 This is common with commercial aircraft. See *Los Angeles Times*, "DC-9 Strategy Helps Northwest" (February 21, 2005): C6.

use value from technically obsolescent inventions is widespread, especially when their utility is entwined with emotional attachments, or with replacement cost considerations. Globalization has, in general, magnified the impact and importance of the use value of many inventions and innovations, particularly for poor nations and for poor people in general. As we will see later in this book, the corporate appropriation of creativity (and of intellectual property in general) is often at odds with the benefits of use of value, particularly for the poorest classes of society.

Social value involves a broader vision of use value, beyond that obtained by individuals or groups, to encompass society at large. This collective definition of use value encompasses both the micro- and the macro-societal dimensions, and it is also increasingly global in scope and reach.[48] Social value is operative regardless of whether market (or exchange) value, and surplus value, are obtained at all. Social value is thus grounded in a social need, or social utility, even when the results of creativity are not commercialized.

An example of social value obtained without commercialization can be found in patents. The overwhelming majority of invention patents are never put to any commercial use. However, they serve as repositories of ideas and knowledge that can help learning. Because of their public (and therefore accessible) status, patents provide many insights on inventions which are important for understanding or learning how new technologies develop. Learning about others' inventions is often necessary to invent or innovate, particularly since existing inventions and innovations often serve as the point of departure for new ideas. Such learning can have considerable social value in itself, especially when its scope and reach is increasingly global. This kind of learning also contributes to the accumulation of codified knowledge that influences creativity. Another example of social value can be found in Open Source software design. Software created through Open Source collaboration has practically no market or exchange value, since it is not commercialized. It is posted freely for everyone to use and revise, and cannot therefore be appropriated, yet it has considerable social value for many millions of people around the world.[49] Open Source software design also has a considerable learning impact for those who experiment with software code, given its global accessibility and the possibility of interacting with others who also seek to experiment and learn.

Corporate appropriation of the results of creativity can influence whether social value can occur, particularly when corporate intellectual property regimes are enforced globally. When corporations control intellectual property, the social value that occurs is likely to be associated with market value. Once the results of creativity are appropriated, those which fail to generate market (or exchange) value (and surplus value as well) stand to be scrapped.[50] Corporate appropriation can therefore eliminate the social value of an invention or innovation, as those

---

48   See the Chapter "Creativity as a Commodity" in Suarez-Villa, *Technocapitalism*.

49   See Chopra and Dexter, *Decoding Liberation*.

50   Letting inventions out of corporate proprietary control is usually not considered, out of concern they might be picked up by competitors. See Choate, *Hot Property*; Joe

that do not generate exchange and surplus value are terminated in favor of the ones that do. Limited resources practically guarantee this outcome whenever corporate appropriation is exclusive (as it is in current intellectual property regimes).

From a critical perspective all forms of value, whether exchange, market, surplus, social or use value, are socially mediated. All forms of value are therefore affected by social factors, such as the relations of power between corporations and society, class relations, socioeconomic inequalities, and the regulatory power of governance. A major feature of technocapitalism and its globalization, however, is the appropriation of the results of creativity by corporate power, and its control over arrangements that lead to market (or exchange) value. Corporate power therefore appropriates whatever market, exchange, and surplus value are obtained. Corporate power also influences greatly to what extent social value may occur, mainly because it sets research agendas, controls the commodification of creativity, and appropriates its results. Corporate power's influence over social value thus sets the stage for major contradictions and pathologies. As we will see later in this book, the globalization of corporate influence compounds those contradictions, with major impacts on life, work, public governance, culture and nature.

Globalization and Dysfunction

The globalization of technocapitalism means that the search for its most valuable resource, creativity, transcends boundaries and restraints. Commodifying creativity therefore acquires a global scope for the technocapitalist corporation, even though it is carried out within the corporate domain. Moreover, as it appropriates the results of creativity, the technocapitalist corporation becomes a powerful entity in the context of globalization. Its power takes up a supranational character that transcends the governance of any nation or locale. Corporate intellectual property regimes that are increasingly global in scope and enforcement magnify that power to an unprecedented extent. Thus, given the contemporary importance of technology, corporate technocapitalism is in a position to impose its influence around the world, particularly on societies with a limited possibility to create new technology.[51]

Anastasi, *The New Forensics: Investigating Corporate Fraud and the Theft of Intellectual Property* (New York: Wiley, 2003).

51 An example is Microsoft and its global hegemony over software. See James Wallace, *Overdrive: Bill Gates and the Race to Control Cyberspace* (New York: Wiley, 1997); Jennifer Edstrom and Martin Eller, *Barbarians Led by Bill Gates: Microsoft from the Inside, How the World's Richest Corporation Wields Its Power* (New York: Holt, 1998). Aggressive strategies have been at the core of many other tech corporations; see Karen Southwick, *Everyone Else Must Fail: The Unvarnished Truth About Oracle and Larry Ellison* (New York: Crown Business, 2003).

Control and Monopoly Power

Appropriating the results of creativity is the key to commodification and to corporate power.[52] Without it, corporatism cannot hope to protect its commodification of that most valuable resource, creativity. Appropriating the results of creativity is the key to corporate intellectual property, and can only be secured through commodification. Intellectual property thus provides corporatism with monopoly rights over a new invention, a phenomenon which is now global and increasingly important. Patents are the most important vehicle for such monopoly rights insofar as technocapitalism is concerned, given their association with new technologies. This monopoly power is now becoming global in scope and reach, as international bodies such as the World Trade Organization gear up for worldwide enforcement by imposing the rules of corporate property on any and all nations.

To sustain its monopoly rights over the results of creativity, corporate power must cast a global net over its intellectual property.[53] This often requires, among other strategies, the co-optation of politicians and of public governance to create laws that protect corporatism's monopoly power over intellectual property, even when those laws harm the public interest.[54] Corruption, done legally or not, is a common outcome as corporate power seeks to protect its appropriation of creativity. Co-optation and corruption of those charged with protecting the public interest is thereby turning corporatism into a shadow government in some nations. Election campaigns end up being funded by corporate interests, covertly or in some cases openly, as public governance becomes an appendage of corporate power.

The global net deployed by corporate power also accounts for the rapid rise of litigation over intellectual property around the world. The range of global corporate intellectual property litigation is increasingly broad and far-reaching. Given the widespread use of genetically engineered seeds, for example, an increasing amount of litigation involves agricultural activities. In some cases, farmers have been taken to court accused of intellectual property infringement, for not preventing pollen from genetically engineered plants from drifting into their

---

52   For most of the nineteenth century, US-based corporations generally did not respect patents or copyrights, and paid little in the way of royalties to inventors, a situation that changed as intangibles gained more importance. See Perelman, "Political Economy of Intellectual Property."

53   The global net is increasingly supported by supranational organizations governed by unelected technocrats. See Qingjiang Kong, *WTO, Internationalization and the Intellectual Property Rights Regime in China* (Singapore: Marshall Cavendish, 2005); Perelman, "Political Economy of Intellectual Property."

54   Microsoft's strategy to try to vanquish Linux software in Africa has included hiring government officials' relatives and paying government contractors large sums to switch to its products. See Steve Stecklow, "Microsoft Battles Low-Cost Rival for Africa," *Wall Street Journal* (October 28, 2008): A1.

crops.[55] Such suits usually claim the defendants benefit from the bioengineered seeds and plants without paying the corporations that own the patents. The drifting pollen is typically carried by winds that sweep over neighboring farms where the patented seeds are used, to farms that do not purchase the engineered seeds. Such intrusive attempts to protect corporate intellectual property may become common, as corporatism tightens its global net to profit from monopoly rights, and drive non-users to consume proprietary products by any means available.

Corporate appropriation of the results of creativity has gained such importance that it is now becoming a major global foreign policy objective for some nations. In the case of the United States, for example, bilateral trade negotiations, including the so-called free trade pacts, typically include demands for corporate intellectual property protection. Not agreeing to the demands introduced by corporations in trade deals can imperil the negotiations. Some enthusiastic supporters of US global hegemony have gone so far as to link corporate intellectual property protection to the need for military threats against nations that refuse to bend to these demands.[56] The "hidden hand" of the market is thus being joined by a "hidden fist" of military power, to make the world "safe" for the corporate appropriation of creativity and of its results. Presumably, we might see in the twenty-first century wars over intangibles, much as the nineteenth and twentieth centuries witnessed wars over tangible resources.[57]

Dysfunctional Inequities

There are two major dysfunctional aspects embedded in technocapitalism's global dynamic. Both are deeply entwined with corporate control and its appropriation of creativity. One resides *within commodification* itself which, as noted earlier in this chapter, is under corporate control. This aspect has significant global implications, particularly for nations with limited possibilities of generating new technology.

---

55 In one specific case, Monsanto, a global corporation that sells genetically engineered seeds and has a considerable number of patents in that field, accused a Canadian farmer of stealing its intellectual property because seeds and pollen from neighboring farms drifted into his land. The judge in the case ruled in favor of Monsanto, despite the lack of any evidence of intent or willful use of the seeds, which had drifted into the accused farmer's property. See Perelman, *Steal this Idea*, pp. 123–24. Such cases can be part of a corporate strategy to induce farmers to buy the genetically engineered seeds to avoid litigation. See Doug Cameron, "Monsanto Says New Seeds Are on Track As Sales Drop," *Wall Street Journal* (January 7, 2010): B7.

56 This view has been been advocated in Thomas Friedman's *The Lexus and the Olive Tree* (New York: Farrar, Strauss and Giroux, 1999), p. 373.

57 See Samir Amin and James H. Membrez, *Liberal Virus: Permanent War and the Americanization of the World* (New York: Monthly Review Press, 2004); James F. Petras and Henry Veltmeyer, *Empire with Imperialism: The Globalizing Dynamics of Neo-Liberal Capitalism* (New York: Palgrave Macmillan, 2005); Noam Chomsky, *Hegemony or Survival: America's Quest for Global Dominance* (New York: Holt, 2004).

The globalization of corporate technocapitalism means that some functions of commodification must be based in certain nations, typically rich ones. Those countries are the ones which have geared up for "fast" accumulation, to an extent that allows them to generate the talents needed by corporatism to invent and innovate on a large scale. Three major functions within commodification discussed earlier in this chapter, fragmentation, disengagement and exchange, are therefore split and contribute to major inequities between rich and poor nations.

Fragmentation is usually a rich-nation operation, dealing with research that involves the exercise of creativity in major ways. This function usually targets invention, and deals with basic research questions that might lead to significant breakthroughs. It is also a very risky function, affected by much uncertainty over outcomes and means. The rich-nation base of fragmentation is part of the reason why technological diffusion is usually hierarchical, with rich nations at the top of the diffusion hierarchy and the poorest ones at the bottom. This condition allows technological diffusion to become part of neo-imperial designs on the part of some rich nations, as we will see later in this book. Imposing obligations that target intellectual property, governance, markets, tangible resources, and any other aspect that suits corporate power and neo-imperial domination, becomes part of the new global game of conquest.

Disengagement is mostly a rich-nation function as well, deployed by corporate power wherever it happens to tap the resources of fast accumulation. Detaching the results of creativity from a creative process (and from those who exercise creativity) is highly linked to fragmentation. The same applies to the alienation of those who exercise creativity from its results, which is also typical of the disengagement function. However, the globalization of technocapitalism and its corporate agents is conferring a worldwide dimension to disengagement. The latter now encompasses the world at large, in the sense that detaching and alienating are not necessarily confined to rich nations where research happens to be undertaken. They now involve other nations as well, as the results of creativity are diffused around the world as products or services, to be used by potentially hundreds of millions of people. Whether they realize it or not, masses of users and consumers in poor nations thereby become "partners" (in a manner of speaking) in the disengagement function.

The exchange function is by far the most global within commodification. Rich, poor and in-between nations are all potential markets for the results of creativity that corporatism appropriates. If anything, poor nations may be targeted intensely, when demand for the results of creativity (in the form of products and services) tapers off in rich nations. This may occur because of the entry of newer products in rich nations, stiffer competition, or market saturation. In some cases, technology products become cheaper over time as they are massively consumed (and produced), and can flood poor-nation markets. Cellular telephones are one such example. Their rapid diffusion to poor nations was aided by the possibility of leapfrogging the conventional telephone and its costly infrastructure.

The split of the fragmentation and disengagement functions with the exchange function deepens the *techno-divide* between rich and poor nations. The latter are primarily targeted for marketing whatever corporatism appropriates, and for manufacturing the products based on that appropriation, at the lowest possible cost. Rich nations, in turn, are where the "brains" of the corporate appropriation machine operate, through the research-based fragmentation and disengagement functions. They are also, nonetheless, markets for those products of corporate appropriation, regardless of where they are produced. Production is a thoroughly global operation nowadays, as numerous nations with low costs vie for corporate investment, often at great expense to themselves by offering subsidies and bending to most any corporate demand. Trade pacts in various areas of the world have lubricated such competition, enshrining corporate demands in treaties from which poor nations may find it very difficult to extricate themselves, if they ever try to do so.

Associated with the deepening techno-divide is the "brain drain" from poor to rich nations. Globalization has made this phenomenon more bountiful than ever for corporate power, as we will see later in this book. Individuals with technologically creative talents now add to the growing brain-drain streams that support the corporate commodification of creativity. Poor nations thus often find themselves pre-empted from benefiting from the talents they paid for (through massive educational and social expenditures) with their scarce resources, as their most talented leave and join corporate research operations in richer nations.[58]

The second dysfunctional aspect involves the *split between commodification and reproduction*. The split between those two elements, discussed previously in this chapter, is deepened by the globalization of technocapitalism and its corporate agents.[59] The commodification of creativity, which remains under corporate control, is itself functionally split, as noted earlier. The reproduction of creativity, a socially mediated phenomenon, is largely outside corporate control. This cleavage between reproduction and commodification has significant implications for the techno-divide between rich and poor nations.

The split between commodification and reproduction further deepens the *techno-divide* between rich and poor. Most poor nations are unable to support reproduction in any significant way, at least at the level needed to generate technological creativity comparable to those in rich nations. Poor nations are largely outside the dynamic of fast accumulation, lacking the resources to generate substantial new tacit knowledge endogenously. Similarly, the accumulation dynamics of infrastructure and capital generally lag far behind those of rich nations. Reproduction therefore ultimately benefits rich nations, compounding their fast accumulation dynamics and the power of their corporations.

These social contexts where reproduction occurs are themselves part of the deepening techno-divide between rich and poor nations. The socio-dimensional

58 See William K. Tabb, *Unequal Partners: A Primer on Globalization* (New York: New Press, 2002), and his *Economic Governance in the Age of Globalization* (New York: Columbia University Press, 2004).

59 For a discussion of the split between commodification and reproduction, see the chapter "Creativity as a Commodity" in Suarez-Villa, *Technocapitalism*.

features of creativity, discussed previously in this chapter, are specific to a social context and to its social relations. However, globalization is largely non-specific, in the sense that it tries to "homogenize" and wipe out specificities that stand in the way of corporate conquest. In this sense, globalization is potentially destructive of any cultural influences on creativity that cannot be co-opted to serve corporate priorities.

This dynamic of global corporate conquest tends to make reproduction itself more uncertain and potentially dysfunctional. After all, the reproduction of creativity relies on rich and diverse cultural influences, many of which may be contrarian to the needs of corporate power. Steamrolling over cultural values or influences that resist corporate power is bound to damage reproduction, thereby shortchanging one of the most important phenomena of technocapitalism. As it conquers peoples and markets through globalization, corporate technocapitalism therefore sows the seeds of its dysfunction, facing contradictions that it cannot hope to resolve except by diminishing human values and social wellbeing.

Conclusion

Intangibles fundamentally support the evolution of capitalism. *Creativity, the most important intangible of technocapitalism, is turned into a commodity for the sake of corporate power and profit.* Much as tangible resources were turned into commodities in previous stages of capitalism, so the commodification of creativity is a major corporate endeavor under technocapitalism.

Commodification is one of the two fundamental phenomena that underpin technocapitalism. It is largely under *corporate* control, and seeks to appropriate the results of creativity on a global scale. *Research is the corporate operation through which such appropriation typically occurs.* Appropriating the results of creativity has therefore become a major vehicle to sustain and expand the global ambitions of corporate power. Intellectual property rights that confer monopoly power, such as patents, are now a very important concern of corporatism. The fact that corporate intellectual property has become a major component of international trade, and an important focus of litigation around the world, underlines the rising importance of creativity as a corporate resource.

Reproduction, another phenomenon underpinning technocapitalism, is inherently *social* and largely outside corporate control. Reproduction regenerates creativity and is increasingly global in scope and reach. It is fundamental for any exercise of creativity, and makes it possible for both socially-acquired and innate talents to be deployed in research. *Reproduction is inherently social because of creativity's intangibility, because of its qualitative character, and because it depends on social contexts and social relations to develop.* Many aspects of reproduction are antithetical to the corporate commodification of creativity, yet they are essential if this intangible resource is to be regenerated and deployed.

The cleavage between those two fundamental phenomena, commodification and reproduction, is a source of major contradictions and pathologies. In the context of globalization, the split between reproduction and commodification deepens the techno-divide between rich and poor nations. Rich nations are most capable to sustain the platform of resources needed by technocapitalism. Fast accumulation and basic research are thus a prerogative of wealthy nations, subject to their global influence, and controlled by their corporate interests. *One outcome of this situation is that corporatism increasingly sets research agendas for technology and science on a global scale.* Deepening the techno-divide between rich and poor, co-opting governments, and setting up global standards that protect its interests are some of the effects. Perhaps then it should not surprise that fueling the neo-imperial ambitions of certain nations, and co-opting supranational organizations that regulate trade, have become important corporate priorities.

In the following chapter we will see how corporatism is itself being transformed by its quest to commodify intangibles and project its influence around the globe. Commodifying intangibles requires organizations that are highly focused on research and on appropriating the results of creativity. Organizational regimes that exploit intangibles increasingly require a global supply of talent that transcends boundaries, governance, and cultures. They must also try to establish an internal apparatus of control that can support research and generate continuous streams of new inventions and innovations. Corporate organizations typical of the twenty-first century will therefore be quite different from those of the past, particularly ones that were mainly concerned with production. Corporatism thus molds itself to the dynamics of technocapitalism, as it seeks to impose its power and priorities around the world.

The New Global Corporatism

The globalization of technocapitalism depends on a new kind of corporatism. The new corporate organizations spawned by technocapitalism are deeply grounded in technology and science through research creativity—a resource that is at the core of this new version of capitalism. Creativity, the most precious resource, becomes a global corporate commodity to be appropriated and exploited on a worldwide scale through new organizational forms.

Despite its distinctive characteristics, the worldwide quest for corporate power and profit of this new era parallels the earlier globalization of industrial capitalism. As the factory production regimes of industrial capitalism sought new frontiers to advance corporate domination, so the technocapitalist corporation's research-driven regime seeks new ground to impose its agendas and priorities. Domination here involves new relations of power on a worldwide scale, based not on production and factory labor processes, but on research, creative power and the appropriation of new ideas. And much as the global power of corporate industrial capitalism planted the seeds of its own dysfunctions, crises and pathologies, so the global relations of power of corporate technocapitalism create new pathologies and crises. As we will see in this chapter, those pathologies are intrinsic to technocapitalism, and are based on its peculiar contradictions and exploitive modes.

The new corporatism depends greatly on the accumulation phenomena discussed earlier in this book. Most of all, the global accumulation of tacit knowledge is directly relevant to this new form of corporate power. Its dependence on creativity and research turns tacit knowledge into an essential asset, to be sought and mined whenever and wherever it may occur. All the more so when it has the potential to generate creativity, and when it can lead to greater corporate power over research. Codified knowledge accumulation is also of importance to the new corporatism, particularly when combined with tacit knowledge. Much as industrial capitalism depended on capital accumulation, the new corporatism depends greatly on the new accumulation modes discussed earlier.

Research in the new corporatist domain typically involves commodifying creativity. Control over commodification is therefore of great importance, given the urgent need to turn the results of creativity into products or services that can obtain surplus value (and, ultimately, profit). The intangibility of creativity, however, introduces contradictions and dysfunctions to the corporate control apparatus, given the elusive, qualitative character of this most precious resource. Unlike the production routines and labor processes of industrial capitalism, which could be quantified and programmed to a great extent, sustaining research and exploiting creativity through commodification require a very different control regime. As we will see in this chapter, that regime creates major quandaries for corporate power, given the high levels of uncertainty and risk that usually accompany research, and the compounding effects of globalization.

Emerging sectors spawned by technocapitalism provide the best examples of the new corporatism. Companies in biotechnology, nanotechnology, bioinformatics and biorobotics, among other new sectors, embody this form of corporatism. Those are organizations that are mostly (in some cases solely) dedicated to research and the appropriation of its results. When production and other operations exist, research is nonetheless the most important function. Genetic decoding companies, for example, are often solely dedicated to research. This involves the deciphering of data used to apply for patents. Their complex research operations usually require specialists from diverse fields, such as bioinformatics, genetics, microbiology, medicine and others, along with lawyers and financiers. Once patents are obtained, they are used to generate revenue by licensing to pharmaceutical and biotech companies on a worldwide basis, which use them to create new products. The genetic decoding companies therefore depend on their research for survival, and usually have no production, marketing or distribution operations of their own.

Globalization affects this new form of corporatism in myriad ways. Among them, for example, is the global character of external networks needed to reproduce creativity, which are largely outside corporate control. Creative talent also needs to be searched for on a worldwide basis, by tapping brain-drain flows, establishing branch operations, or by outsourcing some research activities. Outsourcing, for example, often involves clinical testing of potential new biotech products around the world, in places where costs are low, regulations are weak, and abundant test populations are available. The global scope of corporate technocapitalism is therefore broad and flexible, despite its high research intensity and its dependence on creativity.

The new corporatism and its association with the globalization of technocapitalism will be considered in this chapter. A major phenomenon affecting the organizational ecology of technocapitalism, the decomposition of corporate functions, will help place the emergence of the new corporatism in perspective. As we will see, the new corporatism is part and parcel of the long-term evolution of capitalism, with parallels in the corporate modes of previous versions of capitalism. The commodification of research creativity and the systematized research regimes that support it are major elements of the new corporatism and are supported by the global spread of experimentalism. Pathological tendencies related to the corporate exploitation of creativity and to the experimentalist ethos will be considered, to provide insights on the social effects of this new version of corporate capitalism.

Fast Decomposition and Globalization

Fast decomposition involves *externalizing* (or dismantling) corporate functions through networks. The networks are external to the corporate context and are therefore largely out of the control of corporate power. These networks are now global in scope and scale, enhanced by the spread of communications technology. Fast decomposition therefore places what previously were internal functions outside the domain of any given corporation. As we will soon see, fast decomposition is an unavoidable feature of the technocapitalist dynamic, and is inextricably related to the needs of this new form of global capitalism.

Practically no corporate function is immune to fast decomposition, although research is most likely to remain in-house given its importance for corporate survival. Production, marketing, distribution, technical support, and most every other function is therefore "decomposable" in the global context of technocapitalism. Those functions were usually retained in-house in corporate organizations associated with previous stages of capitalism, when the main resources were tangible and could be commodified and reproduced internally.[1] Keeping functions in-house thus reassured corporate power, allowing it to manipulate labor processes, production or service routines, and day-to-day management. De-skilling of labor, the onset of automation, more repressive management, and a degradation of work in factory and services production were some of the results.[2]

Fast decomposition is network-based and global in scope and reach. Old, established industrial sectors and service activities, whose emergence was closely associated with previous stages of capitalism, are as vulnerable to fast decomposition as the new activities and sectors of technocapitalism. This is already obvious in the increasingly complex web of supply chains, diverse multiple sourcing nets, and the myriad uses of B2B (business-to-business) relations made possible by Internet- and Web-based networks. Fast decomposition is therefore affecting almost all industries and services, from aircraft manufacturing to fast-food service production.[3]

This phenomenon is related to the larger, functional split between the commodification and the reproduction of creativity, that affects the corporate

---

1 Aided by the high degree of vertical integration in the factory regimes of early and middle industrial capitalism, which made it possible to keep tight control over labor processes. See Eric Hobsbawm, *The Age of Capital, 1848–1875* (New York: New American Library, 1979), and his *Labouring Men: Studies in the History of Labour* (London: Weidenfeld and Nicolson, 1964). The character of factory labor processes addressed by Marx in Volume 1, Part III ("The Production of Absolute Surplus Value") of *Capital* [New York: International Publishers, 1967; orig. published in 1867 (Hamburg: Verlag von Otto Meissner)] was made possible by having both commodification and reproduction under internal control.

2 See Harry Braverman, *Labor and Monopoly Capital* (New York: Monthly Review Press, 1974); David F. Noble, *Forces of Production: A Social History of Industrial Automation* (New York: Knopf, 1984). De-skilling and degradation of work advanced from factory production regimes to service production regimes, and continues to do so in our time. See Julie Jargon, "Latest Starbucks Buzzword: 'Lean' Japanese Techniques," *Los Angeles Times* (August 4, 2009): A1.

3 See Michael V. Copeland, "Boeing's Big Dream," *Fortune* (May 5, 2008): 180–91.

organizations typical of technocapitalism. This characteristic feature of technocapitalism, discussed in previous chapters, is both cause and effect of fast decomposition, in a dialectical sense. Together, fast decomposition and the split between commodification and reproduction make corporate power more dependent on external social contexts and, dialectically, they also make those social contexts more vulnerable to corporate intrusion and manipulation. Complicating and magnifying the relations of power of these phenomena is the global scope and reach of corporate technocapitalism. A major outcome of these phenomena is that it is no longer possible for corporations to view themselves as entities separate from society. The old, laissez-faire notion of corporations being apart from society, to look narrowly or solely after their own interest, therefore seems outdated. Corporations are now more a product of society, and of specific social contexts, as fast decomposition makes inroads into most every corporate organization.

Fast decomposition depends greatly on the new accumulation modes discussed in a previous chapter. The accumulation of tacit and codified knowledge are particularly important for fast decomposition. These two accumulation modes are also fundamental for the reproduction of creativity, and for its capacity to generate new ideas. Without them, fast decomposition would be as viable as a rainstorm without water. The reproduction of creativity and fast decomposition are thus inextricably related to each other, through the new accumulation phenomena that involve knowledge, and through the global networks that support both reproduction and the diffusion of knowledge.

Why does fast decomposition occur? The most important driver of fast decomposition is the urgent corporate need to reproduce and gain access to creativity. Intangible resources such as creativity must be reproduced externally because corporate organizations cannot do so internally. The inability of corporations to adequately reproduce and tap those intangible resources in-house, by their own means, is therefore behind the need to externalize functions.

Reproducing creativity typically requires diverse, knowledge-rich interactions which only external, network-supported social contexts can provide. The multidisciplinarity of talents needed to undertake research in the sectors and corporations typical of technocapitalism is also closely related to the need for fast decomposition. The complexity of talents and fields makes it practically impossible to sustain research without external, network-based social relations. Corporate functions which do not directly strengthen or support research thus become more likely to be externalized. This situation is compounded by the expensive and complex experimental hardware usually needed in the sectors typical of technocapitalism. Such hardware often drains resources from other, non-research related corporate functions, and makes it necessary to externalize the latter if doing so reduces costs.

Compounding this scenario are the global competitive conditions which technocapitalist corporations often find themselves in. Aggressive competition means that substantial resources must be devoted to research and development

(R&D) in order to survive. Deploying substantial resources in research is typically the only way to stay "competitive" and stave off threats or predation from other companies. Investing substantial resources in research is all too often also the only way to reduce the risks posed by high failure rates in research. Declining time lags between the introduction of a new product in the market and the entry of rival ones also poses a formidable challenge to technocapitalist corporations, requiring more investment in research to speed up tasks or engage in parallel testing.[4] All this means that externalization of non-research related functions becomes unavoidable, as the necessity to target or conserve available resources for research projects turns into a major corporate priority.

The sectors closely associated with technocapitalism provide the best examples of this dynamic. In biotechnology very high failure rates, often as high as 8,000:1, for compounds created through research, are common.[5] Those failure rates typically occur during testing and the regulatory approval process, before any marketing can occur. Testing and regulatory approval often take as long as five to ten years, and require substantial resources. The high risk and uncertainty involved means that biotech companies typically can only undertake a very narrow set of functions internally, which are usually those closely related to research.

Adding to this scenario of high risk and uncertainty is the fact that most biotech products which receive final approval to be marketed are often unprofitable. In some cases, the products may not work as expected, while in others new rival products that are less costly, more effective, or are promoted by more powerful competitors may enter and prevail in the market. Thus, many biotech corporations have to rely on a narrow set of "hit" products to be able to cover their research costs, let alone generate any profit. In many cases, biotech corporations also seek to be subcontracted for research work from other biotech companies, or from large pharmaceutical corporations in order to cover expenses. Selling or licensing important patents to those pharmaceutical corporations sometimes provide a source of revenue that can support research.[6]

The high risk and uncertainty that are so characteristic of corporate biotech research, and the decomposed nature of this sector, often means that corporations in most fields within biotechnology tend to be small and are highly focused on research. Constellations of small companies, typically interrelated with many other companies, are one of the results. They are often driven and sustained

---

4   Time lag reductions between the introduction of a new product and the entry of rival products is worrisome to corporate power. See Rajshee Agarwal and Michael Gort, "First-Mover Advantage and the Speed of Competitive Entry, 1887–1986," *Journal of Law and Economics* 44(2001): 161–77.

5   Ernst and Young LLP, *Beyond Borders: Global Biotechnology Report* (Palo Alto, CA: Ernst and Young LLP, 2006).

6   See Marilyn Chase, "How Genentech Wins at Blockbuster Drugs," *Wall Street Journal* (June 5, 2007): B1; Ron Winslow and Avery Johnson, "Drug Firms Bet Big on High-Risk Deals," *Wall Street Journal* (March 17, 2009): A1.

by subcontracting agreements with one another, and by relational or mutually supportive arrangements that are network-based, and are grounded in long-standing social contacts and professional interactions. With the spread of biotechnology those constellations of companies are becoming more global, as more nations develop biotech capabilities, and as the companies they spawn insert themselves in the global framework of decomposition.

Older sectors and industries associated with industrial capitalism have also been greatly affected by the decomposition dynamic. Aircraft manufacturing, for example, once a "national pride" industrial sector, which structured many functions in-house and relied greatly on single-nation supply chains, has decomposed globally. Aircraft corporations now concentrate their resources more on research, which typically involves design, and externalize many activities related to production, including the assembly of components, customer technical support, and the manufacture of complex systems such as avionics.[7] Much as occurred earlier in the automotive industry, aircraft manufacturing has thus decomposed substantially, relying on networks of other companies to undertake the functions that were long done in-house or by closely held subsidiaries. The global scope of decomposition in this industry pinpoints the importance of research and its increasing claim on corporate resources. Corporate power thus has little choice but to decompose its domain, as research and creativity become key factors for survival while production and other non-research functions are externalized.

Networks

Networks play a central role in the phenomenon of decomposition. They are *the vehicle* of fast decomposition and are now global in scope and scale. The social mediation, the relations, and the arrangements that are fundamental to fast decomposition are built and sustained through networks. Those networks are typically external to the corporate domain, and are therefore largely outside the control of corporate power.

Why do networks play such an important role in fast decomposition? The *split* between the commodification and the reproduction of intangible resources, that is a hallmark of technocapitalism, is by far the most important cause of their importance. That split, addressed in a previous chapter, makes it unavoidable for the reproduction of intangibles such as creativity to occur outside the corporate realm. Given the impossibility of reproducing creativity internally, under its control, corporate power has little choice but to seek this vital process externally. As we will see later, this fundamental split between reproduction and commodification is behind many of the social pathologies of technocapitalist corporatism.

Networks are essential for fast decomposition because of the *complexity* of this phenomenon and the nature of the intangibles that corporations must use. The complex nature of intangibles needed in research, and the multidimensional character of social relations needed to reproduce creativity and other intangible resources,

---

7   See Copeland, "Boeing."

make it necessary to depend on external networks. Those intangible resources are impossible to access fully through bilateral, inter-corporate arrangements of the sort that were common during late industrial capitalism. External networks embedding a multiplicity of social relations and influences therefore provide a means to deal with the complexity of fast decomposition.[8] Globalization now magnifies the range of those relations and influences, particularly for research programs that are highly dependent on creativity and on its reproduction.

The complexity of fast decomposition is increased by the global scope of the intangibles needed by the technocapitalist corporation, and by the vast (and also global) scale of social relations needed to reproduce them. Access to multidisciplinary talents needed for research creativity in the sectors typical of technocapitalism is increasingly global as well. In many areas of biotechnology research, for example, a vast, worldwide net often has to be cast to find the talents and intangibles needed, and to reproduce them. Many biotech research operations increasingly depend on a combination of talents from multiple fields, such as bioinformatics, molecular biology, medicine, chemistry, biopharmacology, genetic engineering and zoology, among others. The creative talents from those fields often have to be recruited from various nations, especially when very high skill levels are required. The reproduction of the intangibles embedded in those talents often also require a global net of multidimensional contacts, collaboration, sharing, and reciprocity that corporations are unable to provide or understand.

The complexity of fast decomposition is, for example, compounded by the nature of the products created in biotech. Unlike pharmaceutical products, which are usually in pill or tablet form, many biotech products are protein-based therapies of vast molecular complexity, that are injected into patients. The complex molecular structure of the biotech products often requires living cells in bio-reactors, in contrast with the inert ingredients in conventional pharmaceutical products. Deep contrasts in molecular weight between pharmaceutical and biotech products reflect this complexity. The molecular weight of a biotech product-therapy (such as Epogen), for example, is often about 8,500 percent greater than that of a widely used pharmaceutical product (such as Zantac).[9] This kind of complexity is also a factor behind the occurrence of unexpected side effects and deaths.[10]

Software research provides another example of the vast, worldwide net involving intangibles such as creativity. The most effective way to reproduce creativity and generate new knowledge in this field is through Open Source networks. The Open Source software research networks are important because

---

8   The multiplicity of those social relations and influences is largely a product of *network extent*; see the Chapter "Networks as Mediators," in Luis Suarez-Villa *Technocapitalism: A Critical Perspective on Technological Innovation and Corporatism* (Philadelphia: Temple University Press, 2009).

9   James C. Mullen, "Gene Therapy," *Wall Street Journal* (April 27, 2007): A17.

10   See Jeanne Whalen and Jennifer C. Dooren, "Drug Poses Risk of Infection," *Wall Street Journal* (February 20, 2009): B3

they serve as worldwide vehicles for the reproduction of creativity, and because they can do so completely out of the reach of corporate power. They are totally open and free to anyone who wants to join, are non-profit and non-capitalist in orientation, stimulate collaboration and sharing, and require all work to be posted so that it can be freely available to anyone who wants to use it, in or outside the network.[11] Those networks were responsible for the creation of the Linux software, which in some sectors has been displacing Microsoft's software around the world.[12]

The quality and reliability of the Linux software are higher than Microsoft's, because of the vast, worldwide amount and intensity of open, frequent testing by the networks' volunteers, as opposed to Microsoft's profit-driven and control-oriented corporate realm. Microsoft's attempt to control both commodification and reproduction in-house shows the glaring flaws of that corporate model. Microsoft's predominance, it seems, is due to the fact that it was created long before the Linux Open Source network came into existence, because it monopolized its market, and because it has employed hard-ball strategies to destroy or gravely damage corporate rivals.[13] The Linux Open Source network, however, proved impossible for Microsoft to destroy because of its global, open character, its non-corporatist ethos, and because of its formidable capacity to deal with complexity and reproduce creativity.

An example of the rising importance of external networks for research involves parallel experimentation. Parallel experimentation allows for research experiments to occur simultaneously in various laboratories around the world, thus saving time, costs, and allowing faster diffusion of findings.[14] The globalization of communication technologies, and most of all the Internet and the Web, have made this phenomenon possible. Research steps and procedures can therefore be adjusted to take immediate findings into account. Sharing details and interpretations at each step as they occur, have made it possible for researchers to collaborate and share tacit knowledge instantaneously on an unprecedented scale. Such at-distance collaboration has also opened up doors to many possibilities for reproducing creativity, which are typically out of corporate control even when experiments and laboratories are owned or managed by corporate entities.

The intangible resources in question, and most of all creativity, are also external and practically impossible to accumulate internally, within the corporate domain,

---

11   See Johan Söderberg, *Hacking Capitalism: The Free and Open Source Software Movement* (New York: Routledge, 2007).

12   See Söderberg, *Hacking Capitalism*; Peter Wayner, *Free for All: How Linux and the Free Software Movement Undercut the High Tech Titans* (New York: HarperBusiness, 2000).

13   See James Wallace, *Overdrive: Bill Gates and the Race to Control Cyberspace* (New York: Wiley, 1997); Frederic A Maxwell, *Bad Boy Ballmer: The Man Who Runs Microsoft* (New York: Morrow, 2002).

14   See Wesley Shrum, Joel Genuth and Ivan Chompalov, *Structures of Scientific Collaboration* (Cambridge: MIT Press, 2007).

because they are global and mobile. In biotechnology, for example, while many nations may not yet have strong research capabilities, they nonetheless generate researchers who migrate. Their migration is often conditioned by study abroad or by economic and career-related reasons. Once removed from their nations of birth or home culture, many highly skilled researchers often move frequently across nations and between corporate entities.[15] Such mobility, which is unprecedented, makes it difficult for corporate entities to retain, much less accumulate, creative talents in-house for long.

Similarly, in software research accumulating an assemblage of creative talents in-house, that might be comparable to that of Open Source networks, is practically impossible. Even in the rare case where a very rich corporation can muster the resources to assemble a substantial combination of talents in-house, the results will likely be much less desirable than those generated through external networks. The now-legendary flaws found in Microsoft's products, compared to the quality of Open Source (Linux) software, attest to the importance of networks for accessing creativity and providing greater quality.[16]

Another factor supporting the importance of external networks in fast decomposition is that they are more effective for reducing uncertainty and risk than corporate organizations. This happens because external, non-corporate social relations based on networks are more likely to elicit trust and constructive reciprocity than in-house ties. The ties that occur within the corporate domain are all too often based on command-and-control rules over those who must exercise creativity. They frequently involve the sort of calculating behavior that leads to opportunism, concealment, deception, or underhanded schemes between managerial power and those who must exercise their creativity. Interpersonal and professional competition between researchers, usually encouraged by management to divide and rule over employees (or prevent their solidarity against managerial abuses), are often part of corporate command-and-control routines. To a great extent, these symptoms of pathology are a product of the nature of commodification within the corporate domain.[17]

While even under those conditions some trust may occur between some researchers, the kinds of social relations embedded in external networks are nonetheless more likely to help creativity. Those external relations tend to be voluntary, open to change, and can empower self-development to an extent that corporate power, with its obsessive preoccupation with profits, cannot do. From a broader perspective, it must also be taken into account that rising inter- and intra-corporate competition has made distrust and malfeasance a major phenomenon

---

15   See *The Economist*, "Economics Focus: Give Me Your Scientists; Restricting the Immigration of Highly Skilled Workers will Hurt America's Ability to Innovate" (March 7, 2009): 84.

16   See Samir Chopra and Scott D. Dexter, *Decoding Liberation: The Promise of Free and Open Source Software* (New York: Routledge, 2007).

17   See the chapter "Creativity as a Commodity" in Suarez-Villa, *Technocapitalism*.

within the corporate domain. Globalization has contributed to this dynamic by intensifying such competition at all levels of corporate endeavors, internal and external. The high and rising incidence of litigation over corporate theft of intellectual property, over espionage, and the pilfering of ideas as an integral part of corporate strategy are some of the outcomes of this phenomenon.[18]

Finally, globalization has made network extent more important than ever for fast decomposition. Network extent is a composite of features which comprises qualitative and quantitative dimensions, dealing with such aspects as range, accessibility, and composition.[19] Greater network extent is vital for the reproduction of creativity and for accessing this vital intangible of technocapitalism. In general, the greater (or more abundant) the network extent, the more valuable a network becomes for supporting the reproduction of creativity. This nexus between abundance and greater value defies one of the key principles of classical and neoclassical economics: the notion that scarcity leads to greater value.[20] Because it is practically impossible for any corporation to develop sufficient network extent in-house, even in very large corporate domains, external networks provide the best means to reproduce creativity and access this intangible resource.

Globalization has made it easier to achieve greater network extent for creativity because of the myriad opportunities and richer diversity of possibilities that occur as national and cultural boundaries are transcended. The influence of information and communication technologies has been a major factor in this regard, making it easier to diffuse tacit and codified knowledge. Dialectically, however, globalization has also made it possible to use greater network extent to obliterate cultural values that are closely connected with creativity, but are antithetical to corporate control and to the values of corporate power.[21] Those values may, for example, encompass traditions that encourage sharing, collaboration, and that discourage aggressive competition. Those cultural values are usually embedded in social relations that affect creative endeavors involving employment and learning. The destruction of those values in many cultures typically results in alienation, at both individual

---

18   Subcontracting for espionage can become part of corporate competitive strategy, particularly those based on the practices of government intelligence agencies. See Jeremy Scahill, "Blackwater's Bright Future," *Los Angeles Times* (June 16, 2008): A15, and his *Blackwater: The Rise of the World's Most Powerful Mercenary Army* (New York: Nation Books, 2007). Companies such as Blackwater Worldwide provide intelligence-gathering. See Jonathan R. Laing, "The Shadow CIA," *Barron's* (October 15, 2001), http://online. barrons.com/article/SB1002927557434087960.html; *Wikipedia*, "Stratfor," http:// en.wikipedia.org.

19   See the section "Network Extent" in Suarez-Villa, *Technocapitalism*.

20   The notion that greater value is always derived from greater scarcity has been a cornerstone of classical and neoclassical economics. See the chapter "Networks as Mediators" in Suarez-Villa, *Technocapitalism*.

21   See Dan Schiller, *Digital Capitalism: Networking the Global Market System* (Cambridge: MIT Press, 1999); Kevin Robins and Frank Webster, *Times of the Technoculture: From the Information Society to the Virtual Life* (New York: Routledge, 1999).

and collective levels, and in social pathologies that often involve deceit, theft, vandalism and other anti-social actions.

Information and communication technologies have also made it easier to achieve greater network extent rapidly, and to strengthen the reach of corporate power and market capitalism in general. No corner of the world, no matter how remote or impenetrable its culture, can now be considered invulnerable to the reach of corporate power.[22] The new communication technologies have also allowed corporatism to overcome most every obstacle, while at the same time those technologies are closely controlled by corporate capital. One element therefore feeds the other, in a mutually reinforcing way, as corporatism controls, and benefits from, those new technologies in its global quest for profit and power. The times when public governance could keep some economic and social functions out of the control of corporate capitalism therefore seem to have passed into history. The greater network extent provided by globalization thus embeds a great deal of dualism, on the one hand allowing more and better opportunities to reproduce creativity, while on the other it extends the power and reach of corporatism around the world.

Decomposition or Disintegration?

It is important to differentiate fast decomposition from another process typical of prior phases of capitalism. Vertical disintegration was a common feature of middle and late industrial capitalism.[23] It involved externalizing functions, such as manufacturing and service tasks, through bilateral, inter-corporate arrangements. Subcontracting was the usual means for achieving vertical disintegration. The commonly accepted calculus was for vertical disintegration to be pursued until the cost of externalizing functions exceeded the cost of keeping them in-house.[24] Vertical disintegration was therefore assumed to be based on a quantitative decision rule which overshadowed all other aspects.

Networks differentiate fast decomposition from vertical disintegration. The kinds of networks through which fast decomposition occurs are largely outside the control of corporate power, unlike the bilateral, inter-corporate arrangements which were typical of vertical disintegration. Vertical disintegration helped corporate power maintain control over commodification and reproduction, even when in-house corporate activities were externalized, because of the bilateral

---

22   See Schiller, *Digital Capitalism.*

23   See Braverman, *Labor and Monopoly Capital*; Noble, *Forces of Production.*

24   Simplistic as it may seem, this notion was credited with winning the Nobel Prize for economist Ronald Coase ["The Nature of the Firm," *Economica* 4(1937): 386–405]. Coase's precept became a major heuristic for mainstream (neoclassical) economists who tried to explain the rise of outsourcing during the 1990s, to the exclusion of other (often more important) considerations that involve relations of power, internal control, and qualitative issues.

arrangements that were usually employed. Subcontracting was a common target for those arrangements. Whether such subcontracting occurred through formal, contractual vehicles *or* the relational type (based less on contractual grounds), it was usually possible for the subcontracting party to control or specify what the subcontracted would do. The history of industrial capitalism, and the vertical disintegration of industrial and service corporations, provides ample evidence of that key feature.[25] Control over commodification and reproduction was all the more easy to maintain when the subcontracted organization was a subsidiary of the subcontracting company, or when the latter held some stake in the former, as often occurred with the supply chains of industrial and service corporations.[26]

Another contrasting aspect of vertical disintegration is that the resources it involved were usually tangible. All too often, arrangements for vertical disintegration comprised tangible resources, such as raw materials, parts or physical labor. When some intangibles were involved, such as services (accounting or marketing, for example), they typically were for routine or standardized operations rather than research. In the case of fast decomposition, on the other hand, the most important resources are *intangible*, are rich in creativity, and typically have a direct relationship with invention and innovation through research.

Because the resources of fast decomposition are intangible, they are primarily *qualitative* and defy easy or conventional quantification. In contrast, the resources of vertical disintegration were mostly calibrated in quantitative terms, and could be easily or conventionally measured. This occurred because decisions revolved mostly around cost issues, quantitative standards, or established markets. The most important resource of fast decomposition, creativity, on the other hand, is not only qualitative in nature and character, but is quite elusive and often has no markets, at least not the kind that can lead to pre-established outcomes, standards or measures. Uncertainty is a major feature of this intangible resource in a way that makes contractual arrangements (the ones typical of vertical disintegration) difficult or impossible to frame.

Globalization was clearly a dynamic force for vertical disintegration, at least during late industrial capitalism, as outsourcing became a worldwide phenomenon. Processes based on tangible resources were easy to outsource, since outcomes and

---

25   It was most visible in the strategies of large multinational corporations. See Richard J. Barnet, *Global Reach: The Power of the Multinational Corporations* (New York: Simon and Schuster, 1974); Isabel Studer-Noguez, *Ford and the Global Strategies of Multinationals: The North American Auto Industry* (New York: Routledge, 2003); Vincent P. Barabba, *Surviving Transformation: Lessons from GM's Surprising Turnaround* (Oxford: Oxford University Press, 2004). Vertical disintegration in the industrial capitalist corporation, however, did not involve research operations; see George Wise, *Willis R. Whitney, General Electric, and the Origins of US Industrial Research* (New York: Columbia University Press, 1985).

26   See Studer-Noguez, *Ford*; Roger D. Blair and David L. Kaserman, *Law and Economics of Vertical Integration and Control* (New York: Academic Press, 1983).

standards could be pre-established and quantified. Globalization has also greatly affected the intangibles of technocapitalism, such as creativity and knowledge, but in very different ways. One of those ways has been an extraordinary mobility in the migration of talent, usually referred to as the brain-drain phenomenon. Such "brain-drain" of talented researchers is typically unidirectional, toward rich nations, or multidirectional between rich nations.[27] In the case of poor nations, the consequences of brain-drain migration are often grave, as nations badly in need of developing their own technological and scientific capabilities are preempted from doing so. As we will see later in this book, brain-drain migration is closely related to corporate power in the context of technocapitalism, and to its need to secure that most precious intangible, research creativity.

Despite these unfolding global trends, corporatism has been unable to bridge the split between the commodification and the reproduction of creativity, a hallmark of technocapitalism. That split is, above all, what differentiates fast decomposition from vertical disintegration. With vertical disintegration, it was possible for corporate power to keep control over both commodification and reproduction, mainly because the resources utilized were tangible and standardized. With fast decomposition, however, the inability of corporate power to prevent that split creates major challenges to its global capacity to profit, control and exploit.

Challenges and Dysfunction

Fast decomposition poses several major challenges to corporate power. One of them is the longstanding problem of control, which has been a major feature of corporate capitalism since its inception. Fast decomposition and its reliance on external, diverse and relations-rich networks makes it practically impossible for corporate power to control its most important resources, most of all creativity. The globalization of those networks has only made it more complex for corporatism to gain access to those vital resources, despite networks' dualistic role in extending corporate power around the world.

This situation poses a major challenge to corporatism's longstanding propensity to control its environment. Such control has historically been a means for domination, not only over workers but also over the public sphere. Public governance has been a target of this penchant for domination and control since the earliest days of corporate capitalism. Control over its main resources, and of any institutions that affect access to those resources, has traditionally been regarded as essential by corporate power. Such control has been considered a major managerial priority since corporate management became a professional occupation. The ethos of corporatism therefore revolves very strongly around control over its resources,

27   See Michael P. Smith and Adrian Favell (eds.), *The Human Face of Global Mobility: International Highly Skilled Migration in Europe, North America, and the Asia-Pacific* (New Brunswick, NJ: Transaction, 2006); *The Economist*, "Give Me Your Scientists."

yet the character of technocapitalism and its globalization raises a major obstacle to this longstanding objective.

Another problem for corporatism is the dysfunctions that result from its inability to control its main resources, *and* from its attempt to compensate for this vital shortcoming by dominating public governance, and society at large. Among those dysfunctions are the alienation of those who must exercise their creativity in research, and the obsessive attempt to appropriate any and all results of the exercise of creativity. These internal dysfunctions are accompanied by external ones, such as co-opting public governance and officials to serve corporate interests. As we will see later, these problems often get compounded and turn into social pathologies with very negative consequences.

Globalization compounds those dysfunctions by magnifying and projecting them on a scale which recognizes no boundaries, national, cultural or legal. As a result, for example, the quest to appropriate the results of creativity acquire a global dimension. Intellectual property litigation, espionage and theft become more common than ever, and in some cases are an important (and usually covert) component of corporate strategy.[28] Cooptation of public governance then becomes a global project, as no public entity can be considered safe from corporate interference whenever their functions are important to the advancement of corporate power.

Globalization also magnifies another challenge facing corporatism. This challenge is grounded in the relations of power between corporatism and the external networks that are at the core of fast decomposition, and of the reproduction of creativity. This is a direct result of the previously discussed split between commodification and reproduction, which is a hallmark of technocapitalism. Corporatism can thus acquiesce to lose power to external networks and over decomposition, *or* it can limit access to external networks and compromise both the reproduction and commodification of creativity. Decisions made by corporate power on most every aspect of fast decomposition ride on how this challenge is addressed and, as we will see later, the failure to address it and in a socially responsible way is a source of pathology.

Fast, Global Research Regimes

The fast, global research regime is one of the hallmarks of technocapitalism. It is as much a part of this new version of capitalism as the processes of fast accumulation and fast decomposition. Research creativity is the most precious resource sustaining this new form of corporatism, much as production labor

---

28   See Joel Bakan, *The Corporation: The Pathological Pursuit of Profit and Power* (New York: Free Press, 2004); Michael Perelman, *Steal this Idea: Intellectual Property Rights and the Corporate Confiscation of Creativity* (New York: Palgrave Macmillan, 2004).

processes sustained corporate industrial capitalism. As previously discussed in this book, the intangibility of this precious resource, creativity, the fundamental split between commodification and reproduction, and the peculiar character of fast accumulation and fast decomposition, set this new version of capitalism apart from previous eras.

The term *research regime* can be defined as a corporate research apparatus which depends on creativity, on fast accumulation phenomena, and on fast decomposition in order to commodify creativity. Its scope is *global*, meaning that its access to creativity, and its dependence on accumulation and decomposition phenomena, require it to secure its resources from *any* place where their quality can sustain the quest for power and profit. Corporate power must therefore transcend any and all cultural, social, or national boundaries and restraints in order to advance its agenda. As we will see later in this book, this leads to a new form of imperialism, corporate-led and based on technology and science, which is more intrusive and in some ways more harmful than the old versions of empire.

The research regimes typical of technocapitalism require a *systematization* of research, for which creativity is fundamentally important. Systematization therefore means that research is and must be undertaken in a systematic and continuous way, such that streams of inventions and innovations can be generated in the shortest possible time. The systematization of research is deeply entwined with the commodification of creativity. Time pressures, and the need to manipulate all aspects of commodification for the sake of corporate profit and power, thus lead to a sense of urgency which pervades this new form of corporatism.

The *systematized research regime* is at the core of the new kind of corporatism spawned by technocapitalism. Its intensive (or in many ways obsessive) focus on research reflects the ethos of this new source of corporate power. Commodifying creativity is the most important function of the systematized research regime. The organizational apparatus of this new form of corporatism revolves around the commodification of creativity through research, much as corporate industrial capitalism revolved around the commodification of labor through production. As a result, the commodification of research creativity must necessarily lead to exchange and surplus value in order to advance corporate power. Without surplus value, commodification is as useful to corporate power as a ship without a hull is to a sailor.[29]

---

29 The relationship between surplus value and profit has long been debated in Marxian analysis. The earliest treatment of this subject is in Marx's work; see Karl Marx, *Grundrisse: Foundations of the Critique of Political Economy* (New York: Penguin, 1973), section 3: "Capital as Fructiferous Transformation of Surplus Value into Profit," pp. 745–78 (based on his Notebooks I and II dating from 1857–58). The association between surplus value and surplus labor (and, indirectly, between surplus labor and profit) was an important topic in the development of Marxian analysis. See chapter 12, "Surplus Value and Surplus Labor" in Braverman, *Labor and Monopoly Capital*.

The term *fast* refers to the systematized research regime's dependence on fast accumulation phenomena, most of all the accumulation of tacit knowledge. Tacit knowledge, which is fundamental for both reproducing and commodifying creativity, is a major influence on this intangible resource. Tacit knowledge, as discussed earlier in this book, is impossible to generate in any adequate or complete way within the corporate domain, because of the social nature of creativity, the high costs, and the complexity of the new fields that are symbolic of technocapitalism. Tacit knowledge is also very time-sensitive, since it can diffuse rapidly and become codified, thus reducing the possibility of appropriation unless corporate power moves rapidly to secure it (as intellectual property).

The term *fast* must also be associated with fast decomposition and the need to externalize the reproduction of creativity through networks, which provide a rich diversity of social influences that can change rapidly. The systematized research regime therefore depends on the reproduction of creativity, and is partly a product of the fundamental split between commodification and reproduction that drives fast decomposition, as discussed earlier in this chapter. Managing the commodification of creativity internally (a major function of the research regime), while reproduction occurs externally, requires speed in order to appropriate the results. This demand is exacerbated by globalization and its pressures to collapse any cultural or social restraints that stand in the way of greater speed.[30]

Systematized research regimes are typical of the sectors that symbolize technocapitalism. Biotechnology, with its amalgam of new fields, provides some of the best examples of the new corporatism. Companies specialized in genomics research typically depend for their survival on those regimes, to assemble and exploit creative talent from various fields. One of the fields involved is usually bioinformatics, which relies on a combination of expertise from computer science, software engineering and genomics, among other specialties, and require the use of supercomputers to analyze very complex data.[31]

Genetic decoding companies are often the most intensive users of bioinformatics, and tend to be solely or narrowly engaged in research.[32] Gene-decoding research is undertaken for the immediate objective of applying for patents, in order to appropriate decoded knowledge. Patents obtained are archived,

---

30 The case of SAP (Germany's largest software corporation) shows how the pressures for fast research create internal tensions in a global corporation. See Phred Dvorak and Leila Abboud, "Difficult Upgrade: SAP's Plan to Globalize Hits Cultural Barriers; Software Giant's Shift Irks German Engineers, US Star Quits Effort," *Wall Street Journal* (May 11, 2007): A1.

31 See David S. Ross, "Bioinformatics: Trying to Swim in a Sea of Data," *Science* (February 16, 2001): 1260–61; Glyn Moody, *Digital Code of Life: How Bioinformatics is Revolutionizing Science, Medicine, and Business* (Hoboken, NJ: Wiley, 2004).

32 See, for example, Kathryn Brown, "The Human Genome Business Today," *Scientific American* (July 2000): 48–55; Naomi Aoki, "New Alchemy: Patents Aim to Turn Genes into Biotech Gold," *International Herald Tribune* (September 1, 2000): 10.

and are eventually licensed or sold to other companies that can use them in their own research or services. Direct-to-consumer (or personal) genomics and a new kind of medicine based on personal genetics, may well be major future customers of these corporations. Companies such as Invitrogen, 454 Life Sciences, Applied Biosciences, and Ventana are, among many others, the likely corporate clients.[33] The promise of these companies has enticed some pharmaceutical corporations to purchase or acquire major stakes in them.

The systematized research regimens of the gene-decoding companies typically require highly complex knowledge of genomics along with expertise from related fields, such as plant biology, proteomics, biopharmacology or immunology. In addition to highly skilled software and computer engineers, a legion of patent attorneys are employed to research and file patent applications as decoding occurs. The process requires rapid action to preempt competitors from filing patent applications for similar knowledge. By and large, the systematized research regimen therefore provides a framework for the corporate appropriation of creativity that is a fundamental feature of technocapitalism.

Systematization and Commodification

Systematization and commodification are deeply entwined with one another in the technocapitalist research regime. The commodification of creativity can be considered a systematic process, with the paramount objective of appropriating outcomes and extracting surplus value. The exercise of this vital and most precious resource is thus subjected to a regimen of control which compartmentalizes and exploits it, for the benefit of corporate power and profit.

The systematization of the research regimes of technocapitalism has a parallel in the systematization of production regimes under industrial capitalism. The systematized production regimen was mostly concerned with controlling the labor process and appropriating its product. Labor tasks were compartmentalized, standardized, and otherwise manipulated to see that pre-established industrial performance guidelines would be met.[34] Meeting performance goals thus involved little uncertainty, in the sense that almost all aspects could be quantified and programmed. Outcomes could be anticipated because *both* the commodification and reproduction of resources were kept under the control of corporate power, *and* also because the main resources used (raw materials, physical labor) were tangible.[35]

---

33 See *The Economist*, "Getting Personal: A Genomics Merger Highlights the Potential for Personalized Medicine" (June 21, 2008): 76.

34 See chapters 4–6 in Braverman, *Labor and Monopoly Capital*.

35 This made it possible for Frederick Taylor to concoct his models of efficiency in factory work. In a dialectical sense, however, programming was also a result of the Taylorist recipes. See Robert Kanigel, *The One Best Way: Frederick Winslow Taylor and the Enigma of Efficiency* (New York: Viking, 1997).

Automation of labor processes and raw material refinement (or extraction) could thus be implemented on a widespread basis during the middle and late stages of industrial capitalism.[36] Corporate control of both commodification and reproduction, and the tangibility of the resources involved, made this quite feasible. Similarly, the service production regimes of late industrial capitalism (sometimes referred to as "post-industrial" services capitalism) could be automated to a great extent, since both commodification and reproduction were under corporate control, even though in many cases the services marketed might themselves be intangible. Thus, service production regimes in a vast array of sectors, from fast-food operations to airline check-in and medical testing, could be partly or completely automated.

The split between commodification and reproduction, and the *intangibility* of the fundamental resources, however, make it impossible to automate the systematized research regime in a significant way. This means that the systematization of the research regimes of technocapitalism takes up a different character from the systematized production regimes of industrial capitalism (or, for that matter, the systematized service production regimes of so-called "post-industrial" services capitalism).[37] Globalization compounds those differences by making it difficult to transfer the specifics of a systematized research regime from one part of the world to another. At the root of those differences is the split between the commodification and reproduction of creativity (discussed previously), the intangible nature of creativity, and its *qualitative* character. Contributing to creativity's qualitative character is its elusiveness and uniqueness, which make it very difficult to program, standardize, or predict outcomes.

Despite these difficulties and the complexity introduced by globalization, systematization is fundamentally supportive of two major functions of commodification. One of those functions is *fragmentation*. As discussed earlier in this book, fragmentation involves a *compartmentalization* or splitting-up of the exercise of creativity into components. A major effect of this function is to try to turn creativity into a disembodied inventory item, such that it can be standardized as much as possible (futile or even destructive as this might be). This is pursued

---

36   Automation enhanced corporate control over workers who remained, as the threat of unemployment (through automation) induced compliance with corporate demands. See part III, "A New Industrial revolution: Change Without Change," in Noble's *Forces of Production*.

37   Although systematization is largely antithetical to creativity and research, it is quite compatible with production. Systematization will very likely be indispensable when biotechnology becomes an industry, with standard routines and programming. See Christopher T. Scott, *Stem Cells Now: From the Experiment that Shook the World to the New Politics of Life* (New York: Pi Press, 2006); *The Economist Technology Quarterly*, "Organs to Order; Biotechnology: Could the Creation of Replacement Organs, Grown to Order for Particular Patients, Be Just Around the Corner?" (March 11, 2006): 10.

by corporate power in order to exert *control*, in the hope of reducing the inherent uncertainty, and risk of failure, of commodifying creativity.

Systematization supports this corporate exercise of control over commodification by providing systemic guidelines upon which individual and group performance can be judged, no matter how demeaning to researchers this might turn out to be. The systemic dimension here means that those guidelines or criteria affect the entire research regime, to a point where they cannot be disassociated from its operational ethos. Systematization thus potentially ends up creating systemic problems for the technocapitalist research regime, from which it cannot escape unless it compromises the very function and objective of commodification. Such compromises imperil the advancement of corporate power and the prospect of extracting any surplus value. Those problems, introduced by systematization, all too often tend to de-socialize creative processes by demeaning their human qualities and the cultural values that promote solidarity, openness, and sharing.

An example of how systematization demeans those values, and the process of creativity, can be found in the common corporate practice of enthroning comparative and competitive individual performance criteria, in place of independent (and socially-oriented) standards of excellence (or performance), for those who exercise research creativity. The term *independent* here refers to the possibility of setting standards outside the control and objectives of corporate power, even when they oppose or subvert corporate priorities.[38]

Through systematization, corporate power transforms recognition for the exercise of creativity into a *positional asset*, which can only be enhanced through *competition* between those who exercise research creativity. Such competition may be nominally targeted at the exercise of their creativity (or results derived thereof), but all too often spills over into social and personal life, with harmful consequences.[39] For corporate power, the immediate objective of those systemic

---

38   Such independence may nonetheless occur, because corporate power increasingly depends on the integration of diverse social relations (a result of decomposition). See Nick Dyer-Witheford, *Cyber-Marx: Cycles and Circuits of Struggle in High-Technology Capitalism* (Urbana: University of Illinois Press, 1999).

39   The proliferation of obsessive behaviors (and their projection to the societal scale, as a form of collective social psychosis) may be one outcome. Such behaviors all too often seem to be a product of employment conditions, work regime stress, and the pressure to compete. See Lennard J. Davis, *Obsession: A History* (Chicago: University of Chicago Press, 2008). Concern over such behaviors has led to a host of "therapies" which are often promoted by corporate employers, such as the unusual one of requiring employees to simulate death by climbing into a coffin, pretending not to exist (while in a closed coffin), and asking them to plot a way to "start life" over again in the effort to shed behaviors considered negative to productivity and to corporate control over their work regimes. One company in South Korea, for example, required all of its 4,000 employees to undergo this experience; see John M. Glionna, "Dale Carnegie is Not Dead," *Los Angeles Times* (January 4, 2010): A1.

guidelines is to hope that any results obtained from the exercise of creativity can sustain corporate power and profit.

Systematization thus serves as a tool to implement individual or inter-personal competition between researchers as an internal managerial tactic. Systematic in character and aimed at exercising corporate control over those who provide research creativity, it helps fragment research by pitting employees against one another for extrinsic and intrinsic rewards. This effect results from the intimate relationship between commodification and systematization, noted earlier. Corporate power thereby seizes the role of judge and jury in deciding how research personnel perform, setting up formal and informal rules that ultimately reward performance based on how, whether, and to what extent the results of creativity enhance corporate power and profit. This approach is not unlike that employed by industrial corporate management to deal with production workers and control labor processes. This scheme was also used by industrial management to pit labor unions against one another during the heyday of industrial capitalism.[40]

The second major function of commodification supported by systematization is *disengagement*. As discussed previously in this book, disengagement involves *detaching* the results of creativity from those who exercise this most precious resource. Disengagement also involves detaching the results of creativity from the fragmented components of a creative process (which is in turn achieved through the fragmentation function of commodification, noted earlier). The immediate objective of systematization and its support for this function targets the *corporate appropriation* of the results of creativity. The outcomes of the exercise of creativity are thereby turned into corporate property, regardless of whether those outcomes are intangible (as in the case of patents, ideas, processes or formulas) or tangible (as with any organisms, seeds, gadgets or tools).

Systematization supports corporate appropriation in several ways. One of them involves the systematic treatment of any tacit knowledge (derived from the exercise of creativity) as saleable corporate property. The term *systematic* here means that ground rules are applied to the entire operation of the research regime, in a comprehensive or totalistic sense. Sparing no form or type of tacit knowledge, the systematic approach thus considers any form of tacit knowledge generated through the exercise of creativity to be owned by corporate power, regardless of whether any value is eventually obtained or not.

The systematic approach also means that communication of research findings has to be prevented. This applies to any communication destined to be outside the control of corporate power, but in some cases internal communications (which are

---

40   From a broader historical perspective, it was also a major tactic of imperial conquest throughout history, used to pit peoples against one another in a given territory (by manipulating racial, ethnic or cultural differences to stir competition and mutual suspicion, or by pitting economic interests against one another). See Eric Hobsbawm, *The Age of Empire, 1875–1914* (London: Weidenfeld and Nicolson, 1975), and his *The Age of Extremes: A History of the World, 1914–1991* (New York: Vintage, 1996).

under corporate control) may also be included. Given the uncertainty surrounding the technocapitalist research regime, the systematized approach assumes that any and all forms of tacit knowledge generated through the exercise of creativity may conceivably have exchange (or market) value at some point. The systematic approach, which encompasses the entire research regime (in all of its operations, tasks and outcomes), thus promotes an atmosphere of secrecy. Such secrecy is typically enforced, for example, through employment contracts where legally-binding censorship on any communication of research findings is required of employees, under penalty of disciplinary action, loss of income, dismissal, or the potential loss of career.

The systematic application of secrecy and censorship on any outcome of creativity, including tacit knowledge, thus encompasses all research results. It aims, first and foremost, to protect corporate appropriation. Given the high uncertainty and the high risk of failure of research in the sectors symbolic of technocapitalism, the urgency of enforcing such censorship cannot be ignored. Such secrecy is, however, incompatible with the open communication necessary to accumulate tacit knowledge and to reproduce creativity. Thus, systematization in the commodification of creativity (and its research regimes) ends up shortchanging the benefits of research to society at large.

Globalization compounds this association between systematization and commodification in myriad ways. For one, it complicates the association considerably, since secrecy and censorship must be applied anywhere and everywhere a corporate entity happens to have research operations. At the same time, the pressure to appropriate (not to mention the urgency of coming up with saleable research results) increases, given the ever–present need to extract higher profits, satisfy shareholders or investors, and beat competitors on a global scale. Globalization also makes external networks more difficult for corporate power to influence, even when systematization is made to work effectively within the corporate apparatus. In many respects, therefore, globalization makes systematization more difficult, particularly for large, global-scale corporations whose survival depends on research.

The effects of globalization on systematization and commodification are by no means one-way negative, however. Globalization can also make systematization easier to implement, in a dialectical sense. For one, globalization and the unprecedented, intense migratory flows it has triggered make it easier to access talent and ideas to benefit corporate power. The brain-drain flows of talented researchers toward rich nations, or in any case toward corporate research operations, wherever they happen to be, is one example. Such flows of talent, often connected to the internationalization of graduate education in technology and the sciences, can make commodification and systematization easier to achieve.[41] Such talent all too often ends up bonded to corporate power, especially when researchers depend on corporate employment to maintain work visas or legal residency. In this sense

---

41 See *The Economist*, "The Future in Another Country" (January 3, 2009): 43.

globalization, its migratory flows, and residency or immigration requirements enforced by certain (mostly rich) nations end up becoming an important support for corporate power.

World as Corporate Laboratory

Much as the corporations of industrial capitalism found it necessary to reach around the globe to consolidate and extend their power, the technocapitalist corporation seeks to turn its research regimes into a global project. No aspect of social relations, culture, nature or life can be spared, no part of the globe can be overlooked, so long as they have potential to sustain the new corporatism's quest for profit and power. The tools for this grand scheme of conquest are, of course, technology and science, made to serve corporate power through research and the exploitation of research creativity. Through technology and science, the new corporatism seeks to breed a homogenization of societies, cultures and existence, a kind of techno-social functionalism aimed at advancing its power over all things human, over life and over nature itself.

Experimentalism is the existential platform supporting this grand scheme of conquest, and is defined here as technological and scientific inquiry whose overarching objective for being is commercial. It therefore involves experimentation for the sake of corporate power and profit, as opposed to experimentation for its own sake or for the sake of attaining new knowledge. Experimentalism thus symbolizes the ethos of technocapitalism and of the new corporatism it spawns.[42]

In praxis, corporate experimentalism encompasses systematization and commodification, and provides the rationale for their existence. Systematization, which may not occur at all when experimentation is undertaken for its own sake (or merely for the sake of obtaining new knowledge), thus becomes an integral part of the experimentalist platform. Programming and manipulation of research, which are part of the process of systematization, also become a necessary element of corporate experimentalism. The praxis of experimentalism therefore covers the whole spectrum of experimental methods, activities, and procedures needed to support the commodification of research creativity.

Experimentalism had its parallels in previous versions of capitalism. Under industrial capitalism, for example, its counterpart might be referred to as *productionism*. This represented the ethos of a capitalist era when corporate power and profit were grounded in the production of manufactures or services. Labor processes, raw materials, management, and practically every major aspect of corporate power thus revolved around production, and around the need to make it ever more efficient, such that surplus value could be extracted.[43] Under mercantile capitalism, *mercantilism* might be considered to have represented the ethos of an era where merchandise trade (of raw materials, simple tools, or slave labor)

---

42   See the chapter "Experimentalism" in Suarez-Villa, *Technocapitalism*.
43   See Braverman, *Labor and Monopoly Capital*.

sustained companies' power and profit.[44] In this sense, therefore, experimentalism has parallels within the general framework of capitalism, even though its essence is of a quite different character from previous versions of capitalism.

Much as industrial and mercantile capitalism cultivated superfluous or unnecessary consumption as a means to extract profit, technocapitalist experimentalism seeks to create needs that are often unnecessary or wasteful. Thus, for example, some biotechnology and biopharmaceutical corporations seek to make life-long customers of people with no symptoms, for treatments that are costly and unnecessary. Genomics and proteomics, for example, provide the opportunity to test humans for genetic "errors" that might trigger diseases. Biopharmaceutical corporations then develop medications and treatments that turn those genetic errors off, so long as the medications are taken, even when there are no symptoms and no real indication that any illness can or will occur.[45] Much as industrial products or services found customers who did not need them, some products of corporate experimentalism can therefore be expected to target "illnesses" which do not really exist, or "patients" who do not suffer them.[46] Thus, in some fields, superfluous "pathological conditions" are being "identified" which seem guided more by corporate profit motives than by any need to protect or advance human well-being.[47] The rising global scope of technocapitalist experimentalism means that these tendencies are to acquire a worldwide dimension, as corporatism seeks every possibility to expand its reach for profit, regardless of need.

Several aspects of corporate experimentalism that influence its rising global profile need to be taken into account, if we are to understand its effects. The *first* aspect is that the globalization of corporate experimentalism is partly a result of the split between the commodification and reproduction of creativity, considered previously in this book. That functional split means that a shift of power out from the corporate domain occurs, through external networks. As discussed previously, those external networks are largely outside the control of corporate power. This dynamic is generally impossible to avoid if creativity is to be reproduced adequately, through the rich diversity and regenerative possibilities that external, societal networks provide. Those external networks, however, are increasingly *global*, and must be so for reproduction to occur effectively, and to generate the

---

44   See, for example, Beaud, *History of Capitalism*. Trade, rather than production, was therefore the prime mode of capital accumulation.

45   See Erick Schonfeld, "Beyond the Genome," *Business 2.0* (July 2003): 94–00.

46   A medication or treatment which may not be needed may thus be made to seem necessary through clever advertising that targets psychological vulnerabilities, or through a redefinition of normal conditions as illnesses. See H. Gilbert Welch, Lisa Schwartz and Steven Woloshin, *Overdiagnosed: Making People Sick in the Pursuit of Health* (Boston: Beacon Press, 2010); Sally Satel, *One Nation Under Therapy: How the Helping Culture is Ignoring Self-Reliance* (New York: St. Martin's Press, 2005).

47   The field of psychiatry offers an interesting case. See Ron Grossman, "Psychiatry Manual's Secrecy Criticized," *Los Angeles Times* (December 29, 2008): A19.

sort of cutting-edge research creativity needed by the highly complex fields that are symbolic of technocapitalism.

The functional split between commodification and reproduction, and the overarching need for corporate power to access and appropriate creativity wherever it may be found, also establishes new relations of power. Those relations of power involve the colonization by corporate experimentalism of any part or place in the world that can be a significant source of creative talent. That colonization can be of several kinds. One involves the setting up of corporate subsidiaries or branches in nations and locales that are sources of creative research talent. This can also include corporate take-overs of companies based in those locales and nations.

Another kind involves promoting or tapping into the global brain-drain that draws talent away through the global migratory networks, usually from poor (or less well-off) nations toward the richer ones. As noted previously in this chapter, those global brain-drain flows often allow corporate power to find talented individuals who will provide their creativity at less cost (by their acceptance of lower salaries), and also under some form of tacit bondage to the hiring corporation, because of residency restrictions (which require employment) or work-visa regulations. Individuals who run afoul of those residency or work-visa restrictions by quitting their employment, or refusing to submit to corporate conditions and lower compensation, will find themselves deported or with a status similar to that of fugitives. The relations of power that these arrangements involve thus typically favor corporate power. They also often involve the cooptation or corruption of governance, so that laws and regulations favorable to corporate power are enacted in the receiving nations or locales.[48]

Subcontracting or outsourcing some research operations abroad may also provide advantages. While corporate experimental research is typically shrouded in great secrecy, and is legally protected by censorship over researchers and over the results of their creativity, some activities closely linked to research might nonetheless be outsourced. Such activities may involve clinical trials, for example, where testing (especially of humans) is undertaken in poor countries by local subcontractors. Pharmaceutical and biotech corporations can thereby reduce the high cost of research by globalizing clinical testing operations. Typically about half of all drug trials by the global pharmaceutical industry, for example, are conducted today in poor or middle-income nations. The number of countries where such tests are conducted more than doubled during the past decade, and their costs are substantially lower than they would be in most every rich nation.[49] Drug trials in

---

48   Bribery by some of the world's largest technology corporations is often part of a strategy to influence laws and regulations. See *The Economist*, "The Siemens Scandal: Bavarian Baksheesh" (December 20, 2008): 112.

49   Seth W. Glickman et al., "Ethical and Scientific Implications of the Globalization of Clinical Research," *New England Journal of Medicine* 360(2009): http://content.nejm.org/content/full/360/8/816; Shirley S. Wang, "Most Clinical Trials Done Abroad," *Wall Street Journal* (February 19, 2009): D3.

poor or middle-income nations usually cost less than half what they would in the US or western Europe, and have fewer safeguards for the people who participate.[50]

A *second* aspect that needs to be taken into account in the globalization of corporate experimentalism involves *creative power*, or the potential for the exercise of creativity by individuals or groups in a systematized research regime.[51] Experimentalism seeks to exploit creative power any way it can, and most of all in ways that can further corporate power and profit. Functionally, a prime objective of corporate management is to harness creative power to commodification and systematization, such that any results can be appropriated. Appropriation by corporate power is therefore a fundamental step on the road toward extracting surplus value from research, without which the technocapitalist corporation cannot survive.

Creative power also had parallels in previous phases of capitalism. Its counterpart under industrial capitalism and its systematized production regimes was labor power.[52] Labor power in the *productionist* regimes of industrial capitalism was fundamental for the industrial corporation. Its exercise allowed corporations to appropriate products obtained through labor processes in manufacturing or service production. Labor power was thus the fundamental component of the labor process and of factory production under industrial capitalism, much as creative power is fundamental to research processes and the systematized research regimes of technocapitalism.

Despite the parallels, a fundamental difference between experimentalism and productionism can be found. The underlying purpose of experimentalism and of creative power in the systematized research regime is to *create value*. As discussed earlier, this is done by commodifying research creativity through systematized research regimes. In contrast, the purpose of productionism in the systematized production regimes of industrial capitalism was to *add value*.[53] This occurred by transforming tangible resources through the use of labor power, and associated labor processes, in manufacturing or service production regimes.

A *third* aspect influencing the rising global profile of experimentalism is its inherently *reductionist* approach to research. This is not reductionism for the sake of achieving technological or scientific knowledge, but reductionism for the sake

---

50   Shirley S. Wang, Geeta Anand and Jeanne Whalen, "Scrutiny Grows of Drug Trials Abroad," *Wall Street Journal* (December 1, 2008): B1. At the same time, it has become more difficult to find patients for clinical trials in rich nations; see Shari Roan, "Clinical Research Lacks for Patients," *Los Angeles Times* (March 14, 2009): A1.

51   See the chapter "Experimentalist Organizations" in Suarez-Villa, *Technocapitalism*.

52   The analysis of labor power in factory production was part of Marx's critique of capitalism. See pp. 293–310 (sections "Labour Power as Capital," "Labour Process Absorbed into Capital," and "Production Process as Content of Capital") in Marx, *Grundrisse*.

53   Adding value was enshrined as a performance indicator in the "value-added" statistics reported by census agencies around the world.

of corporate profit and power.[54] In this sense, the reductionism of technocapitalist experimentalism reflects, and is a part of, the agenda of corporate power.

Reductionism for the sake of corporate profit and power is part of the commodification of creativity. In particular, reductionism is central to the *fragmentation* component of commodification. In that part of the larger process of commodification, reductionism supports the aim of corporate power and its control over commodification by narrowing researchers' vision of the exercise of their creativity.[55] Research tasks are thus in and of themselves "reductionized", usually in a very narrow way, along with the scope of knowledge that is to be applied to research. Similarly, reductionism narrows down considerably researchers' awareness of their rights (as employees and providers of creativity), of the social implications of their exercise of creativity, of their exploitation by corporate power, of the corporate appropriation of the results of their creativity, and of the potential value (social, economic, human) of what they create. Such "reductionization" of the exercise of creativity in research is very important for corporate power to maintain its control over commodification.

Reductionism is also helpful for corporate power to appropriate the results of the exercise of creativity, and to thereby disengage researchers from what they create, once the fragmentation phase is over. The *disengagement* function of commodification therefore relies deeply on the reductionist character of experimentalism, enabling corporate power to sustain and expand its control. Experimentalist reductionism helps corporate power in this function by making the alienation of those who exercise creativity less noticeable. Very narrow focus, a hallmark of reductionism, thus works wonderfully to make those subject to corporate power ignore their alienation as creativity providers, and the corporate appropriation of their creativity. Corporate attention can thus be shifted toward the extraction of surplus value through marketing, licensing, and other commercial schemes. Reductionism, coupled with commodification and systematization, is therefore vital for the research regimes of corporate technocapitalism because of its support of corporate control.

Related to the reductionist character of corporate experimentalism is a *fourth* aspect that influences the rising global profile of this phenomenon. This aspect involves corporate power's quest to set global technological *standards* that others will have to follow. The overarching purpose of this objective is to set the rules that will most strongly favor a powerful corporation's quest for power and profit, by imposing rules that others must conform with whenever they sell products or

---

54   See James A. Evans, "Reports: Electronic Publication and the Narrowing of Science and Scholarship," *Science* 321 (July 18, 2008): 395; Rosie Mestel, "Gene Therapy Undergoes a Reevaluation," *Los Angeles Times* (November 12, 2002): A1. Reductionism's pervasive influence on most every field of academic research has also invaded the corporate domain.

55   This kind of reductionism has parallels in the narrow Taylorist practices of factory production regimes. See Braverman, *Labor and Monopoly Capital*; Kanigel, *One Best Way*.

services in the targeted category. The standards typically involve a very profitable technology created or appropriated by corporate power. A secondary objective is to make it more convenient to use a given technology, in order to make products compatible across an entire sector. Publicizing this aspect may make the corporate standards-setting objective attractive to regulators, politicians and the public, and give a false impression of altruism to what is in fact a very self-serving scheme. Setting the rules of the technological game by imposing standards on a global scale is therefore another aspect of corporate experimentalism.

Globalization no doubt allows corporate power to set standards on an unprecedented scale. The world thereby becomes the locus of a competitive power struggle, in which the vital issue at stake is the monopoly of technological and scientific authority by corporate power.[56] Setting standards thus involves relations of power, domination, and corporate hegemony over entire global segments involving new technologies. Since globalization has made it easier to bypass national governance, the setting of standards can now largely ignore national priorities and any associated cultural values.

One of the most important examples connecting global standards-setting with corporate hegemony and monopoly control is that of Microsoft. Enabled by its early rise toward monopoly over operating software, at the dawn of the personal computer (PC) revolution [and later, the rapid growth of (IBM) PC-compatible hardware], Microsoft tacitly established Windows as the world standard, before most people around the world ever knew what software was.[57] Thus, this early domination of a new technology allowed Microsoft to accumulate incalculable power and profits over the years, becoming one of the world's richest corporations in a relatively short span. By setting the standards (in a tacit way, through monopoly control), Microsoft thus came to "own" a technology upon which countless applications were made by other companies (using Windows as the platform), all of whom depended on Microsoft and had to pay royalties to it. To be able to improve their products, those "application" companies then also had to pay Microsoft to have access to any new versions of the Windows software code. Not doing so meant that their competitors (who would pay Microsoft for the new code) would have an advantage over them.

Other examples of standard-setting have involved fierce, winner-take-all battles between rival corporate entities or between groups of corporations. The case of Blu-ray versus HD DVD (High Definition Digital Video Disc) for the video disc technology standard and, several decades earlier, corporate battles involving an earlier generation of video-recording technology, VHS versus Betamax, revealed

---

56 Monopoly of scientific authority through standards-setting involved national governments; see Pierre Bourdieu, "The Specificity of the Scientific Field and the Social Conditions of the Progress of Reason," *Social Science Information* 14(1975): 19–47. Globalization and the rise of technocapitalism, however, have transferred standards-setting to the corporate realm.

57 See Wallace, *Overdrive*.

how important and profitable it was to set standards.[58] A more recent example is the battle for wireless network standards, also known as "fourth generation" (4G) networks: WiMAX versus LTE. The main rival corporations in this battle were INTEL (from the computer hardware sector, the world's largest microchip company) supporting WiMAX, versus Ericsson (from the telecommunications hardware sector), supporting LTE.[59]

At stake, accompanying the setting of a major standard, was INTEL's drive to impose its power and interests on the telecommunications hardware sector (where Ericsson is a major player). INTEL also got various other major corporations with convergent interests, such as Google and Sprint Nextel (a wireless telecommunications provider) to join its quest, among other companies. A major common objective of imposing WiMAX by the INTEL-led camp was to turn wireless broadband data communications into a global commodity, with INTEL providing the hardware (microprocessors), Google providing the search engine services, and other associated companies taking up compartmentalized roles with this new technology. With globalization, these battles inevitably end up setting standards that acquire a worldwide scope, accompanied by unusual opportunities to greatly advance corporate power and profit.

The rising global profile of corporate experimentalism is thus creating a new social and economic reality that intrudes into most every aspect of life, work, human relations, and into nature itself. The global collapse of restraints and borders, social, cultural and national, is both cause and effect of this dynamic. Never before in history has the global spread of a new social and economic mode advanced so rapidly or so intrusively. To the extent that the new corporatism imposes its power by setting standards, spreading its reductionist vision of research, technology and science, exploiting creative power, and manipulating governance, it generates social pathologies that are no longer confined to nations, continents or locales. Those pathologies, as we will see in the following section, are now global and spare practically no corner of the globe, no culture, no national identity, and no aspect of nature that can be harnessed to the corporate quest for power and profit.

Global Dilemmas and Pathologies

The new corporatism embodies dilemmas and contradictions that can be linked to major social pathologies. The dilemmas are grounded in corporatism's need to control the intangible resources and exploitive processes upon which its survival depends. Those resources and processes have acquired a global scope through

---

58 See Dave Owen, "The Betamax vs. VHS Format War," www.mediacollege.com/video/format/compare/betamax-vhs.html (2008); Robin Harris, "Blu-ray vs. HD DVD: Game Over," http://blogs.zdnet.com/storage/?p=149 (June 20, 2007).

59 See *The Economist*, "Culture Clash: As 'third generation' (3G) networks proliferate, the focus shifts to 4G," (July 19, 2008): 76.

the breakdown of restraints (social, cultural, regulatory) that has accompanied the expansion of corporate power.

The dilemmas and contradictions of technocapitalism, and their global scope, are quite different from those of previous eras of capitalism. They are grounded in the character of the resources that are vital to this new form of capitalism (which are intangible), the exploitive processes (which are based on research rather than production), and the relations of power between corporatism and society that now intrude into most every aspect of life and nature. The use of technology and science on a global scale, as major vehicles for corporate power and profit, are at the root of this phenomenon. Throughout its history, corporate capitalism has sought to invade, colonize, and impose its realities upon most any aspect of human existence from which it can extract power and profit. The dilemmas and pathologies created by the new corporatism are therefore part of the global expansion of the corporate domain of capitalism.

What makes those dilemmas and pathologies of greater concern to humanity is that they now have major potential effects on the human species in a biological way, on practically any form of life, and thereby on most any aspect of nature, not to mention human societies, cultures, and all economic endeavors.[60] Thus, capitalism is no longer limited to structuring production, to the exploitation of raw materials and labor, or to setting the rules of public governance. Capitalism is now becoming deeply entwined with nature, with life, and with the genetic future of the human species, as it harnesses technology and science to extract power and profit from its new colonial domain. The new domain that technocapitalism colonizes is thus fraught with major issues for the future of humanity as a viable species, for global society and its capacity to sustain human relations, for a global economy that can promote social justice, and for the need to maintain the ecological viability of the planet.

Two major dilemmas underlie the question of how the new corporatism addresses those challenges, or whether it can do so at all without introducing major social pathologies. The dilemmas are grounded in the character of the exploitive processes, in the appropriation which those processes are geared to support, and in the nature of the intangible resources upon which the new corporatism depends. Thus, although the dilemmas are grounded in those seemingly functional aspects, they (the dilemmas) and the processes on which they are grounded create new realities. Whether those realities are pathological depends on the relations of power between corporatism and society, and on whether the contradictions they embed can be resolved to favor human needs and social justice on a global scale.

The first dilemma deals with reproduction and commodification. *Corporatism can constrain the reproduction of creativity* (which increasingly operates at a global scale) *and thereby shortchange commodification, or it can let reproduction operate*

60 One of the means for such effects is genetic engineering. See Finn Bowring, *Science, Seeds, and Cyborgs* (London: Verso, 2003); Antoinette Rouvroy, *Human Genes and Neoliberal Governance: A Foucaldian Critique* (London: Routledge-Cavendish, 2007).

freely (out of its control), *through external global networks, and risk losing control over both the commodification and reproduction of creativity.* This dilemma results from the fundamental split between commodification and reproduction, which is a hallmark of technocapitalism, and also from the need to decompose corporate functions on a global scale, as discussed earlier in this chapter.

Shortchanging or losing control over the *commodification* of creativity is disastrous for the global corporate quest for power and profit. It compromises not only the possibility of extracting surplus value from the results of creativity, but also possibly the very survival of the corporate entity. Constraining the *reproduction* of creativity compromises not only creative power, but also the quality of creativity, the results obtained through commodification (if not the very process of commodification itself), and ultimately the exchange (market or otherwise) of the product or service involved, along with its opportunity to generate surplus value.

The second dilemma faced by the new corporatism involves appropriation. *Corporatism can appropriate the results of creativity as a means to secure power and profit on a global scale, and thereby shortchange their benefit to society, or it can let the results of creativity be freely available* (out of its control) *to society and lose power and profits, if not compromise its very survival.* This dilemma results from the imperative to sustain and advance corporate power and profit through appropriation, in the context of global capitalism. Appropriation, a major objective of the commodification of creativity, thus sets the new corporatism up against society's interests.

Globalization affects these dilemmas by providing a context that transcends nation-states, cultures, locales, social relations, and the kind of restraints that have accompanied a sense of identity and community. This global context amounts to a new reality, grounded in the new corporatism's entwined existence with technology and science. Technological invention and innovation, achieved through the commodification of creativity, thus pave the road to corporate power on a global scale, without regard to place, identity, culture, or governance. Much as industrial capitalism globalized its factories, its labor processes and its production regimes, thus creating new realities through its power, so technocapitalism globalizes its experimentalist corporate culture and research regimes, creating new realities that take its new form of capitalism deeper into life and nature on a worldwide scale.

Predation Worldwide

Many of the pathologies that arise from these dilemmas involve predation. Predatory strategies partly result from the pressure to bypass the process of reproduction (related to the first dilemma). More generally, they may also be seen as a response to the permanent state of urgency under which the new corporatism operates.[61] Urgency is a major factor of the *fast* culture of the new corporatism,

---

61   See Karen Southwick, *Everyone Else Must Fail: The Unvarnished Truth About Oracle and Larry Ellison* (New York: Crown Business, 2003).

of its systematized research regimes, and of the pressure to compete by finding expedient shortcuts to extract surplus value. Competition is therefore entwined with the pathologies of predation.[62]

Efforts to reduce the risk and uncertainty inherent to research regimes are also behind predation. Risk and uncertainty are major sources of anxiety to corporate power, which often justify predation, especially when the chances of getting away with it are judged to be favorable.[63] The risk of *not* engaging in predation must also be taken into account, since they might be considerable when a research program's success is very uncertain. Thus, forgoing predation may be seen as having a cost in and of itself, to the extent that opportunities for success may be lost.

Many acts of corporate predation are, in any case, not illegal, and the moral or ethical consequences (if any occur) tend to be very temporary and often lead to little or no material harm to the perpetrator.[64] Whether there is any such harm is often also a matter of power. A powerful and richer corporate entity can more easily get away with predation against a weaker one, being better able to shoulder any contingencies that result, such as litigation, adverse judgments, or punitive compensation.

An increasingly common pathology involves corporate espionage.[65] Espionage against competitors to extract company secrets, such as new and potentially valuable research findings, is part of this tendency. Clearly, globalization now offers more opportunities for this sort of pathology than ever before, as the corporate ecology of high-tech (and especially technocapitalist) corporations expands, even in nations that not long ago were considered inadequate for these businesses. Many of those nations have little or no regulation and legal frameworks that sanction corporate espionage. Adding to this trend of malfeasance are the consulting services which

---

62 Some contemporary recipes on competitive corporate strategy are indicative of the sort of mindset which often drives corporate power. Two of the world's best-known corporate consultants, who are top executives of one of the world's top consulting firms, for example, provided the following set of "hardball strategies" as an overarching guide: (1) "Devastate rivals' profit sanctuaries" (p. 67), (2) "Plagiarize with pride" (p. 68), (3) "Deceive the competition" (p. 68), (4) "Unleash massive and overwhelming force" (p. 70), and (5) "Raise competitors' costs" (p. 71); see George Stalk Jr. and Rob Lachenauer, "Hardball: Five Killer Strategies for Trouncing the Competition," *Harvard Business Review* (April 2004): 62–71.

63 The chances of getting away with highly aggressive predation seem to have improved substantially, with the emergence of private contractors to spy, steal data, or co-opt employees of rival companies. See Scahill, *Blackwater*; Tom Engelhardt, "Blackwater's Noble Gas," *The Nation* (February 20, 2009), www.thenation.com/blogs/notion/410194.

64 Individuals are often blamed for such actions, thus (partially or wholly) lifting responsibility from a corporate entity. See Bakan, *The Corporation*. In other cases, subcontractors hired to perform such acts can be blamed if their malfeasance is exposed.

65 See Adam L. Penenberg and Marc Barry, *Spooked: Espionage in Corporate America* (Cambridge, MA: Perseus, 2000); Hedieh Nasheri, *Economic Espionage and Industrial Spying* (Cambridge: Cambridge University Press, 2005); Bakan, *The Corporation*.

use the kind of tactics employed by government intelligence agencies, and are often run by former intelligence agents.[66] Such services can be subcontracted in a way that leaves no "paper trail," or other evidence for any law-enforcement agency to track down, and are often arranged for in nations or locales that have no laws against them.

Espionage is also done by employing or bribing competitors' employees. Bribing may be risky and its benefits tend to be temporary, but can provide advantages if the data received is fundamentally important. The greater risk is usually incurred by those who are bribed, given the potential damage to their careers, reputation or employment through firings, demotions, or legal action. Hiring away or raiding competitors' research departments can sometimes be costly and counterproductive, especially when it ends up raising costs (salaries, benefits) for the raider. Nonetheless, it can produce advantages if the hired employees can help the receiving company, or if their departure can cripple their former employer's research program.

For the raided company, however, the loss of research secrets can be devastating.[67] Partly for this reason, technocapitalist companies typically include research secrecy clauses in their employment contracts, which prohibit disclosure of research findings to anyone outside the employer's site, and in many cases also within the corporation itself. Clearly, this culture of internal and external secrecy is at odds with the diffusion of knowledge, and most of all tacit knowledge, and presents a serious contradiction to the accumulation processes discussed earlier in this book.

Reverse engineering is another common predatory tactic. It is surreptitious in character and praxis, and is often aimed at making patent infringement undetectable. In many cases, the objective may also involve copying or improving a design, process or method created by the targeted party. The advantage to the perpetrator lies in shortcuts that can save research costs and time, and thus simplify the internal pressure to exercise creativity. This form of predation can therefore simplify the process of commodification, or even replace it altogether, for the perpetrator. In this way, it reduces the considerable risk and uncertainty that often accompanies basic research and the commodification of creativity. More disturbing is that reverse engineering can be carried out on a regular basis, as a matter of strategy and operational practice, and seems to be increasingly common in companies that have R&D units with close links to production.[68] This allows findings obtained through reverse engineering to be rushed to production, in order to introduce the pilfered innovations rapidly, such that they can undercut competitors' products.

A third form of predation can occur through second-mover research. This strategy involves tweaking others' ideas or intellectual property, without permission or licensing. Development (the "D" in R&D), as opposed to basic research, is the key aspect of second-mover research, although the dividing line between the two

66   See Scahill, *Blackwater*; Laing, "Shadow CIA."

67   Justin Scheck and Lauren Pollock, "Former H-P Executive Pleads Guilty: Malhotra Could Get Jail Time for Stealing IBM Trade Secrets," *Wall Street Journal* (July 14, 2008): B8.

68   Carl Hoffman, "The Teardown Artists," *Wired* (February 2006): 136–39.

may blur depending on the project.[69] Malicious second-mover research is most opportunistic whenever the idea, method or process pilfered is not "owned" (in a legal sense, as intellectual property in the form of a patent, for example) by anyone. This makes it more likely that the predator will get away with it, particularly if the victim is weaker, or asymmetric relations of power favor the perpetrator.

Certain inter-corporate arrangements aimed at reducing the uncertainty of reproducing creativity, and its dependence on external networks, can embed second-mover research, reverse engineering, and espionage. Those inter-corporate arrangements can, for example, be in the form of research unit-to-research unit (R2R) cooperation between two or more companies, joint ventures, or strategic alliances. Reverse engineering, malicious second-mover research, and espionage in such cases involves a betrayal of trust between the corporate parties involved. For that reason, those arrangements are all too often short-term, and while they might pretend to benefit all participants in some way, can be used by a perpetrator-participant to siphon new (tacit) knowledge and research findings from partners.[70]

The relations of power within the R2R, strategic alliance, or joint venture arrangement may determine how predation occurs. Weaker participants are likely to be most vulnerable whenever the relations of power within the arrangement are very asymmetrical. Highly asymmetrical relations of power are not uncommon, for example, between biotech companies (which are often in great need of capital to support their research) and large pharmaceutical corporations (which need new, patented or patentable research findings). The biotech companies are also highly vulnerable because of the extreme risks and uncertainty they face in research, where the odds of a new compound being approved for marketing are often over 8,000:1 against.[71] In such arrangements, it is difficult to see how a weaker company can avoid being preyed upon if a powerful participant is determined to use predation. This is all the more likely when a weaker participant rejects takeover or buy-out attempts by the more powerful partner.

---

69 As most corporations place greater emphasis on Development in their R&D operations, the incidence of second-mover "research" is rising. See Pat Choate, *Hot Property: The Stealing of Ideas in an Age of Globalization* (New York: Knopf, 2005); Nasheri, *Economic Espionage*; *The Economist*, "Out of the Dusty Labs: Technology Firms Have Left the Big Corporate R&D Laboratory Behind, Shifting the Emphasis from Research to Development. Does it Matter?" (March 3, 2007): 74–6. Motivation for corporate second-mover schemes involves the assumption that imitation is more profitable than undertaking original research; see William L. Baldwin and Gerald L. Childs, "The Fast Second and Rivalry in Research and Development," *Southern Economic Journal* 36(1969): 18–24.

70 See Wilma N. Suen, *Non-Cooperation: The Dark Side of Strategic Alliances* (New York: Palgrave Macmillan, 2005); Julia Mengewein and Shirley S. Wang, "Swiss Firm Files Claim Against J&J," *Wall Street Journal* (February 25, 2009): B2.

71 See Ernst and Young, *Beyond Borders*; see Daniel Costello, "Amgen Needs Mojo Working: A Series of Missteps and Problems With its Top Sellers Put the Drug Maker On its Heels," *Los Angeles Times* (March 12, 2008): C1.

The ultimate benefits of predation through inter-corporate arrangements, if it can be carried out successfully, without detection or without negative consequences for the perpetrator, can be considerable. The long chain of uncertainty and risk from the reproduction of creativity through its commodification, all the way to marketing a product, can be reduced substantially, along with costs and time. The risks to such predation, however, can also be significant. The rapid rise of inter-corporate litigation is testimony to how often, or how easily, such predation can go wrong. Perhaps it should not surprise that the time horizons for inter-corporate collaborative arrangements are usually very short-term, narrowly focused on specific research projects or tasks, and often operate with substantial distrust between participants.[72]

Globalization has expanded the possibilities for those inter-corporate arrangements. Joint ventures, strategic alliances, and R2R arrangements are possible worldwide, more easily than ever. Telecommunications, the Internet, and the Web have made it easier to communicate and structure those arrangements at a distance. In many cases, R2R links modeled on B2B (business-to-business) networks—common among many decomposed industrial and service corporations—can expand the possibilities of finding partners as well as targets of predation. Many nations also lack legal safeguards against this form of pathology, leaving any enforcement (if such can occur) up to the relations of power between the corporate actors involved.

Appropriation Pathologies

A second set of pathologies arises from pressures to appropriate the results of creativity. Appropriation is of fundamental importance to the new corporatism.[73] It is key to extracting surplus value from the exercise of research creativity, and it is also vital for corporate survival. In the context of technocapitalism, where corporate survival depends on research creativity, appropriation gains paramount importance in corporatism's strategic quest for power and profit.[74]

One form of appropriation pathology involves the exploitation of those who provide their creativity. Exploitation occurs through the corporate *confiscation* of the results of creativity. Such confiscation is typically grounded on employment, and whatever salary and benefits corporate power grants to the individuals who

---

72   See Suen, *Non-Cooperation*; Choate, *Hot Property*.

73   Appropriation, although fundamental, is not the only preoccupation of corporate power. Beyond making decisions on appropriation, all other means for extracting profit and power must be brought into play, according to the best-known academic on corporate strategy: "...simply making that set of choices will not protect you unless you're constantly sucking in all of the available means to improve your ability to deliver," (p. 154), Keith H. Hammonds, "Michael Porter's Big Ideas," *Fast Company* (March 2001): 150–55.

74   Appropriation must be considered the prime vehicle to profitability; see the Chapter "Experimentalist Organizations," in Suarez-Villa, *Technocapitalism*.

provide their creativity. That sort of compensation is typically a very small fraction of the ultimate, accumulated surplus value that a corporation will derive from appropriation. Although many results of creativity may not end up generating surplus value, those that do typically do not compensate their creators justly, in comparison with the rewards that their creativity bring to corporate power.[75]

This form of confiscation or tacit theft, perpetrated on employees who provide their creativity, is all the more poignant when compared with the lavish compensation and benefits that corporate executives get. Compensation for the twenty highest-paid corporate executives in the US, for example, has averaged over 36 million dollars per year during the past decade. Executives of Wall Street investment banks have received as much as 67 million dollars in annual compensation in recent times.[76] Compensation for chief executives of Fortune 500 companies during the past decade averaged close to 400 times the compensation of an average employee, compared to 20 times in the 1960s.[77] Adding insult to injury, the kind of retirement benefits that employees get from corporations are typically dismal compared with the multi-million dollar "golden farewell" retirement pay-outs that corporate executives receive. A retirement lump-sum payout to a corporate chief executive was reported to be 85 million dollars, for example, and such awards seem very likely to go higher over time.[78]

The enormous difficulties for employees to claim their rights or confront abuses cannot be underestimated. A former US Secretary of Labor, for example, noted that even in the best circumstances, employees' chances of forming a union or similar employee-rights organization is about one in five.[79] Employees who try to organize are usually subject to intimidation and threats. Whistleblowers who report corporate abuse or malfeasance to authorities usually have little chance of being protected

---

75   See Perelman, *Steal this Idea*; Choate, *Hot Property*; J. Rodman Steele, *Is this My Reward? An Employee's Struggle for Fairness in the Corporate Exploitation of His Inventions* (West Palm Beach, FL: Pencraft, 1986); *Science*, "Letters: The Problem with Patents," 308(April 15, 2005): 353. Patent infringements against individual inventors by corporations have become more common and easier to perpetrate; see Michael Hiltzik, "Defending Patent Takes Toll on Inventor: Through Reexamination, Patent Rights Can Easily Disappear," *Los Angeles Times* (June 15, 2011): B1.

76   Aaron Lucchetti and Matthew Karnitschnig, "On Street, New Reality on Pay Sets In," *Wall Street Journal* (January 31, 2009): C1; Susanne Craig, "Goldman Officer Quits; Got $67.5 Million in '07," *Wall Street Journal* (February 18, 2009): C1.

77   See Robert B. Reich, "CEOs Deserve their Pay," *Wall Street Journal* (September 14, 2007): A13. Reich nonetheless argued that such disparities are "deserved", even though most corporate executives do not meet the objectives that they set for their own companies. See, for example, Phred Dvorak, "Poor Year Doesn't Stop CEO Bonuses," *Wall Street Journal* (March 18, 2009): B1.

78   Mark Maremont, "How Some Firms Boost the Boss's Pension," *Wall Street Journal* (January 23, 2009): A1.

79   Robert B. Reich, "Power in the Union," *Los Angeles Times* (January 26, 2009): A13.

from reprisals.[80] Those who refuse to bend to corporate threats are typically fired, even when doing so is illegal. In the rare cases when a corporation is fined for such firings, the penalties imposed by courts are insignificant and do not deter abuse.[81]

Globalization now provides more opportunities than ever for this form of exploitation and theft. Tapping brain-drain flows makes it easier to find creative talent that will bend to the will of corporate power. In many cases, individuals employed through global brain-drain flows will be placed in competition with home-based talent, to limit the latter's compensation and to make them more submissive to corporate power. Residency and work-visa requirements in rich countries are important supports of this global system of exploitation and confiscation. Those regulations typically prevent foreign employees from claiming their rights (or switching employers), for fear of deportation or of being black-listed by potential employers.

Outsourcing research tasks or opening branches in less developed nations also creates opportunities for this form of exploitation. Lower salaries, fewer benefits, and a lack of employee rights most certainly translate into lower operational costs for corporate power. Opportunities to exploit and confiscate the results of creativity proliferate, as underemployment and unemployment provide abundant applicants. Less developed nations with science and technology institutions that produce reasonably qualified graduates are prime targets for this worldwide corporate exploitive strategy.

Another type of pathology related to appropriation is *co-optation*. Co-optation involves corporate strategies aimed at corrupting or making others bend to the interests of corporate power. It can target other corporate entities, public governance, or academic researchers and practicing professionals. This pathology is grounded in the relations of power between the new corporatism and those who can affect its quest for profit and hegemony.

An example of cooptation of corporate entities can be found in the case of generic pharmaceuticals and biotechnology. Large pharmaceutical and biotech corporations that hold soon-to-expire patents try to co-opt generics manufacturers to delay the introduction of their cheaper, rival products. In one case, a major pharmaceutical corporation got a generics manufacturer to keep a cheaper generic off the market for twenty months. The additional time obtained (for the medication about to lose patent protection) generated about twenty-two billion dollars in revenue for the owner of that product.[82] In another case, fifteen US states sued a major European pharmaceutical corporation for paying ninety million dollars to an American generics manufacturer to delay the introduction of a cheaper rival to a best-selling heart medication.[83]

---

80   Jennifer Levitz, "Whistleblowers are Left Dangling: Technicality Leads Labor Department to Dismiss Cases," *Wall Street Journal* (September 4, 2008): A3.

81   See Reich "Power."

82   Avery Johnson, "Pfizer Buys More Time for Lipitor," *Wall Street Journal* (June 29, 2008): B1.

83   *The Economist*, "Prescription Drugs: Protection Racket" (May 19, 2001): 58.

Beyond payments, the threat of lawsuits against generic manufacturers can also play a role in getting recalcitrant companies to bend. Sometimes, filing lawsuits and seeking out-of-court settlements with generics manufacturers can be conditioned to their delaying introductions of cheaper products. In one case, for example, a delay of seven months for a high-selling medication generated almost four billion dollars in revenue for the company holding a soon-to-expire patent.[84] Whenever such tactics are successful, society is harmed by preventing the availability of cheaper substitutes, most of all to the poor.[85]

As much as 60 billion dollars' worth of patented medications lose their patent protection every year, and face immediate competition from generic rivals.[86] This situation translates into much lower revenues and profit for corporations that lose patent protection but, on the other hand, it provides lower prices to consumers as generic substitutes arrive. A European Union report, for example, found that generic medications enter European markets at prices that average about 25 percent less than those with expiring patents, and drop an additional 40 percent after two years.[87] The threat of drastic losses in revenue for corporations that hold about-to-expire patents, has thus become a powerful incentive to co-opt those who can diminish this challenge.

Cooptation of governments, public officials, and politicians is another type of pathology related to appropriation. Cooptation and corruption in this area can involve a wide range of pressures and measures. De-regulation or creating laws that make it easier for corporations to appropriate the results of creativity are the usual vehicles.[88] For example, laws that limit lawsuits brought by employees against corporate entities are one vehicle. Others can make it easier to fire employees who oppose corporate policies on appropriation, or corporate censorship over research

---

84   *The Economist*, "Pharmaceuticals: Patently Absurd" (December 6, 2008): 82; Jonathan D. Rockoff, "How a Drug Maker Tries to Outwit Generics," *Wall Street Journal* (November 18, 2008): B1.

85   Thomas M. Burton, "Left on the Shelf: Why Cheap Generic Drugs that Appear to Halt Fatal Sepsis Go Unused," *Wall Street Journal* (May 17, 2002): A1.

86   *The Economist*, "The Pharmaceutical Industry: The Bitterest Pill" (January 26, 2009): 62–3. Pressures on the corporate quest for profit associated with patent expirations has led some large pharmaceutical companies to try to produce biotech generics, also known as "biosimilars." See *The Economist*, "Pharmaceuticals: All Together Now" (July 26, 2008): 73–4; Jonathan D. Rockoff and Ron Winslow, "Merck to Develop Biotech Generics: Its First Copycat Drug Would Compete with Amgen's Aranesp and is Scheduled for Launch in 2012," *Wall Street Journal* (December 10, 2008): B1.

87   *The Economist*, "Patently Absurd."

88   Political lobbying is a common vehicle of co-optation. See Robert G. Kaiser, *So Damn Much Money: The Triumph of Money and the Corrosion of American Government* (New York: Knopf, 2009); Alicia Mundy, "Political Lobbying Drove FDA Process," *Wall Street Journal* (March 6, 2009): A1.

results.[89] In other cases, cooptation involves influencing politicians and regulatory agencies to allow marketing of insufficiently tested products.

The most egregious effects of cooptation can be found among pharmaceutical and biotechnology corporations, where harmful medications have caused an unprecedented number of injuries and deaths.[90] In the US over a period of four months, an independent monitoring group reported 21,000 injuries and 4,825 deaths from harmful medications, amounting to a 300 percent increase in deaths from the previous four-month period, and a 38 percent increase in injuries from the previous year's quarterly average.[91] These figures, alarming as they may be, are nonetheless only a fraction of the total number of cases involving harmful effects. Because the reporting of such cases is purely voluntary, it is considered that this kind of data represents less than ten percent of the total of harmful effects caused by medications.[92]

Another symptom of this pathology is the record amounts paid by pharmaceutical and biotech corporations over litigation against harmful products. One such case in the US involved a payout of 20 billion dollars to victims of weight-control diet products by a major pharmaceutical corporation.[93] Other cases involved payouts by corporations of 4 billion dollars to victims of a well-known pain reliever, and over one billion dollars to patients harmed by one of the best-known anti-psychotic medications. Litigation that seeks compensation for victims of harmful products nonetheless faces rising obstacles, as corporations seek every possible way to obstruct victims' right to sue.[94] Such ploys include, for example,

---

89   Ricardo Alonso-Zaldivar, "FDA Scientist Says He Faces Retaliation: Star Witness Who Criticizes His Agency's Drug Safety Record Contends He's Under Pressure to be 'Exiled' to a Different Job," *Los Angeles Times* (November 25, 2004): A26.

90   In the US, this has been partly attributed to the "partnership" of the main regulatory agency with pharmaceutical and biotech corporations. See David Willman, "How a New Policy Led to Seven Deadly Drugs," *Los Angeles Times* (December 20, 2000): A1; Alicia Mundy, "FDA Memos Undercut Stance on Pre-Empting Drug Suits," *Los Angeles Times* (October 30, 2008): A3. Unexpected side effects seem to be one of the outcomes of this "partnership"; see Ricardo Alonso-Zaldivar, "Drug Linked to Traffic Mishaps," *Los Angeles Times* (May 25, 2008): A20; Lisa Girion, "Lawsuit Targets Botox Maker: Allergan is Alleged to Have Failed to Warn About the Dangers of the Anti-Wrinkle Drug," *Los Angeles Times* (July 10, 2008): C1.

91   Institute for Safe Medication Practices, "Adverse Drug Events," www.ismp.org; Thomas H. Maugh II, "Side Effects of Prescribed Drugs Reach Record," *Los Angeles Times* (October 23, 2008): A12.

92   Maugh "Side Effect."

93   Alicia Mundy and Shirley S. Wang, "In Drug Case, Justices to Weigh Right to Sue," *Wall Street Journal* (October 27, 2008): B1; Alicia Mundy, *Dispensing with the Truth* (New York: St. Martin's, 2001).

94   Mundy and Wang "Drug Case"; David G. Savage, "Right to Sue Drug Makers is Affirmed: The Supreme Court Says FDA Approval of a Medicine is No Shield," *Los Angeles Times* (March 5, 2009): A1.

attempts to induce politicians to pass legislation limiting compensation amounts, or appealing every judicial decision to cause litigation costs to mount for victims, along with the hope that adverse judgments will be overturned.

Another example of co-optation involves bribing public officials to obtain government contracts. Such contracting is an important source of revenue for many tech research-intensive corporations. One of Europe's largest technology corporations, highly reliant on research and with a very diverse range of products and services, reportedly paid 805 million dollars over six years to government officials in various nations to win government contracts.[95] So customary was this practice, that the corporation set up "cash desks" in its own offices, where containers could be filled with up to a maximum of one million euros, in order to win contracts for its telecommunications hardware unit alone. Over a period of four years, some 67 million dollars were paid off in cash through those "desks." For other cases, the same corporation placed bribe funds, amounting to hundreds of millions of dollars, in special bank accounts that were kept off the company's ledgers. Illicit payments to foreign officials continued for many years, even after that corporation's home country outlawed such bribes.

Co-optation also involves researchers and professional practitioners. Typically, this vehicle of pathology involves corporate payments for academic researchers to endorse or publicize products whose testing they oversee.[96] In the first place, many studies of medications' effectiveness are financed by the same medications' manufacturers.[97] Although there is no pre-requirement that results be favorable to the products being tested, there is a tacit incentive for researchers to show positive results.[98] Moreover, there is no legal requirement that researchers or the corporations that finance such studies publish *negative* results. Positive results are thus about five times more likely to be published than negative ones.[99] This can

---

95   US Department of Justice, "Siemens AG and Three Subsidiaries Plead Guilty to Foreign Corrupt Practices Act Violations and Agree to Pay $450 Million in Combined Criminal Fees," (December 15, 2008), www.usdoj.gov/opa/pr/2008/December/08-crm-1105.html; see also *The Economist*, "Siemens Scandal."

96   See Jerome P. Kassirer, *On the Take: How America's Complicity with Big Business Can Endanger Your Health* (New York: Oxford University Press, 2005), and his "Tainted Medicine," *Los Angeles Times* (April 6, 2008): M6.

97   Marcia Angell, *The Truth About the Drug Companies: How They Deceive Us and What to Do About It* (New York: Random House, 2004).

98   Reprisals on researchers that do not play along with the interests of the corporations that fund the studies is not uncommon. See Cynthia Crossen, "A Medical Researcher Pays for Challenging Drug-Industry Funding," *Wall Street Journal* (January 3, 2001): A1.

99   See *The Economist*, "Absence of Evidence: Do Drug Firms Suppress Unfavourable Information About New Products?," (November 29, 2008): 82. In most cases, negative results are not published (or submitted for publication) because the corporations involved "bury" them. See *Washington Post*, "Drug Maker Buried Antipsychotic Study: AstraZeneca Knew Long Ago that the Pricey Seroquel Caused Significant Weight Gain, Documents Show," reprinted in *Los Angeles Times* (March 18, 2009): A18.

lead to the belief that new medications are better than they actually are, or that they are more effective than the products they replace.[100] Not publishing negative results can also lead to ignorance of potential side effects or deaths.[101]

Financial links between researchers and corporations that manufacture products have become so common in the US that they seem normal. A limited survey conducted by one of the most important medical journals, for example, found that more than one-third of researchers in charge of trials at medical schools and hospitals, had financial ties to pharmaceutical or medical device companies.[102] Major research journals have in many cases overlooked financial ties between authors they published and the corporations whose products they tested in their work.[103] In numerous cases, company-hired ghost-writers have drafted articles for publication, touting the benefits of certain medications while excluding indications of troubles or deficiencies.[104] This kind of collusion between researchers and corporate power now seems all too acceptable and may

100   One of the more interesting cases involved the controversy over "aspirin resistance" by people who take aspirins to prevent heart attacks. See David Armstrong, "Aspirin Dispute is Fueled by Funds of Industry Rivals," *Wall Street Journal* (April 24, 2006): A1.

101   Robert L. Hotz, "What You Don't Know About a Drug Can Hurt You: Untold Numbers of Clinical-Trial Results Go Unpublished; Those that are Made Public Can't Always Be Believed," *Wall Street Journal* (December 12, 2008): A16; *Washington Post*, "Drug Maker."

102   Denise Gellene, "Financial Ties Found Among Clinical Trials," *Los Angeles Times* (November 30, 2006): A22. In one case, an eminent anesthesiology researcher reportedly fabricated twenty-one medical studies that showed positive benefits from painkillers and were published in well-known anesthesiology journals. See Keith J. Winstein and David Armstrong, "Top Pain Scientist Fabricated Data in Studies, Hospital Says," *Wall Street Journal* (March 11, 2009): A12.

103   Ron Winslow and Rachel Zimmerman, "High Blood Pressure: A Medical Journal, Doctors Sever Ties," *Wall Street Journal* (July 29, 2005): B1; *Science*, "The Undisclosed Background of a Paper on Depression Treatment," (August 4, 2006): 598. Curiously, the leading US medical journal, itself a strong advocate for public disclosure of financial ties between researchers and the corporations whose products they test, was caught in a scandal involving just such ties in an article it published. The scandal also involved the journal's suppression of whistleblowers' information that called attention to the problem. See *The Economist*, "Medical Journals and Ethics: Pity the Messenger; A Leading Journal Unveils a Controversial Policy on Financial Disclosures," (March 28, 2009): 90–91; David Armstrong, "Medical Group Seeks Probe of Its Journal," *Wall Street Journal* (March 28, 2009): A4; *The Economist*, "Scientific Journals: Publish and Be Wrong; One Group of Researchers thinks Headline-Grabbing Scientific Reports Are the Most Likely to Turn Out to be Wrong" (October 11, 2008): 109.

104   David Armstrong, "How the New England Journal Missed Warning Signs on Vioxx: Medical Journal Waited Years to Report Flaws in Article that Praised Pain Drug," *Wall Street Journal* (May 15, 2006): A1; Anna Wilde Mathews, "At Medical Journals, Writers Paid by Industry Play Big Role," *Wall Street Journal* (December 13, 2005): A1.

not even result in any harm to reputations. Never before has corporatism enjoyed such close association with academic researchers, at the expense of society and the public interest.

Co-optation of researchers at the US government's pre-eminent agency for medical research, the National Institutes of Health (NIH), reveals how deep and widespread the collusion between researchers and corporate power can become. More than half of NIH scientists were thought to have violated the agency's policies on conflict of interest involving corporate links, according to one internal survey.[105] In one case, a NIH researcher served as consultant and witness for a major pharmaceutical and biotech corporation, testifying in favor of a product seeking approval, despite the fact that US laws prohibit federal employees from representing an external (non-governmental) party before a government agency.[106] The medication in question went on to generate 859 million dollars in sales for its manufacturer, over the first five years of sales. Later, the researcher in question was found to have engaged in "serious misconduct" but received no penalty from the agency.[107]

Orientation of research strategies to ignore preventive measures and instead target expensive remedies that favor corporate interests, is another outcome of the co-optation of research by corporate power. Cancer research has, for example, long been targeted toward trying to find "cures" that are grounded in corporate research, and in the corporate quest for greater profit through expensive products. Preventive, low-cost measures that would target avoidable causes of cancer, such as contaminants in food, water, air and soil, or ingredients in pesticides and household products, have been neglected. It should not surprise, then, that the lack of interest in prevention by the US's most important cancer research organization is associated with guidance from individuals in key corporate executive positions, who serve in its boards or as its top officers.[108] Corporate executives and corporate board members from the pharmaceutical, oil, steel and chemical industries, or from investment banking, have long succeeded one another as heads of that

---

105   David Willman, "NIH Inquiry Shows Widespread Lapses, Lawmaker Says," *Los Angeles Times* (July 14, 2005): A23. A NIH researcher was found to have taken 285,000 dollars in payments from a pharmaceutical company connected to his research; see David Willman, "NIH Scientist Charged with Conflict," *Los Angeles Times* (December 5, 2006): A11.

106   David Willman, "Drug Trials with a Dose of Doubt," *Los Angeles Times* (July 16, 2006): A1.

107   David Willman, "NIH Audit Criticizes Scientist's Dealings," *Los Angeles Times* (September 10, 2006): A1.

108   The National Cancer Institute's lack of interest in preventive measures has long been criticized, while the American Cancer Society has been found to have financial ties to manufacturers of polluting chemicals, and to pharmaceutical corporations that produce cancer medications. See Samuel S. Epstein and Quentin D. Young, "An Ounce of Prevention: Billions are Spent on Finding Cures, Little on Keeping Cancer from Occurring," *Los Angeles Times* (August 31, 2003): M1.

organization, orienting its policies and program toward the interests they favor, and from which they derive their wealth.

Corporate hiring of a very well-known researcher is usually sufficient to attract positive attention to products. The "marquee" scientists hired are usually based at a top-tier university or elite research center, and are paid to promote a product to practitioners through seminars.[109] Travel to those seminars is typically paid for by the sponsoring corporation. Practitioners usually do not have the time to review all the details of the research, and are all too often persuaded by the reputation and advice of the "marquee" scientist to prescribe the product. In the case of physicians, moreover, pharmaceutical and biotech corporations can finance the costs of continuing medical education needed to keep licenses to practice.[110] This association between corporate interests and practitioners is compounded by the pharmaceutical corporations' access to databases on physicians' prescription habits. The data allow corporations to target promotional campaigns at doctors who do not prescribe their products often enough.[111] Such databases also allow corporations to follow up over time, to determine whether changes in prescription habits occur, and to approach physicians directly to promote products.

Payments to researchers who bend to corporate cooptation can be quite high. One researcher at a top university, for example, received 19 million dollars over five years from one of the US's largest manufacturers of spinal devices, to induce surgeons to use that corporation's products.[112] In another case, a researcher at a top university received more than 8 million dollars when the company he advised was taken over by a major corporation, and subsequently received almost 300 thousand dollars per year to promote its products.[113] Another case involved a researcher (also at a top university) who received 1.6 million dollars

---

109   See Linda Marsa, "The Rising Health Costs of Capitalism's Invasion of the Science Lab," *Los Angeles Times* (December 20, 1998): M1, and her *Prescription for Profits: How the Pharmaceutical Industry Bankrolled the Unholy Marriage Between Science and Business* (New York: Scribner, 1997); Kassirer *On the Take*.

110   See Angell, *Truth About Drug Companies*.

111   Such corporate promotional efforts may in part be responsible for the widespread over-prescription of certain products in the US. See Mary Engel, "Deadly Bacteria Defy Antibiotics: Hospitals Are Vulnerable to New Drug-Resistant Strains, and Experts Fear the Toll Could Rise," *Los Angeles Times* (February 17, 2009): A10.

112   David Armstrong and Thomas M. Burton, "Medtronic Paid this Researcher More than $20,000—Much More," *Wall Street Journal* (January 16, 2009): A7; David Armstrong and Thomas M. Burton, "Medtronic Product Linked to Surgery Problems," *Wall Street Journal* (September 4, 2008): A1. Later, it was found that the son of a federal judge who ruled in favor of that company had long been linked with it through the law firm in which he was a partner; see Thomas M. Burton, "Judge's Son had a Link to Medtronic," *Wall Street Journal* (February 13, 2009): B1.

113   Keith J. Winstein, "Harvard Anti-Aging Researcher Quits Shaklee Advisory Board," *Wall Street Journal* (December 26, 2008): B1.

in payments over seven years to promote certain medications for children.[114] Practitioners also often receive payments for prescribing medications, in the form of honoraria, travel grants, or support for continuing education to renew licenses.[115] Such payments or support are typically not disclosed to patients who receive prescriptions for the products involved.

The third type of pathology related to appropriation involves *censorship* of research results. This pathology is closely related to the fundamental split between the commodification and the reproduction of research creativity, that is a hallmark of technocapitalism. It is also closely linked to the intangibility of creativity. Both of these features are great sources of anxiety, since they complicate greatly corporatism's quest for appropriation. The risk that any research results might leak out of the corporate domain and end up in the ears (or worse, the labs) of competitors is extremely disturbing to corporate power. All the more so when one considers that research costs alone can sometimes be as high as hundreds of millions of dollars for a single new product. As a result, corporatism seeks tight intellectual controls over those who exercise creativity, and over whatever they divulge about its exercise.

Such control over people and their creativity contrasts with the kind of control exercised by corporate power under industrial and mercantile capitalism. In those prior versions of capitalism, the most precious resources were tangible.[116] Raw materials, labor power and physical capital engaged in industrial or service production were used according to preconceived performance rules. Most important, because commodification and reproduction could both be sustained within the corporate domain, control over them was seldom at risk.[117] Physical control was usually sufficient to prevent their loss. Moreover, those resources could be easily measured, graded, or exchanged in standardized or pre-established ways.

---

114   Jennifer Levitz, "Drug Researcher Agrees to Curb Role," *Wall Street Journal* (December 31, 2008): B3.

115   See Gregory Zuckerman, "Biovail is Paying Doctors Prescribing New Heart Drug," *Wall Street Journal* (July 21, 2003): C1; Rhonda L. Rundle, "Industry Giants Push Obesity Surgery," *Wall Street Journal* (March 31, 2008): A1; David Armstrong, "Unions Say CVS Pushed Costly Drug to Doctors," *Wall Street Journal* (November 14, 2008): B1. Research results that cannot be approved by the FDA have nonetheless been promoted to doctors; see Ann Davis, "Tactic of Drug Makers is Raising Questions About Use of Research: Studies of Alzheimer's Pill, Too Limited for FDA, Are Aired to Doctors," *Wall Street Journal* (January 7, 2002): A1.

116   This can explain why intellectual property was so undervalued. See Michael Perelman, *Steal this Idea: Intellectual Property and the Corporate Confiscation of Creativity* (New York: Palgrave, 2002), and his "The Political Economy of Intellectual Property," *Monthly Review* (January 2003): 29–37.

117   See Braverman, *Labor and Monopoly Capital*; Noble, *Forces of Production*.

The technocapitalist corporate apparatus, however, requires intellectual and personal control in order to appropriate the results of creativity.[118] Corporate censorship is thus grounded on corporatism's unavoidable need to control an intangible quality, whose character is qualitative and very difficult, if not impossible, to measure, standardize or quantify. Claiming intellectual property, by disengaging those who provide creativity from its results (through commodification), is a major aspect of this type of pathology. Doing so depends greatly on confiscating the results of creativity such that corporate appropriation can occur, as noted earlier, *and* on co-opting any entities or individuals that might facilitate both confiscation and censorship.

This form of pathology damages society in various ways. It prevents, for example, the communication and diffusion of tacit knowledge that is a vital ingredient of the reproduction of creativity. In this regard, corporate power can end up damaging a fundamental process upon which it depends. Such damage occurs because of the split between reproduction and commodification, discussed earlier in this book, and the importance of external social influences on the reproduction of creativity. The open and free diffusion of research findings, and of tacit knowledge, are of vital importance for technology and science to benefit society.[119] Impeding such diffusion can, for example, prevent the timely treatment of diseases, the saving of lives, and a timely resolution of technological problems upon which human well-being depends.[120] Timely learning and practice are thus shortchanged, and human advancement is compromised, in order to benefit corporate power. Diffusion, if or when it occurs, happens on terms set by corporate power. Those terms typically favor corporate appropriation and intellectual control over employees' exercise of creativity.

Another vehicle of corporate appropriation is the patent system. Patent filings and awards are, however, considered a public record in many nations. This means that details of such filings and awards are typically open and available to anyone. Patent awards thus defeat secrecy and censorship, but they confer two important, albeit temporary, advantages. One of those advantages is monopoly power (typically lasting about 20 years) for the idea (embodied or represented by a gadget, material, method, organism, process or formula) that receives a patent award.[121] The second advantage is the power a patent award confers to

118 It must be noted, however, that research secrecy and censorship have spread beyond technocapitalist corporations, as creativity and intellectual property acquire greater value than ever. See Dan Neil, "Chrysler Needs a New Jolt," *Los Angeles Times* (January 11, 2009): A1.

119 See Hotz "What You Don't Know"; Kassirer "Tainted Medicine; Angell *The Truth.*

120 Biotech corporations that had decoded the staph bacterium's genome and held it as intellectual property, for example, refused to share such knowledge. See Marlene Cimons and Paul Jacobs, "Biotech Battlefield: Profits vs. Public," *Los Angeles Times* (February 21, 1999): A1.

121 Invention patents in the US are awarded to individuals. Patents awarded to an employee must, however, be assigned to the corporate employer, even when the invention was generated externally. See Steele, *Is This My Reward?*

litigate, and to intimidate through the threat of litigation, against anyone who is thought to infringe a patent. This threat can serve as an important deterrent, particularly when the relations of power are asymmetrical, and the patent holder is a powerful corporation with ample resources to litigate and coerce.

The rise of wasteful litigation is therefore one of the outcomes of corporate appropriation through patenting. Claims of patent infringement, combined with those of corporate predation victims who seek redress, account for hundreds of billions of dollars of litigation every year. The annual litigation budget of one global technology corporation alone, Intel, has been estimated to be close to one billion dollars.[122] Mostly, that budget covers costs from patent and other intellectual property infringement suits sought by the corporation, or filed against it. The exponential rise in litigation has turned intellectual property law into the highest-paid legal specialty in the US. In many ways, the astronomical increase in this kind of litigation reflects the rising importance of creativity as the prime resource of technocapitalism.

The overwhelming importance of research creativity is also reflected in the rising influence of corporations over universities, and the worldwide dimension of that influence. This aspect, discussed earlier in this book, is part of the appropriation pathology, as the frantic search for research results that can generate profit takes corporatism ever more deeply into academia.[123] A major point of conflict and contradiction involves the corporate need to enforce censorship over research. Academic research is and must, by nature, be open, to be shared and diffused as widely as possible. Without it, universities cannot fulfill their prime societal mission of reproducing creativity and generating new knowledge that leads to learning, as a way to benefit humanity.

Corporatism's survival, however, depends on the censorship of research results as a means to safeguard them and the surplus value they generate. The diametrically opposed aims of academic research and of corporate appropriation inevitably lead to a destruction of academic freedoms, and of open sharing and diffusion, that are vital to reproduce creativity in an academic setting. Universities are therefore on the losing end of this contradiction and of the conflict it generates. Their need for funding, even in public institutions that historically depended on the state, nowadays trumps considerations of independence or the right to contrarian intellectual expression. Actions speak louder than words and propaganda, whenever one looks deeply at the priorities

---

122   Robert P. Colwell, *The Pentium Chronicles: The People, Passion, and Politics Behind Intel's Landmark Chips* (Hoboken, NJ: Wiley-Interscience, 2006); Perelman "Political Economy" p. 34; Brian W. Kelly, *Chip Wars: Intel vs. AMD; Intel vs. IBM* (Scranton, PA: Lets Go, 2005).

123   See Bernard Wysocki Jr., "Ivory Power: Once Collegial, Research Schools Now Mean Business," *Wall Street Journal* (May 4, 2006): A1; Marc Bousquet, *How the University Works: Higher Education and the Low-Wage Nation* (New York: New York University Press, 2008).

of university executives, who all too often try to model themselves after their corporate counterparts.[124]

A common compromise, whenever university and corporate research are fused together, is to seek patents jointly as a way to diffuse research findings openly (since details given in patent filings and awards are considered public record). This tactic, however, greatly defeats universities' social mission of safeguarding openness and free diffusion, since research results are inevitably turned into property through patenting. Such appropriation is the cornerstone of litigation, as noted before. Universities are therefore put in the position of becoming global handmaidens of corporate power, supporting (and to some extent sharing) in its appropriation schemes. In a very real way, to preserve their favor as recipients of corporate donations, universities are therefore also adopting many of the ways and culture of corporatism.

Conclusion

Technocapitalism is spawning a distinctive new form of corporate organization. Grounded in technology and science through the exploitation of research creativity, the new organizations are projecting their power on a worldwide scale. Their quest for profit and power transcends boundaries and restraints, as most any aspect of human existence, life and nature become targets for corporate colonization.

The quest for global hegemony of the new corporatism is based on the *commodification* of creativity, which is under corporate control, and on the *reproduction* of this most precious resource, which is largely outside its control. *The split between these two fundamental phenomena, commodification and reproduction, along with the intangible qualities of creativity, set the stage for major contradictions and pathologies as technocapitalism acquires a global dimension.* Those contradictions and pathologies, and the dilemmas they pose to corporate power, are hallmarks of the new version of capitalism that technocapitalism represents, and of the new corporatism which it engenders.

The ethos of the new corporatism is based on a mode of social and economic praxis that can be referred to as *experimentalism*. Experimentalism involves, first and foremost, the harnessing of technological and scientific research for corporate power and profit. *Its ethos is diametrically opposed to the notion that new knowledge and research discoveries should be pursued for their own sake, to be shared and diffused freely for the primary benefit of humanity and society.* In the experimentalist ethos, new knowledge and research findings are worthy

124   See John Hechinger and Rebecca Buckman, "The Golden Touch of Stanford's President: How John Hennessy's Silicon Valley Connections Reap Millions for the University—and Himself," *Wall Street Journal* (February 24, 2007): A1; Rick Wolff, "The Decline of Public Higher Education," *Monthly Review* (February 16, 2007): www.monthlyreview.org/mrzine/; Bousquet, *How the University Works*.

only if they advance corporatism's global quest for profit and power. As corporate experimentalism advances its reach over societies and cultures around the world, it creates a new reality based on the domination of corporate priorities over all.

The global spread of corporate experimentalism is associated with another phenomenon of technocapitalism. This involves the need to decompose corporate functions and structures, which thereby become external and out of the control of corporate power. *Fast decomposition* is thus one of the phenomena accompanying technocapitalism and the new corporatism it spawns. Networks that are external to the corporate domain are the vehicles of decomposition, and they pose significant contradictions to the traditional corporatist quest for power and control. The re-configuration of the ecology of corporatism that decomposition encompasses, based on networks and the externalization of corporate functions, is closely related to the split between commodification and reproduction, noted earlier. Fast decomposition, a hallmark of technocapitalist corporatism, thus becomes a source of pathology in the new global reality that technocapitalism imposes.

A major internal aspect of corporate experimentalism is the emergence of systematized research regimes as the most important organizational mode. By and large, the systematized research regime is to technocapitalism what factory production regimes were to industrial capitalism. Appropriating the results of creativity is a major objective of the systematized research regime. Control over the commodification of creativity is essential for this objective, and it is also crucial for extracting any surplus value out of creativity. Such appropriation and control take up a global scope, as corporate technocapitalism spreads its tentacles into most any area that can advance its agenda. Through globalization, the new corporatism thus aims to tap and control any source of creativity whenever and wherever they occur. Exploiting the brain-drain flows of talent, along with the worldwide deployment of research activities, is also part of this grand scheme of expansion and conquest.

The sustainability of the new corporatism nonetheless remains an open question, as does the sustainability of technocapitalism itself. Although the new corporatism provides capitalism with an extended lease on time, it is likely that its many contradictions, dilemmas, and pathologies will provoke deeper crises than those humanity faced over the past three centuries. As the globalization of industrial capitalism sowed the seeds of its contradictions, crises and dysfunctions on an unprecedented scale, the globalization of technocapitalism promises deeper social pathologies than those humanity has encountered before. Corporatist technology and science seem poised to guarantee that those pathologies will have a lasting effect on global society, on its inequalities and injustices, and on humanity's link to life and nature.

The Haves and the Have-nots

Inequalities have been part of the reality of capitalism since its earliest times. They have played a major role in the evolution of capitalism, in the struggles against its injustices, and in its global schemes of domination. Inequalities are also very much a part of technocapitalism and of its advancing global reach.

The inequalities generated by technocapitalism are deeply entwined with its phenomena. Those inequalities are tied to the phenomena of fast accumulation, of the new corporatism and its research regimes, of the commodification of creativity, and of the global relations of power that this new version of capitalism imposes. The inequalities of technocapitalism are also deeper and farther-reaching than those found in previous stages of capitalism, because of their deep roots in technology and science. Technocapitalism's quest to re-engineer human existence, life and nature for the benefit of corporate power and profit, may thus lead to injustices the likes of which humanity has never experienced.

Technocapitalism's global relations of power revolve around accumulation and the corporate appropriation of that most precious resource, creativity. Those relations of power impose a chasm between the nations, peoples and cultures that have the means to sustain technocapitalism and those that do not. This cleavage between *the haves* and *the have-nots* will therefore be fundamental for understanding social injustice, and its association with a new kind of global hegemony that will likely be a hallmark of the twenty-first century. The cleavage between haves and have-nots is also likely to make inequalities, their permanence and their intensity, more poignant than those of any prior stage of capitalism.

The dimensions of inequity and domination will be noticed through the new sectors associated with technocapitalism. Advances in biotechnology, nanotechnology, biopharmacology and other emerging sectors will be used to sustain the new global reality imposed by technocapitalism. Since many advances in these new sectors will have military and surveillance applications, they will likely enforce the new global order and its inequalities in ways that humanity has never experienced before. This situation has some parallels in the use of new technologies under industrial capitalism, many of which served corporate priorities, cultural hegemony and military conquest. The new global reality imposed by technocapitalism, however, promises to create deeper and more pervasive global inequities, because of its grounding in technology and science, and its need to create a new global order based on corporate power.

The chasm between haves and have-nots, the character of inequalities and their role in sustaining technocapitalism will be explored in this chapter. The permanence of inequalities and their importance for corporate technocapitalism will be considered first, along with their association with a new form of global domination that is deeply grounded as much on technology and science as on corporate power. Major aspects of globalization that sustain inequality and corporate power will be taken into account, along with the cultural-ideological construct that tries to justify this new reality. The new global divides created by technocapitalism will be taken up in the final part of this chapter, to place the emerging new order of domination and inequity in perspective.

Haves versus Have-Nots

The struggle between have and have-not peoples, cultures and nations is a multi-dimensional phenomenon. It involves domination, social class differences, cultural values, emancipation, identities and human dignity as much as it does technology and science, or social and economic advancement. In this struggle, which will be a hallmark of the twenty-first century, technology and science along with corporate capitalism become more than ever a part of the social fabric, of the governance of society, and of the problems that humanity must grapple with.

The scope and scale of this struggle means that no corner of the earth is likely to be spared from its effects. These effects will therefore transcend previous struggles between haves and have-nots in the industrial capitalist era, when industrial might and modernization were seen as keys to advancement. In that era, factory and service production regimes, and the exploitation of labor and raw materials, penetrated the social fabric of many nations and cultures, setting the ground for greater inequality, for new modes of class conflict, and for a stronger subservience of governance to corporate capitalism. The globalization of technocapitalism not only compounds those effects in deeper and more intrusive ways, but also changes the terms of human social existence, life and nature.

We are thus at the beginning of an era in which a new version of capitalism and its corporate apparatus engender new forms of global inequality.[1] The new inequalities and conflicting interests are multidimensional, given the depth and reach of technology and science into most every human endeavor, into life, and into nature itself. Their dimensional scope is therefore not solely technical, economic or organizational, but is also social, political, cultural, ecological and

----

1   The new forms of inequality transcend and comprise longstanding concerns over social class injustices and struggles. Thus, longstanding treatments of social class inequality or labor struggles such as Stephen A. Resnick and Richard D. Wolff's *Knowledge and Class: A Marxian Critique* (Chicago: University of Chicago Press, 1987) and Harry Braverman's *Labor and Monopoly Capital: The Degradation of Work in the Twentieth Century* (New York: Monthly Review Press, 1974), continue to be part of the new reality imposed by technocapitalism.

socio-psychological, in the sense that they seek to establish a new reality that is all-encompassing.

Elements of Inequality

In a fundamental way, the new reality and the global inequalities that technocapitalism imposes rest on control of the main resources of this new era, by a new form of corporate power. In this new reality, the struggle between the haves and the have-nots is grounded in three major elements that are closely associated with this new kind of corporate power.

A major element is the *global relations of power*, which heavily favor nations that can control the fast accumulation phenomena and the most precious resource of technocapitalism, creativity. Controlling fast accumulation and the main resource of technocapitalism, technological creativity, depends on corporate power. Fast accumulation, the new corporatism and its research regimes are therefore at the root of new global relations of power. Without the new corporatism, its research regimes and the nodes of power they embed, technocapitalism would be as baseless as industrial capitalism without the factory system.[2]

The relations of power place cultures and nations that are at the vanguard of technocapitalism in a dominant position with respect to societies, cultures and nations that cannot sustain fast accumulation. The mechanism of global power is therefore heavily tilted in favor of those who control and sustain fast accumulation. However, fast accumulation is not sufficient, in and of itself, to place a society, culture or nation at the vanguard of technocapitalism, or to allow it to become dominant in this new era.

Another element, related to the first one, involves *appropriation*. Appropriation in the context of technocapitalism is a key to exploitation. And, what sort of appropriation distinguishes technocapitalism as a new version of capitalism? Corporate appropriation of the results of creativity, whatever they might be, as in the case of patents, ideas, formulas, processes, methods, copyrights or any other form of creative outcome, all of which are typically intangible. This kind of appropriation is far different from that exercised under industrial capitalism, which typically involved control over raw materials, capital, and the products of labor.[3]

2　The factory system had its roots in the Industrial Revolution and the emergence of *anonymous* capital (capital obtained from providers who had little or no relation to the industrial capitalist who would use it). See Michel Beaud, *A History of Capitalism: 1500–2000* (New York: Monthly Review Press, 2001); Eric Hobsbawm in *The Age of Capital: 1848–1875* (London: Weidenfeld and Nicolson, 1975).

3　Corporate appropriation under industrial capitalism might thus be considered *simple* in the sense that it involved commodities that could be readily measured and traded. Such appropriation was based on the physical (or tangible) character of the resource. This aspect

Corporate intellectual appropriation on a global scale is therefore a major element of the struggle, and of the inequalities associated with technocapitalism.[4] As we saw earlier in this book, the vehicle for appropriation is the corporate research regime. The key to the research regime's appropriation is the commodification of the results of creativity, such that surplus value can be extracted by corporate power. Thus, appropriation on a global scale is closely related to the relations of power that are implicit in the process of commodification, and in the extraction of surplus value. Appropriation is therefore part and parcel of the commodification of creativity, without which the technocapitalist dynamic cannot be sustained.

As a source of global inequality, appropriation rests on commodification, on the corporatist research regime in both its organizational and exploitive dimensions, and on the larger phenomenon of fast accumulation. Societies, cultures and nations that cannot generate, sustain and control those components of technocapitalism become the have-nots. The complexity of the inequalities between haves and have-nots in the context of technocapitalism are difficult to comprehend, not only because of the abstract nature of technology and science, but also because of the long-term character of fast accumulation, the intangible and qualitative character of the main resource, and the high risk and uncertainty that accompany research.

As a result, long-standing recipes for reducing inequality tend to have little relevance given the new reality set by technocapitalism. Policies that effectively targeted production, industrial expansion, and the trade of industrial commodities seem inadequate to deal with the global inequalities engendered by technocapitalism and its corporate apparatus.[5] The ultimate targets of those policies, modernization and industrial might, now seem less important, in an era when intangibles, qualitative features, corporate research and intellectual property influence so much the question of who rules global society.

---

made it possible to analyze processes of industrial capitalism in a systematic way. See Karl Marx, *Grundrisse: Foundations of the Critique of Political Economy* (New York: Penguin, 1973), pp. 401–50 ("Section Two: The Circulation Process of Capital").

4   Intellectual property started to gain increasing importance during late industrial capitalism, and most of all during its so-called "post-industrial" or services-oriented phase. See Michael Perelman, *Steal this Idea: Intellectual Property Rights and the Corporate Confiscation of Creativity* (New York: Palgrave Macmillan, 2004); Neil W. Netanel, ed., *The Development Agenda: Intellectual Property and Developing Countries* (New York: Oxford University Press, 2009).

5   One the most important policies during industrial capitalism was import substitution. See Raúl Prebisch, *Change and Development: Latin America's Great Task* (Washington: Inter-American Development Bank, 1970); Albert O. Hirschman, *The Strategy of Economic Development* (New York: Norton, 1958). Import substitution was heavily engaged in the Soviet Union starting in the 1920s through five-year plans; see Sanda Alexandridi, *L'Industrialisation de l'U.R.S.S. par le Plan Quinquennal* (Paris: Presses Universitaires de France, 1934).

The third major element of global inequalities under technocapitalism involves *neo-imperial means of domination*. These means are multidimensional and intrude upon most every aspect of society not only at the macro level, including the social, political, economic and military spheres, but also at the micro level, involving human existence and our relationship with life and nature. Thus, the kind of neo-imperialism that the haves can wield against the have-nots is much more complex than the imperialist frameworks of the past.[6]

The neo-imperialist reality of technocapitalism is more complex not only because it is deeply grounded in technology and science, but also because it is based on new organizational frameworks typified by the new corporatism and its research regimes, and on the multidimensional, long-term phenomenon of fast accumulation. Resisting the neo-imperial framework that accompanies technocapitalism may therefore be practically impossible with the vehicles of resistance used against prior versions of imperial domination.[7]

A key aspect one must not lose sight of in the neo-imperial reality set by technocapitalism is the totalizing role of technology and science. Their all-encompassing character is due to the inextricable marriage of technology with corporate power, and to its effect on human existence and nature. Thus, for example, a biotech corporation that creates genetically engineered seeds makes it easier for large agricultural corporations to profit, while driving small farmers out of business.[8] The genetically engineered seeds replace natural seeds, making the biotech corporation predominant in its market segment. A lifetime window of one crop, engineered into the seeds, means that farmers must purchase new seeds periodically. If not, farmers must pay royalties to the biotech corporation for every crop. Special fertilizers that must be used with the engineered seeds, and that alter soils and ecologies, make it practically impossible to return to the natural seeds. A continuous stream of profits is therefore "engineered" into the seeds. Natural seeds are thus eliminated from usage, not only because they require more care, have a higher risk of being damaged by the vagaries of nature, or have lower yields, but also because they mix with the genetically engineered ones and the resulting crops cannot provide a natural substitute.

The biotech corporation in question then becomes dominant on a global scale, shielding its research-driven aim of greater profit and power (its main objective)

---

6   Accumulation of tangible resources played a central role in imperialist strategy. See Samir Amin's *Accumulation on a World Scale* (New York: Monthly Review Press, 1974); Paul A. Baran, *The Political Economy of Growth* (New York: Monthly Review Press, 1957); John Bellamy Foster, "The Imperialist World System: Paul Baran's Political Economy of Growth After Fifty Years," *Monthly Review* (May 2007): 1–16.

7   Resistance to neo-imperialism and neoliberalism has so far lacked a common vision and strategy. See Leo Panitch and Colin Leys (eds.), *Global Flashpoints: Reactions to Imperialism and Neoliberalism* (New York: Monthly Review Press, 2008).

8   See Marie-Monique Robin's documentary, "The World According to Monsanto" (Ottawa: National Film Board of Canada, 2008).

with propaganda that touts a seemingly altruistic goal of eliminating famines, hunger or malnutrition.[9] All the corporation's propaganda says so, trumpeting the importance of its genetically engineered seeds. Through its engineered seeds the biotech corporation creates a new reality, one which makes farmers subservient to the corporation as a customer.[10] Farmers must pay a lot every year to purchase the genetically engineered seeds, the special fertilizers, or the royalties, often going into debt. Small farmers that cannot pay or have too much debt may then go out of business, and their land may be taken over by large agricultural corporations that can afford to purchase the engineered seeds.[11]

The new reality created by the biotech corporation thus involves not only a replacement of farmers who cannot pay for its genetically engineered seeds, but also a modification of the ecology of farming and of food itself. Global usage of the genetically engineered seeds or special fertilizer means that multiple organisms that depended on the natural seeds or the soils are cast out of the environment, since the engineered seeds or the fertilizer cannot be part of their food chain. The disappearance of those organisms in turn causes the extinction of other organisms, as the use of the genetically engineered seeds creates a ripple effect throughout the natural ecology of entire nations and continents. Moreover, the long-term effects of the genetically engineered seeds on human health are not well known since simulations of long-term usage are all too often incomplete. Those simulations cannot take into account every possible factor or combination of factors that may occur over the long term.[12]

The biotech corporation thus gains global clout not only because of its profits but also because of its effect on the profitability of many other companies, such as the agricultural corporations that use its genetically engineered seeds. Speculators purchase the biotech corporation's shares, and as shareholders they therefore have a vested interest in promoting the corporation's technology and its global profitability. In the case of the customers (agribusiness corporations), the genetically engineered seeds increase their profitability and their "shareholder

---

9   See Marianne Kaplan's documentary, "Deconstructing Supper" (Oley, PA: Bullfrog Films, 2002); Robin, "World According to Monsanto."

10   Farmers who are not "customers" and end up with the engineered seeds in their crops (because of wind or water) may be sued by the biotech corporation. See Perelman, *Steal this Idea*, p. 123.

11   See Robin, "World According to Monsanto"; Dominic Clover, *Monsanto and Smallholder Farmers: A Case Study on Corporate Accountability*, IDS Working Paper (Brighton, UK: Institute for Development Studies, University of Sussex, 2007). Not paying royalties can lead to costly lawsuits for farmers; see John W. Miller, "Monsanto Loses Case in Europe Over Seeds," *Wall Street Journal* (July 7, 2010): B1.

12   A key aspect is the assumption of "equivalence" criteria in testing genetically engineered seeds, through which regulatory agencies assume the engineered seeds to be "equivalent" to natural ones in their long-term development. See Robin, "World According to Monsanto."

value". For shareholders, increasing profitability and the biotech corporation's global market become paramount priorities.

In this emerging reality, which can readily be observed today in various parts of the world, governments get co-opted by the biotech corporation, and politicians who resist find themselves discredited, as propaganda campaigns meant to degrade them are orchestrated by the biotech corporation or its corporate customers. Since politicians are bound to be elected (a common prerequisite for political legitimacy in contemporary global society), the propaganda campaigns targeting them find "allies" and political capital in the form of opponents. Similarly, researchers, public agencies or citizen groups that raise questions about the genetically engineered seeds are muzzled as the biotech corporation exercises its clout over media (most of which may be controlled by large news corporations) and over regulatory agency officials.[13]

Intellectual appropriation of the technology behind the genetically engineered seeds by the biotech corporation, in the form of patents, allows this corporate control over agricultural sectors and crops to expand worldwide. Seed types whose patents expire are replaced by other newly patented seeds which may provide improvements over those losing patent protection. In many cases the improvements may be marginal (though patentable), but nonetheless fulfill the paramount objective of extending corporate appropriation. A prime function of the systematized research regime and its commodification of creativity, after all, is to keep patentable results flowing even when improvements are marginal. Thus, the connection between the systematized research regime and this process of appropriation is an intimate and mutually reinforcing one.[14]

The newly patented seeds aim to sustain the biotech corporation's profits and its hold over its global market segment. In many cases, by the time patent protection expires, the natural alternative (natural seeds) may well be a historical memory, known only through biological history books, and there may be little or no chance of returning to the natural seeds. All crops in that market segment are therefore likely to be using the genetically engineered seeds, since nature (through wind, water and soil) may unavoidably mix seeds and crops.[15]

---

13 Such campaigns may be orchestrated by powerful customers (global agri-business corporations, for example) whose profits and power are at stake. See James B. Lieber, *Rats in the Grain: The Dirty Tricks and Trials of Archer Daniels Midland* (New York: Four Walls Eight Windows, 2000); Kurt Eichenwald, *The Informant: A True Story* (New York: Broadway Books, 2000). Corporate campaigns may also include suppressing information on dumping of toxic chemicals or pesticides. See Dennis Love, *My City Was Gone: One American Town's Toxic Secret, Its Angry Band of Locals, and a $700 Million Day in Court* (New York: Morrow, 2006).

14 The systematized research regime is a fundamental vehicle for corporate appropriation on a worldwide scale, as discussed in the previous chapter.

15 See Perelman, *Steal this Idea*, p. 123.

The high cost of research, along with various related patents the biotech corporation holds, will likely preempt other companies from trying to compete.[16] A locked-in customer base or "walled garden" thus emerges, and the biotech corporation achieves monopoly power over entire crop segments. In any case, the seeds that lose patent protection (and therefore become generic) will be touted as less effective by the biotech corporation's propaganda, thereby dissuading those who might use them. Not employing "best practice" methods and technology, in this case meaning the latest (patent-protected) genetically engineered seeds, may keep customers from using the generic versions. After all, no agricultural corporation (the customer) seeking to enhance its own shareholders' value would want to be seen as sub-optimal, or as a user of technology that is not "cutting-edge." Propaganda, free samples of the new patent-protected seeds, foregoing price increases during introduction, and other tactics may insure that the new seeds are adopted quickly. Also, once the new patent-protected seeds start to be used by any customer, it may be impossible to return to the now-generic seeds, since the new ones may neutralize the generic ones, making it impossible to cultivate with them after a switch is made.

This dynamic of technologically-grounded corporate power and domination is now being played out around the globe. The government of the nation that houses the biotech corporation plays active handmaiden to the corporation's aim of spreading its tentacles all over the world. After all, what are embassy commercial attachés for? Politicians, usually in office temporarily (as election cycles come and go), accommodate to the corporate demand to expand markets abroad. After all, what are campaign contributions for? And, are exports (intangible in the form of patent licenses, or tangible in the form of seeds) not good for the home nation's economy?

Regulatory agency officials seek to get testing and approval of any new genetically engineered seeds quickly. After all, this will greatly improve the chances of their corporate employment once they leave the regulatory agency. And, moreover, the biotech corporation may, because of its global clout, come to be closely associated with the nation that houses its headquarters, with the global image and power that the government tries to project (technological proficiency a most likely one), and with national pride. Governments are thus enlisted in the technocapitalist corporate game of global domination. After all, what is government good for if it does not support the profit, power, and global presence of a biotech corporation headquartered in its territory? Does that corporation not pay taxes, contribute money to politicians, and otherwise support the national image?

Perhaps it should not surprise that the interlinking of these elements, along with the overwhelming influence of technology and science in this corporatist domination

---

16   See Christopher Then, "A Danger to the World's Food: Genetic Engineering and the Economic Interests of the Life-Science Industry," in Matin Qaim, Anatole Krattiger and Joachim von Braun (eds.), *Agricultural Biotechnology in Developing Countries: Towards Optimizing the Benefits for the Poor* (Amsterdam: Kluwer, 2000).

dynamic generates pathologies. Those pathologies are multidimensional: social, ecological, political, human, biological, ethical, environmental and economic. Because of their multi-dimensionality and their grounding in technology and science, they go deeper and encompass more than any previous pathology of capitalism.

The multi-dimensionality of these pathologies has attracted the attention of a scientist noted not only for the excellence of his eco-systemic research, but also for his critical views of contemporary capitalism. Richard Levins has explained how the crises and pathologies of contemporary capitalism have also become crises and pathologies of nature, thereby providing an understanding of the likely character of future crises in this century.[17] His *eco-social distress syndrome* is grounded in the interrelationship between capitalism, its damage to the earth's eco-systems, and the crises faced by humanity in its relationship with society, life and nature.

These crises and the resulting damage to nature can be considered part of the emerging technocapitalist system. They are as much a result of this emerging version of global capitalism as the social inequalities that divide the haves and the have-nots. In the new reality being imposed by technocapitalism and its corporate apparatus, ideology, actions and effects cannot be separated from one another. All of them are linked and complex, and the chasm between the have and have-not nations, peoples and cultures is part of their collective dynamic. The effects generated by the harnessing of technology and science to corporate capitalism will therefore be part of an eco-social distress syndrome that threatens not only our eco-systems but also the very existence of humanity on earth.

Features of Distress

The chasm between the haves and the have-nots exhibits several features which deserve our attention. They are as much part of the eco-social distress phenomenon that technocapitalism feeds as they are its effects. One feature involves the aggravation of *contradictions and conflicting interests* between social classes, between cultures, and between nations around the globe. These conflicts involve those who dominate the fast accumulation of technocapitalist resources and those who do not.

---

17   See Richard Levins, "Living the 11th Thesis," *Monthly Review* (January 2008): 29–37; Richard Levins and Richard Lewontin, *The Dialectical Biologist* (Cambridge: Harvard University Press, 1985), and their *Biology Under the Influence: Dialectical Essays on Ecology, Agriculture, and Health* (New York: Monthly Review Press, 2007). The conceptual scope of Levins' work has broad applications as corporate technocapitalism expands its frontiers. A major one is the oceans' ecology and its potential for corporate profit and power. See Bob Drogin, "A Deep Dive Into the Great Mysteries of Life: A Sea Catalog-in-Progress Has Already Upended Scientists' Views," *Los Angeles Times* (August 2, 2009): A1. All ocean species that have some potential for corporate profit and power stand to be genetically decoded and appropriated.

The contradictions and conflicts underlie the emergence of a new global order, based on the harnessing of technology and science to corporate capitalism *and* the coupling of this phenomenon with social domination. This form of domination is different, however, from that found in prior cultural and class struggles. Past struggles were typically grounded in the ownership and control of capital, labor, raw materials or land. Thus, social struggles often revolved around labor processes, the use of capital, resource exploitation, land tenure or factory production regimes.[18] The new global order and its class conflicts are grounded instead in access to new knowledge and in the appropriation of technological creativity.

A second feature of distress involves the *control of technological and scientific authority* by corporate power in order to benefit itself.[19] An important way to seize this authority is the setting of technological standards to serve corporate interests. Another vehicle, often combined with the setting of standards, is corporate influence over regulation. Standards-setting and regulatory influence can occur in various ways. In agro-biotechnology, corporate pressure to adopt equivalence criteria that assume genetically engineered plants develop in the same way as the natural specimens they replace is one example.

This kind of standard-setting, which is relevant to food-related regulation, may in fact *not* be based much on long-term knowledge of the genetically engineered plants' effects, or how they actually develop, but on assumptions concocted to favor the rapid introduction and marketing of those and plants.[20] Since it may take a long time and be very costly to find out the effects such genetically engineered products have, this assumption can help corporate profitability greatly. For the regulatory agencies that accept this assumption as a standard for testing

---

18   Factory production regimes, in particular, engendered a vast array of inequities, injustices and struggles. See Braverman, *Labor and Monopoly Capital*; David F. Noble, *Forces of Production: A Social History of Industrial Automation* (New York: Knopf, 1984).

19   Control over scientific authority is often the product of struggle between corporations, as explained in Pierre Bourdieu's "The Specificity of the Scientific Field and the Social Conditions of the Progress of Reason," *Social Science Information* 14(1975): 19–47.

20   This is consonant with the findings that much data and great research rigor often have no effect in changing beliefs; see Harry M. Collins and Trevor J. Pinch, "The Construction of the Paranormal: Nothing Unscientific is Happening," in Roy Wallis, ed., *On the Margins of Science: The Social Construction of Rejection Knowledge*, Sociological Review Monograph 27 (Keele, UK: Department of Sociology, University of Keele, 1979); Evelleen Richards, *Vitamin C and Cancer: Medicine or Politics?* (London: Macmillan, 1991). Corporate pressures can also impede change; see Robin "World According to Monsanto"; Lieber, *Rats in the Grain*. In academia, vested interests also often impede change; see Harry M. Collins, "An Empirical Relativist Programme in the Sociology of Scientific Knowledge," in Karin Knorr-Cetina and Michael Mulkay (eds.), *Science Observed: Perspectives on the Social Study of Science* (London: Sage, 1983); Bruno Latour and Steve Woolgar, *Laboratory Life: The Social Construction of Scientific Facts* (Beverly Hills, CA: Sage, 1979).

and approval, its simplicity may be rather convenient given the need to make decisions in a timely way, all the more so when corporate pressures are brought to bear on agency officials and the politicians who oversee the agencies.[21] For the corporations, pressing to have this standard accepted is of paramount importance given the limited time window of patent protection for the engineered plants, the high cost of research to create them, and the need to market and extract profits quickly. The corporation's shareholders must also be taken into account, since they expect quick and strong returns on their investment, and such returns are typically linked to compensation for the executives who command the corporation. Thus, a self-reinforcing web of influence, pressures, action and long-term effects (which may be potentially harmful to humanity and nature) occurs, with corporate power driving the process.

Standards-setting does, of course, vary between technology sectors. In the communications sector, standard-setting may involve a tie-in with a corporation's existing hardware. Coalitions with smaller companies may be arranged by the most powerful rivals vying to impose a standard.[22] Since the products do not involve food or human health in any direct way, regulatory oversight may be minimal. In such cases, the relations of power may be decisive, as large corporations and their coalition partners battle for their standard. Standard-setting may therefore involve strategies for capturing customer preferences, splintering the rival corporation's coalition, or otherwise compromising its profitability, public image and market share by various tactics. Some of these tactics may involve predatory schemes, as discussed in the previous chapter.

In very new sectors the standards may be set by powerful corporations that establish an early presence.[23] In nanotechnology, for example, its use for surveillance and social control requires interlinking with communications and software technologies. Transmissions of data gained through surveillance may occur continuously (in real time) thus posing the need to encrypt the data to keep it secret. Given the extremely small size of nanotech devices, their potential detection may not be a major problem, in contrast with past spying and surveillance devices (such as eavesdropping microphones and micro-transmitters), which could be detected on plain sight by searching. For nanotech surveillance, therefore, setting

---

21 See Robin, "World According to Monsanto"; David Willman, "NIH Inquiry Shows Widespread Lapses, Lawmaker Says," *Los Angeles Times* (July 14, 2005): A23, and his "How a New Policy Led to Seven Deadly Drugs," *Los Angeles Times* (December 20, 2000): A1.

22 See Robin Harris, "Blu-ray vs. HD DVD: Game Over," http://blogs.zdnet.com/storage/?p=149 (June 20, 2007).

23 Microsoft provides one of the best examples. See Wayne R. Dunham, *The Determination of Antitrust Liability in U.S. v. Microsoft: The Empirical Evidence the Department of Justice Used to Prove Its Case* (Washington: U.S. Department of Justice, Antitrust Division, 2004); William H. Page and John E. Lopatka, *The Microsoft Case: Antitrust, High Technology, and Consumer Welfare* (Chicago: University of Chicago Press, 2007).

encryption standards may become a paramount objective for corporations that operate in this sector.

Software corporations moving into nanotech surveillance may thus set encryption standards linked to their existing products, such that nanotech-enabled spying can become one more "application" for their customers. Holding patents on the software platform and the encryption formulas would help the standards-setting objective. A powerful corporation that sets the data encryption standard for nanotech surveillance may then move into nanotech hardware as it seeks to expand its market presence by diversifying. Standards-setting and diversification of market niches therefore often go hand in hand as the power of the standard-setter grows.[24] The standard-setter can then gain a virtually unassailable position, by diversifying its market niches such that anti-monopoly regulators cannot act against it on the basis of single-market dominance.

A third feature of distress and inequality is *cultural* in character, and involves creating new attitudes and strategies. These may not necessarily favor a corporate entity specifically, but corporate power and its domination of society, life and nature in general. These strategies and attitudes can set up justifications for inequality and domination of the have-nots by the haves. Such justifications allow concerns over social injustices to be masked or waived altogether by the public, by policy-makers, and most of all by corporate power.

The most important example of this feature of distress is the imposition of a culture of *competitism* on a global scale. This culture is now built into the rules of meta-national organizations that impose rules on nations around the world. The World Trade Organization (WTO), the International Monetary Fund (IMF), the World Bank and others are some of the organizations that have enshrined competitism as a major instrument of policy.[25] Such enshrinement is often subtle, but can come out bluntly in times of crisis.[26] Nations that refuse to accept the rules usually find themselves marginalized or cast out of the world's trade and finance networks. Credit becomes hard to obtain, financial flows may be obstructed, and their possibility of accumulating the resources they need may be impaired.

What does competitism involve and why is it so important for corporatism? At the core, competitism involves imposing competitive performance criteria in place of independent standards of excellence that are based on trust, solidarity and

---

24   See Dean Takahashi, *Opening the XBox: Inside Microsoft's Plan to Unleash an Entertainment Revolution* (Roseville, CA: Prima, 2002).

25   See, Lori Wallach and Patrick Woodall (eds.), *Whose Trade Organization? A Comprehensive Guide to the WTO* (New York: New Press, 2004); Richard Peet, *Unholy Trinity: The IMF, World Bank and WTO* (London: Zed, 2009).

26   The International Monetary Fund (IMF) has long been a prime instrument. See David Harvey, "Neo-Liberalism as Creative Destruction," *Geografiska Annaler* 88B(2006): 145–58; James Marson and Alexander Kolyandr, "Ukraine Defies IMF Warnings: International Aid Is in Jeopardy After Increases in Minimum Wage, Pensions," *Wall Street Journal* (October 31, 2009): A9.

reciprocity.[27] In so doing, competitism tries to undermine the autonomy, cultural identity, and the self-worth of those who refuse to submit to its domination. Systemically, this is done by demeaning (or worse, destroying) cultural values that do not fit, are incompatible with, or oppose its ethos. Competitism's fostering of rivalry, competitive criteria, and cut-throat tactics destroys trust, social bonds and non-competitive standards of value and self-worth. Social recognition is thus transformed into a positional commodity that can be realized only in the context of competition for social status, domination and economic gain.[28]

The point is often made that competitism affects corporate power negatively, through the vanquishing of a specific corporation by other corporations. This argument, however, misses the fact that competitism favors corporate power *generally* even though specific companies are driven under in the competitist game. After all, in the game of competitism a corporation that is driven under is replaced by another corporation (or various others).[29] The game of competitism thereby continues, regardless of who happens to be dominant or vanquished, and corporate power is even enhanced more through it, by giving the impression that it has no security or permanent lease on markets. But the issue here is not the fortunes or vagaries of survival of a specific corporation, or even that of various corporations, but the predominance of corporate power in general, as a social force. Whether corporate power comes from the winner or the vanquished corporation is largely irrelevant to this argument. A vanquished corporation's power will be replaced by another's (or by others'). It thus matters little which corporation specifically dominates. Through the competitist game, corporate

---

27   This is obvious in the competitive recipes provided in the management literature. See George Stalk Jr., Robert Lachenauer and John Butman, *Hardball: Are You Playing to Play or Playing to Win?* (Boston: Harvard Business School Press, 2004). The fact that onr of the world's best-known business schools publishes such work may reflect how much competitism pervades management education and the corporate psyche. In their "Hardball: Five Killer Strategies for Trouncing the Competition," *Harvard Business Review* (April 2004): 62–71; these authors recommend five strategies: (1) "Devastate rivals' profit sanctuaries," (2) "Plagiarize with pride," (3) "Deceive the competition," (4) "Unleash massive and overwhelming force," and (5) "Raise competitors' costs." The article concludes by promoting "a hardball state of mind" that must be internalized deeply and applied "at home."

28   Business economists long extrapolated these features of competitism to the case of nations and the global economy. See Michael E. Porter, *Competitive Advantage: Creating and Sustaining Superior Performance* (New York: Free Press, 1985).

29   Competitism can lead to oligopolistic (or even monopolistic) conditions, as the American experience with deregulation in various economic sectors shows. See Robert W. McChesney, *The Political Economy of Media: Enduring Issues, Emerging Dilemmas* (New York: Monthly Review Press, 2008); *The Economist*, "Technology and Antitrust: Here We Go Again; Will the Computer Industry Ever Escape Its Antitrust Problems?" (May 9, 2009): 63–4.

power is always dominant, no matter which specific entity happens to be exercising it.[30]

The strategies, attitudes and actions associated with the culture of competitism are all around us. Cut-throat competitive strategies at all levels: individual, corporate, national, cultural, racial and inter-class (as opposed to cooperation and solidarity), free trade (as opposed to fair trade), treating economic endeavors as war (as opposed to opportunities to form social bonds and trust), treating most any action that damages others but extracts advantage for the perpetrator as a triumph, and considering opportunities to exploit as god-sent occasions to be seized by any means, are a few examples of what this new reality means. This incomplete repertory of attitudes and actions can be seen throughout the social spectrum of many nations around the world, in popular media and culture, in governance, in social behavior, and increasingly even in academia.[31]

The ideological substance of competitism is grounded in neoclassical (mainstream) economic dogma, in neoliberal thought, in neoclassical economics' colonization of business education during the past four decades, and in its increasing influence over governance, popular culture and social behavior. The advancement of neoclassical economic precepts and their deep connections with neoliberalism is a history that remains to be told.[32] Although this history remains outside the scope of this book, its effects on American society are all around us. Existential fragility and emptiness, oppressive management, economic insecurity, destructive hedonic decision patterns, anti-social behavior, and widespread social alienation are some of the effects.[33] More alarming is that this panorama of cultural pathology is now spreading around the world.

---

30   When competitism is extrapolated to the case of nations, corporate power is also dominant; see Porter, *Competitive Advantage*. It is hard to think that a business economist would recommend that nations compete in the global economy through anything other than corporate entities.

31   Treating business competition as "war" is now common in the management literature. See C. Kenneth Allard, *Business as War: Battling for Competitive Advantage* (Hoboken, NJ: Wiley, 2004); *The Economist*, "Business Books: Kicking Ass in an Unflat World" (November 3, 2007): 77–8.

32   The longstanding connection between neoliberalism and neoclassical economics is probably best expressed in Milton Friedman and Rose Friedman, *Capitalism and Freedom* (Chicago: University of Chicago Press, 1962). Associated precepts such as privatization and deregulation have become guiding principles of meta-national organizations. See Bob Davis, "Report on World Bank Sees Deregulation Bias," *Wall Street Journal* (June 13, 2008): A6; Barbara Garson, "True Believers at the World Bank," *Los Angeles Times* (May 30, 2005): B11.

33   The dehumanizing effects of this phenomenon are all around us. See Tim Kasser, *The High Price of Materialism* (Cambridge: MIT Press, 2002); Avner Offer, *The Challenge of Affluence: Self-Control and Well-Being in the United States and Britain Since 1950* (Oxford: Oxford University Press, 2006). Perhaps it should be of great concern that neoclassical economics has long been one of the most popular majors in American

The three features of distress discussed in this section are central to the domination dynamic of the haves over the have-nots. In many ways, being a have-not means experiencing more contradictions and conflict with little chance of resolving them, being subject to standards set by the most powerful, and having no choice but to follow competitive precepts that have nefarious social consequences. All of these features are macro-societal in the context of technocapitalism's globalization, and they help sustain the relations of power that generate inequality and injustice.

Fast Neo-Imperialism

Enforcing the relations of power that sustain technocapitalism requires an apparatus of domination and control that is neo-imperial in character and praxis. This apparatus of domination extends the longstanding features of imperialism and neo-imperialism, by harnessing technology and science to corporate power to an extent never seen before in human history. As we will see later, the close association of technology with corporate power also has a military dimension—a necessary element to enforce the new global relations of power.

Fast accumulation provides the fundamental platform of support for this new era of empire-building. The accumulation of knowledge and of technological infrastructure therefore take up a very important role in this game of domination. They are a fundamental social source of creativity and of creative power, as discussed previously in this book. The accumulation of knowledge and of technological infrastructure thus provide a foundation of power for the new corporatism and for the globalization of "fast" neo-imperialism that is part of the new reality.

This new game of global domination, *fast neo-imperialism*, promises to reach deeper into human existence, life and nature than any previous version of

---

universities (and also in many universities around the world). All too often, it seems that the precepts learned in class are turned into a "what-to-do" guide for most any situation in life, work, social relationships and even romance. In romance, for example, treating dating as a business venture (based on widely diffused neoclassical economic precepts) has become common; see Robert McGough, "If You Can't Get a Man With a Gun, Big Bucks Might Work," *Wall Street Journal* (December 16, 1998): A1. In business schools, whose curriculum neoclassical economics colonized starting four decades ago, the precepts of this discipline pervade the professional training provided in MBA degree programs. Many of those precepts are turned into "best practice" recipes for management, thus creating substantial imitation effects. See Sumantra Ghoshal, "Bad Management Theories Are Destroying Good Management Practices," *Academy of Management Learning and Education* 4(2005): 75–91. At the level of communities, the negative effects are also palpable; see Stephen A. Marglin, *The Dismal Science: How Thinking Like an Economist Undermines Community* (Cambridge: Harvard University Press, 2008), and comments in my review of Marglin's *Dismal Science*, published in *Growth and Change* 41(2009): 533–41.

capitalism. It is also all-encompassing in its influence on humanity, more so than any prior era of capitalism could be. Under industrial capitalism, imperialism and neo-imperialism revolved around the conquest of raw materials and labor power, the use of factory and service production regimes as vehicles for exploitation, and the achievement of tangible products that could obtain power and profit.[34] Fast neo-imperialism, however, involves the appropriation of creativity, the use of systematized research regimes as exploitive vehicles, and the achievement of intangible results for extracting profit and power. These elements of the new era are bound up with technology and science through corporate experimentalism as a tool for appropriation. The different character of this new mode of capitalism therefore introduces new features in the longstanding framework of imperialism.

Three longstanding features can be found in the history of imperial and neo-imperial domination.[35] One of them involved a division between center (the haves) and the periphery (the have-nots). The game of domination was thus geared toward accumulation in the center. This longstanding feature is also part of fast neo-imperialism, but it reaches farther and deeper than previous versions of imperial domination. Whereas in the past the center (the haves) were the imperial dominators (as nations), and involved their own governments, their military, and their corporations as wealth extraction vehicles, under fast neo-imperialism this dynamic goes further to involve scientific establishments, educational institutions, meta-national organizations, and the rise of a new militarism based as much on technology and science as on raw firepower and physical aggression.

A second longstanding feature of imperialism and neo-imperialism placed the nations at the center on top of the global hierarchy of power, in an economic, political, military, social, and cultural sense.[36] Under fast neo-imperialism, however, this hierarchy is more flexible. As a result, the hierarchy can be fragmented, giving the appearance that some self-organization is possible. Certain nations that are not quite at the top of the hierarchy, and their corporate entities, may thus exercise much influence over certain "niches" of technocapitalism. Those niches can involve sectors such as bioinformatics or advanced software, for example, or specialized nanotech applications for textiles and auto parts.[37]

34 See Eric Hobsbawm, *The Age of Empire, 1875–1914* (London: Weidenfeld and Nicolson, 1987), and his *Industry and Empire: An Economic History of Britain* (London: Weidenfeld and Nicolson, 1968); Amin, *Accumulation*.

35 They apply to imperialist (nineteenth century British empire, for example) and neo-imperial systems. See Eric Hobsbawm, *Industry and Empire: From 1750 to the Present Day* (London: Penguin, 1999). A neo-imperialism based on the imposition of neoliberal policies and ideology is the topic of David Harvey's *The New Imperialism* (Oxford: Oxford University Press, 2003).

36 See Amin, *Accumulation*; Baran, *Political Economy*; Hobsbawm, *Age of Empire*.

37 New military technologies, such as those involving bioengineering, biomimetics and nanotechnology will most likely be monopolized by the nation with the greatest power in the hierarchy. See William J. Hennigan, "Military Seeks Lethal Arms in a Tiny Package," *Los Angeles Times* (May 31, 2011): A1.

The hierarchy of fast neo-imperialism therefore conveys some appearance of mobility (up or down) based on opportunism. In this way, the hierarchy of fast neo-imperialism seems less rigid than previous hierarchies of imperialism, and more capable of rapid evolution as conditions shift. Fast neo-imperialism is "faster" than previous forms of imperialism and neo-imperialism, because it can adjust more quickly, patch-up its vulnerabilities, and re-compose itself to continue the game of domination.

A third longstanding feature of imperialism and neo-imperialism involved the global ascendance of capital.[38] This is a process that started with the globalization of mercantile capital and was followed by industrial capital (in both its factory- and service-based modes).[39] This globalization of capital is now considered to be about complete with the integration of China and the nations of the extinct Soviet bloc into the global framework of capitalism. The global ascendance of capital is therefore part of the support platform for fast neo-imperialism. With the world now practically integrated in the framework of capitalism, the conditions are thereby set for the rise and spread of a new mode of capitalism—the globe's ground has therefore been fertilized for the planting of the seeds of technocapitalism and of fast neo-imperial conquest.

Beyond these three longstanding features and the new modifications introduced by fast neo-imperialism, there is a new dimension that will likely become a hallmark of technocapitalism and of the twenty-first century. This is the emerging *global ascendance of technological and scientific creativity as a tool of conquest* and of corporate power. Thus, in many respects technological and scientific creativity seems destined to take a place alongside capital as a worldwide vehicle for neo-imperial domination. Such creativity is thereby set to be a major economic, political and military resource in its own right, as it becomes ever more entwined with fast neo-imperialism and the new corporatism.

The global ascendance of technocapitalism, of its apparatus of fast accumulation, of the new corporatism, of its main resource (creativity) and of fast neo-imperialism, can be seen as an attempt to overcome (or at least ameliorate) a major problem of capitalism and of its unfettered globalization. This problem involves slow long-term growth in the center (the haves) in the current global order, which includes the nations most capable of sustaining fast accumulation.[40] Those nations and cultures are at the top of the fast neo-imperial hierarchy, and only through the deep harnessing of technology and science to corporate capitalism (that technocapitalism represents) can they have any hope of overcoming the problem of stagnation or slow growth.

---

38 See Amin, *Accumulation*; Hobsbawm, *Industry and Empire*.

39 See Beaud, *History of Capitalism*.

40 See Philip Armstrong, Andrew Glynn and John Harrison, *Capitalism Since 1945: The Making and Breaking of the Long Boom* (Oxford, UK: Blackwell, 1991); David Harvey, *A Brief History of Neoliberalism* (Oxford: Oxford University Press, 2005).

The attempt to overcome the problem of slow long-term growth through financialization, with loose monetary policies, unfettered speculation and high indebtedness, seems to have run its course.[41] This wild and perilous adventure that started in the early 1980s was seriously damaged with the financial crisis that started in 2007. As a remedy for long-term slow growth it was a fantasy grounded in neoliberal ideology and legitimized through neoclassical economic precepts. The fantasy may have made much money for those lucky enough to pull their billions out before crisis struck, but its consequences have shown that it cannot be a sustainable remedy for slow growth.

As a potential generator of growth, technocapitalism therefore seeks to sustain the dominance of the center (the haves) through fast neo-imperialism. The methods to be employed to sustain this dominance will be deeply grounded in technology and science. Their all-encompassing nature and their effects on human existence, life and nature may make the effects of previous imperial adventures pale by comparison. The new methods, which are likely to be based on bioengineering, nanotechnology and other sectors symbolic of technocapitalism, will impose a new reality—one which we do not yet fully understand.

Inequality and Power

Inequality is part of the new reality imposed by technocapitalism. Fast neo-imperialism, corporate experimentalism and fast accumulation are technocapitalism's vehicles for global domination, but the inequalities these vehicles help create have a more disturbing aspect. This is that the global sustenance of technocapitalism, of its new corporatism, of fast accumulation, and of fast neo-imperialism depend greatly on the *permanence of inequalities* between the haves and the have-nots. Those inequalities, which occur in many dimensions, between cultures, between social classes, between peoples and between nations, are therefore as much a part of the new reality imposed by technocapitalism as the systematized research regimes, the experimentalist ethos, or the commodification of creativity.

The permanence of global inequalities between the haves and the have-nots is essential for technocapitalist corporatism for one very practical reason. Global inequalities help keep research costs down, thereby sustaining profits. And profits are, after all, fundamentally related to corporate power and survival. Keeping research costs down is therefore of fundamental importance to the technocapitalist corporation. The very expensive nature of research, and its high risk and uncertainty require continuous, unflinching efforts to keep costs down by all means. This is where the importance of the have-nots comes into the calculus of the new corporatism. When there are many have-not nations or peoples around, there is always the possibility of reducing research costs greatly.

---

41   John Bellamy Foster, "The Financialization of Capital," *Monthly Review* 59(April 2007): 1–12.

Outsourcing and Inequality

The possibility of reducing research costs through inequalities, and through their permanence, occurs in two ways. One of them involves the outsourcing of research activities to have-not nations, as noted previously in this book. Research outsourcing has and will become increasingly important in reducing costs because of the very expensive nature of research in the emerging sectors associated with technocapitalism. In particular, research tasks associated with clinical testing, which often involve great risk both in terms of potential success and the personal health of the test subjects, are a major target for outsourcing.[42] This is the case, for example, in biopharmacology, genomics, proteomics and genetic engineering.

Outsourcing of human testing to have-not nations is already booming for research-oriented corporations in biotechnology and biopharmacology.[43] It is likely to increase substantially as these companies try to reduce costs and speed up research and testing by every means possible. However, other kinds of testing in sectors with much risk to individual and public health are also starting to be outsourced. In nanotechnology, for example, where extremely small particles pose risks to human and animal organs, safety tests and trials are also moving toward have-not nations.

Beyond testing and trials, core research activities are also increasingly targeted for outsourcing. Laboratories supported by governments, along with companies in have-not nations, are taking up core research tasks subcontracted out by corporations from the "have" nations. This kind of outsourcing is often geared toward the more dangerous tasks, but it is now also targeting relatively simple (but expensive) core activities that can be undertaken away from the corporate mother labs. This kind of outsourcing also transfers risk to the have-not nations, thus eliminating potential legal liabilities for the outsourcing corporation.

The benefits for the receiving have-not nations are usually quite limited, since they obtain little or no real technology transfer, in the sense that the isolated research tasks they are subcontracted for do not add up to the whole of any new technology. The actual learning of a new technology, or the development of the underlying creativity and knowledge, is therefore missing. The complexity and abstract quality of the new technologies associated with technocapitalism also make it very difficult for them to be picked up through the practice of research.[44]

---

42   See Shirley S. Wang, "Most Clinical Trials Done Abroad," *Wall Street Journal* (February 19, 2009): D3; Seth W. Glickman et al., "Ethical and Scientific Implications of the Globalization of Clinical Research," *New England Journal of Medicine* 360(2009): http://content.nejm.org/content/full/360/8/816.

43   Wang, "Most Clinical Trials"

44   Learning by doing in biotech, nanotech or any other field of research associated with technocapitalism requires a lot more background knowledge and preparation (many years of advanced study and possibly a doctorate) to be able to make the transition from repeating research tasks to being truly creative, compared to the fields associated with

What happens is that the most important pieces of the larger puzzle of the technology are never revealed to them, and they cannot therefore replicate or learn them in order to launch themselves independently.

This situation is designed to be that way, so that the have-nots cannot become competitors of the corporations that subcontracted them. The main research elements of the technology are therefore kept under the control of the corporation (in its "have" nation home base) that subcontracted them, in order to safeguard its appropriation of that technology. Thus, the labs or companies subcontracted in the have-not nations may become little more than narrow specialists for certain research tasks, that never add up to any learning of a new technology, in any complete sense. Their role in research outsourcing may actually turn out to be more disadvantaged than that of the offshore sweatshops and factories in old-tech industries (such as textiles, apparel or auto parts), since at least the old-tech subcontractors often get to learn a whole technology on their own.[45]

Brain Drain Conquest

The second important way in which permanent inequality helps reduce research costs is through brain drain flows of research talent migrating out of have-not nations. These flows have become increasingly important for the "have" nations that are building a substantial profile in the new sectors associated with technocapitalism. The United States in particular, which is at the vanguard of technocapitalism, depends greatly on brain drain flows out of have-not nations.[46] This is partly a consequence of the deficient quality of American primary and secondary school science education.

Thus, by the time they reach university the vast majority of American students are woefully deficient for undertaking any study in technology and science fields.[47] The very abstract nature of cutting-edge technology and science education today, their complexity, the high level of concentration and persistence required, and

industrial capitalism. See John D. Bernal, *Science and Industry in the Nineteenth Century* (London: Routledge and Paul, 1953); Noble, *Forces of Production*.

45   See Rongping Mu, *Technology Transfer from Germany to China: Case Studies on Chinese Carmakers and Parts Suppliers* (Berlin: Technische Universität, 2001); Richard Li-Hua, *Technology and Knowledge Transfer in China* (Aldershot, UK: Ashgate, 2004).

46   *The Economist*, "Give Me Your Scientists: Restricting the Immigration of Highly Skilled Workers Will Hurt America's Ability to Innovate" (March 7, 2009): 84; Michael P. Smith and Adrian Favell (eds.), *The Human Face of Global Mobility: International Highly Skilled Migration in Europe, North America, and the Asia-Pacific* (New Brunswick, NJ: Transaction, 2006).

47   The US has long ranked below all other "have" nations, and even below some have-not nations, in high school science and math performance. See Stephane Baldi, *Highlights from PISA 2006: Performance of U.S. 15-Year-Old Students in Science and Mathematics Literacy in an International Context* (Washington: National Center for Education Statistics, 2007).

the personal sacrifices (in terms of social and private life) that must be made mean that even the relatively few university-level students with the requisite knowledge often do not take up study in these fields. At the same time, widespread American cultural values that favor get-rich-quick and other hedonic mindsets also shortchange the possibility of attracting more students to technology and science fields.

It therefore seems fair to say that much of the United States' capability for sectors associated with technocapitalism is being built on the back of brain drain flows. Such flows come in two main forms. One of them occurs through the large number of foreign students who undertake graduate education in technology and science fields.[48] The importance of this kind of flow may become obvious to any casual observer who visits technology and science departments at any American university. It is common to see that as many as 90 percent of all graduate students in technology and science fields in American universities are foreign, having completed their undergraduate education abroad (usually in have-not nations). The vast majority of them typically stay in the US after completing their degrees in science and technology fields, and either go on to work for research-oriented corporations (of the technocapitalist mold) or enter academia as faculty and researchers.

The cost of their primary and secondary schooling, and their undergraduate university education is borne by their home (have-not) countries, thus relieving the US of this kind of very expensive, long-term and complex investment. Most of those foreign students will stay in the US indefinitely, thus building their careers there, for their entire professional lives or at least a large portion of them.[49] This means that they also become major creativity providers to American technocapitalist corporations.

American universities thereby become very important partners in the dynamic of technocapitalism, of its new corporatism, of fast accumulation and of fast neo-imperialism.[50] All these components of the technocapitalist apparatus are

---

48   See Teresa B. Bevis, *International Students in American Colleges and Universities: A History* (New York: Palgrave Macmillan, 2007); Richard B. Freeman, Emily Yin and Chia-Yu Shen, *Where Do New US-Trained Science-Engineering PhDs Come From?* (Cambridge, MA: National Bureau of Economic Research, 2004).

49   In the US, immigrants made up about two-thirds of the net additional individuals with science and engineering doctorates between 1995 and 2006. In American universities and research laboratories, about half of all scientists and engineers with doctorates are immigrants. See *The Economist*, "Give Me Your Scientists."

50   The influence of technology corporations in American universities now seems stronger than ever, for obvious reasons. They are repositories of immigrant students in science and engineering fields who will be recruited to work in corporate research labs once they graduate. Also, universities are repositories of much tacit knowledge that can be used in research. Despite the negative effects of this trend, few critical works have addressed it. See Jennifer Washburn, *University, Inc.: The Corporate Corruption of American Higher Education* (New York: Basic Books, 2005); Alan P. Rudy, *Universities*

thus bound together in fundamental ways. They feed and support one another by the permanence of global inequalities between the haves and the have-nots. They cannot be separated from one another without breaking down the system of technocapitalist accumulation and global power.

Another form of brain drain flow involves international migration of technological and scientific talent from have-not toward "have" nations. This kind of flow, which is now global and growing rapidly, involves already educated individuals in technology and science fields, most with graduate-level diplomas, and in many cases also research experience. The have-not nations where these flows originate thus finance their entire education, and the "have" nations that receive them are thereby relieved of the need to educate them, from the primary level all the way through university. This represents an enormous subsidy from the have-not to the "have" nations.[51]

Although it is sometimes argued that the remittances of brain drain migrants back to their home (have-not) nations help offset the costs incurred by those nations, such arguments ignore the fact that remittances are typically directed to family members for private ends. They have little or no effect on social or collective spending, of the type (educational, health, infrastructure and other) that allowed the brain drain emigrants to gain talents in technology and science. Any "trickle-down" of such remittances to support vital social expenditures is typically quite weak or inexistent. This distinction between the *social* nature of public spending, and the *private* character of remittances is lost on arguments that favor brain drain migration.[52] Moreover, remittances usually do not pay taxes that can help offset the public sums expended in the education, health, and other support for potential emigrants, or for those who already emigrated. Brain drain emigrants who return also often end up working for foreign corporations based in the "have" nations, or set up their own enterprises, avoiding the kinds of positions that contribute most to build up creative talents for research, as in education, or in public services that directly support technology and science.

The migratory brain drain flow benefits greatly the technocapitalist corporation. Research costs are reduced by employing immigrant researchers, who are typically held in a sort of bondage to their employer by virtue of their visa status. Changing employers is often a perilous undertaking, since visa regulations may discourage it. Those regulations may also tacitly allow reprisals by their corporate

---

in the Age of Corporate Science: The UC Berkeley-Novartis Controversy (Philadelphia: Temple University Press, 2007).

51   This subsidy is still largely unquantified. A related issue is the debt that have-not nations supposedly owe the "have" nations; see Paulo Nakatani and Rémy Herrera, "The South Has Already Repaid its External Debt to the North: But the North Denies its Debt to the South," *Monthly Review* (June 2007): 31–6; Steven Hiatt, ed., *A Game as Old as Empire: The Secret World of Economic Hit Men and the Web of Global Corruption* (San Francisco: Berrett-Koehler, 2007), p. 19.

52   See *The Economist*, "Economics Focus: Drain or Gain?" (May 28, 2011): 80.

employer. These reprisals may take the form of notification to the authorities about a "violation" of the visa's requirements when the employee is in the process of changing jobs, or before he can find another employer that can provide the necessary documentation to prevent deportation. This aspect alone often acts as a perverse incentive to make employees stay with an abusive corporate employer. The entwined nature of visa regulations and this sort of bondage is part of the fast neo-imperialist apparatus of domination of the haves over the have-nots.[53]

Fast Militarism

Sustaining global inequalities can require military force. After all, when meta-national organizations fail to bring the have-nots into line, and the have-nots organize themselves well enough to resist, only force (or its threat) can further the goal of conquest.[54] Fast neo-imperialism, however, relies on a different kind of military force from that used in past imperial and neo-imperial conquest. This new kind of military force may be called *fast militarism*, as it is deeply entwined with the new technologies that technocapitalism provides.

Fast militarism is an emerging phenomenon that will likely be closely associated with the twenty-first century and with technocapitalism. Its most important characteristic is the rapid, very violent and clever use of force to conquer whoever happens to be targeted. Speed, great violence and highly sophisticated technologies are therefore at the core of this new form of conquest.[55] Violence

---

53 In the case of the US, the tailoring of visa requirements to serve the needs of corporate power has long been part of the politics of immigration. See Jane Guskin and David L. Wilson, *The Politics of Immigration: Questions and Answers* (New York: Monthly Review Press, 2007).

54 The doctrine of preemptive war may acquire special relevance in this regard. See James M. Cypher, "From Military Keynesianism to Global-Neoliberal Militarism," *Monthly Review* (June 2007): 37–55; Ernest Haberkern, "Prophets of the 'Permanent War Economy'", *Monthly Review* (May 2009): 62–4. Preemptive war is implemented through a global system of military bases: the US reportedly has bases in 70 nations around the world, with the total number of bases (of one type or another) said to number more than one thousand; see Chalmers Johnson, *The Sorrows of Empire* (New York: Metropolitan Books, 2004); James Mann, *The Rise of the Vulcans* (New York: Viking, 2004). Preemptive war will likely be highly intrusive, given the new technologies that technocapitalism can provide. See Nick Turse, *The Complex: How the Military Invades Our Everyday Lives* (New York: Metropolitan Books, 2008).

55 The high brutality of this new form of warfare may be difficult to imagine but perhaps Michael Scheuer's "Break Out the Shock and Awe: If We Want to Defeat Our Enemies, We Have to be Willing to Use Lethal, Overpowering Force," *Los Angeles Times* (March 9, 2008): M1, and his *Marching Toward Hell: America and Islam After Iraq* (Prince Frederick, MD: Recorded Books, 2008) can provide some insights on the mindset. See also Andrew F. Krepinevich, *Seven Deadly Scenarios: A Military Futurist Explores War in the 21st Century* (New York: Bantam Dell, 2009); Philip Bobbitt, *Terror and Consent: The*

here includes not just past forms of military strategy, but also new ones enabled by biotechnology, nanotechnology, biopharmacology, genetic engineering, advanced software and biomimetics.

This marriage of technology, military power and corporatism made possible by technocapitalism may likely revolutionize warfare in the twenty-first century. The *techno-military-corporate complex* that underpins fast militarism may be at the service of fast neo-imperialism in more versatile, clever and innovative ways than any previous military power at the service of imperialism could ever be.[56] Its impact on warfare will likely surpass the effects of the introduction of gunpowder centuries ago, or perhaps even air power and nuclear weapons in more recent times. The have-nots who resist may thereby be more effectively conquered and submitted to the new global order imposed by technocapitalism and its vehicle of fast neo-imperialism.[57] In this way, fast militarism may become a formidable tool to insure the permanence of inequities between the haves and the have-nots.[58]

Wars for the Twenty-First Century (New York: Knopf, 2008). The connection between the new warfare and economic domination is quite explicit in Bobbitt's book. He believes that the nation-state is now being supplanted by the "market state." Such states will be required to deregulate and privatize in a massive way (along neoliberal lines), thereby outsourcing most of their operations to private contractors. Warfare, intelligence and defense would be among these outsourced operations.

56 This techno-military-corporate complex is largely a product of the intimate connection between the US military and the advance of high-tech during the twentieth century. See David Hambling, *Weapons Grade: How Modern Warfare Gave Birth to Our High-Tech World* (New York: Carroll and Graf, 2005); Christophe Lécuyer, *Making Silicon Valley: Innovation and the Growth of High Tech, 1930–1970* (Cambridge: MIT Press, 2006).

57 The global execution of fast militarism may largely occur through the use of warfare contractors. See Jeremy Scahill, *Blackwater: The Rise of the World's Most Powerful Mercenary Army* (New York: Nations Books, 2007); Suzanne Simons, *Master of War: Blackwater USA's Erik Prince and the Business of War* (New York: HarperCollins, 2009). [Blackwater Worldwide changed its name in 2009 to Xe Corporation after atrocities in Iraq, and overpayments of tens of millions of dollars from the US government, attracted unwanted attention; see Yochi J. Dreazen, "Audit Finds that U.S. Overpaid Blackwater," *Wall Street Journal* (June 16, 2009): A6]. Warfare outsourcing and training services are also becoming important revenue sources for other companies long engaged in providing military technology, such as Lockheed Martin, Northrop Grumman, BAE Systems, and L-3 Communications Holdings; see, for example, August Cole, "Defense Firms Look to Fill Gaps as U.S. Policy Shifts," *Wall Street Journal* (March 2, 2009): A4.

58 The importance of military power for sustaining American global economic domination was argued in Thomas Friedman's *The Lexus and the Olive Tree* (New York: Farrar, Straus and Giroux, 1999): "The hidden hand of the market will never work without a hidden first—McDonald's cannot flourish without McDonnell Douglas, the designer of the F-15. And the hidden fist that keeps the world safe for Silicon Valley's technologies is called the United States Army, Air Force, Navy and Marine Corps. Without America on duty, there will be no America Online." (p. 373) (also quoted in Perelman, "Political Economy

The tools of fast militarism might seem to have come out of some science fiction volume on futuristic warfare, but the reality is that all the technologies to undertake this kind of warfare are already available, or are well on the way. Only scientific ethics and economic cost stand in the way of producing and deploying them. However, these barriers can be counted on to collapse as knowledge of these technologies advances and the imperative of conquest and profit becomes ever more urgent. As a restraint, ethics seems no more durable than other social and cultural obstacles that at one time or another stood in the way of the Industrial Revolution, of the factory system, or of mass production.

All such restraints collapsed as the imperial calculus of profit and power made it clear that substantial gains could be extracted. The cost barrier may be more technical but no less surmountable, given the magnitude of the gains to be extracted. Did the cost of developing thousands of nuclear weapons not seem prohibitive at the time the first atomic bomb was being developed? Or, for that matter, gunpowder-based artillery at the time gunpowder was introduced? Or, fleets of military aircraft at the time the first machine gun was mounted on a biplane? Cost barriers have a way of collapsing quickly whenever the calculus of profit and power indicate substantial gains can be reaped through military conquest.

From biotechnology and genetic engineering, we should not be too surprised if fast militarism comes to depend on bioengineered humanoids or on (also engineered) organisms that are expendable (in a political sense) but can do the kind of fighting that human soldiers have done.[59] This possibility might seem objectionable to many people, but was the introduction of carpet bombing during World War II not also objectionable to many? Or, before that, the use of gas in trench warfare during World War I? After all, a major political constraint on warfare involves the loss of soldiers, and who would rather lose a relative or friend in war rather than an engineered humanoid? If human history is any indication, ever more barbaric and unjust ways of making war seem to become justifiable whenever the calculus of power and profit indicate greater gains ahead.

From nanotechnology, the development for warfare of minute (perhaps invisible) devices that can kill, neutralize or be used for surveillance seem a very real possibility. After all, if nanotech devices can circulate in human arteries to monitor physiological functions or dispense medications and thus save lives, they can also be used to kill. The only questions are how, in what numbers, and at what economic cost nanotech devices will be deployed to kill or maim those who resist. For espionage, nanotech devices may prove to be the most important breakthrough in hardware ever, given their capacity to be invisible, and to transmit

---

of Intellectual Property"). For insights on American military strategies and concerns see Andrew Bacevich, *The New American Militarism* (New York: Oxford University Press, 2005).

59 Advances in cloning have reached the point where the design of human-like creatures for warfare and other highly dangerous activities is within reach. See Thomas H. Maugh II, "Stem Cell Success, Ethics Quandary," *Los Angeles Times* (July 24, 2009): A1.

large amounts of information with the aid of software and telecommunications. For armor, nanotech is already being used to create practically indestructible plates, panels and protectors that can be used in warfare.

From biopharmacology, behavior modification "therapies" for conquered populations (or perhaps those about to be conquered) may be used to make them more receptive to the impositions of the conquerors. Conversely, biopharma "therapies" might also be used to diminish conquered populations' capacity to resist conquest.[60] After all, conventional pharmaceuticals have already succeeded in adjusting the behavior of tens of millions of people around the world. Pharmaceuticals that change the behavior of pet animals have also experienced considerable growth in recent times. However, fast militarism is likely to have better pharmacological tools at its disposal. More effective and precise "therapies" than those we already have can be expected from the kind of biopharmacology that technocapitalism is spawning.[61]

From biomimetics, an emerging field that attempts to imitate living organisms through mechanics, through nanotechnology or through the bio-engineering of creatures with similar capabilities, we can expect warfare applications. Biomimetics is, for example, already being used to create mechanical robots with movements and physical structures similar to those found in lobsters, to scour the deeper ocean floor.[62] Might we not expect the knowledge and creativity found in this emerging field to create more rapid and effective weaponry? For example, the rapid movement of military vehicles through very difficult terrain, such as swamps, deserts, jungles or mountains has always been a challenge. Through biomimetics, it is likely that the difficulties posed to military vehicles by such terrain may be largely overcome. This would mean that the mobile characteristics of certain species (gazelles, roadrunners, lizards or crabs, for example) well suited for difficult terrain might be incorporated in the design of tanks, armored carriers, robotic field artillery, and most any kind of landed military vehicle.[63]

---

60   Biopharmaceutical substances that increase feelings of trust may become one of the weapons (water supplies or food being a potential vehicle for distribution). See Michael Kosfeld et al., "Oxytocin Increases Trust in Humans," *Nature* 435(June 2, 2005): 673–76; Robert Lee Holtz, "Researchers Find Trust to be a Hormonal Affair," *Los Angeles Times* (June 2, 2005): A18.

61   A vehicle for distribution may involve digital pills, whose action can be adjusted at any time depending on circumstances. See Don Clark, "Take Two Digital Pills and Call Me in the Morning," *Wall Street Journal* (August 4, 2009): A6.

62   See *The Economist*, "Biomimetic Materials" (January 29, 2009): http://www.economist.com/sciencetechnology/displayStory.cfm?story_id=13013043.

63   Landed military vehicles have usually been variants of civilian vehicles, built on platforms designed for trucks, automobiles or tractors. The increasing use of robots and drones in warfare and their combination with biomimetics, advanced software and telecommunications provides another new avenue of weaponry for fast militarism. See P.W. Singer, "The American Killing Machines," *Los Angeles Times* (January 30, 2009): A23; Peter Pae, "A Mini-Missile is Tested in the Mojave," *Los Angeles Times* (April 20, 2009):

From advanced software, we can expect cyber-warfare capabilities that can cripple a targeted nation's networks. Not only the networks of the Internet and the Web, but practically any kind of network that involves vital functions.[64] Thus, telecommunications, utilities (electricity, water supply, gas, drainage), fuel, defense, public health, radio-television broadcasting, rail and air traffic control networks, among others, can be targeted and crippled. All of these networks utilize software for control purposes, and the ways to disrupt them have now become a major component of military strategy.[65]

The targeted nation could thereby find its vital activities paralyzed until it gives in to demands. In any case, rebuilding those networks after they are crippled may be something that can only be undertaken with financing from the "have" nations that mounted the attack. In this way, the hand of fast militarism supports the hand of finance and reconstruction. After all, whatever is destroyed has to be rebuilt, thus creating profitable opportunities for corporations from the "have" nations.[66]

The spectrum of possibilities for fast militarism and the techno-military-corporate complex with which it is closely associated therefore seems quite diverse. As instruments of war, the new technologies spawned by technocapitalism may well push the envelope for warfare further than any prior military innovations. Can we possibly expect that such technologies may not be used for conquest whenever the gains to be obtained by a conqueror justify their use? All the more so when not only the conquest of natural resources (the objective of much past imperialism) but also the conquest of human resources (entire populations) with substantial creativity to be exploited, are part of the new game of imperialism?

New Global Divides

The permanence of global inequalities creates new global divides between the haves and the have-nots. These divides encompass not only conventional,

A1; Noel Sharkey, "The Ethical Frontiers of Robotics," *Science* 322(December 19, 2008): 1800–1801; *The Economist*, "Military Drones: Robo Raider; A New Drone Emerges With the Ability to Fight Back" (July 17, 2010): 85.

64   See Siobhan Gorman, August Cole and Yochi Dreazen, "Computer Spies Breach Fighter-Jet Project," *Wall Street Journal* (April 21, 2009: A1; Siobhan Gorman and Julian E. Barnes, "Cyber Combat: Act of War," *Wall Street Journal* (My 31, 2011): A1.

65   Siobhan Gorman and Yochi J. Dreazen, "New Military Command to Focus on Cybersecurity," *Wall Street Journal* (April 22, 2009): A2; Julian E. Barnes, "Military Unit Created for Cyberspace Operations," *Los Angeles Times* (June 24, 2009): A16.

66   Militarism, post-war reconstruction, and corporate welfare are closely linked; see Pratap Chaterjee, *Halliburton's Army: How a Well-Connected Texas Oil Company Revolutionized the Way America Makes War* (New York: Nation Books, 2009); Paul Richter, "Where is the $6.6 Billion? Cash for Iraq Projects May Have Been Stolen, Auditors Say," *Los Angeles Times* (June 13, 2011): A1; Joel Millman, "The Hunt for Weapons of Mass Corruption," *Wall Street Journal* (June 13, 2011): A6.

longstanding concerns over income, health, education and other socioeconomic aspects, but they also comprise dimensions that are particular to the emergence of technocapitalism as a new global phenomenon. Those divides therefore now comprise creativity, knowledge, fast accumulation, research regimes, and the corporate apparatus of technocapitalism.

Behind these global divides is the ever more urgent corporate appropriation of creativity and of its results, in whatever form they happen to be. This aspect, *corporate appropriation*, therefore transcends every dimension of the globalization of technocapitalism, of the permanence of inequalities and of fast neo-imperialism. Appropriation, which is at the heart of the corporatist quest for profit and power, pervades and influences every aspect of the new global reality that technocapitalism imposes. Appropriation, as might be recalled, is also the main objective of commodification in the technocapitalist corporation's systematized research regime.

One global divide involves *fast accumulation*—in particular, the accumulation of knowledge and of technological infrastructure—the elements most closely associated with the emergence of technocapitalism. These two elements of fast accumulation are a major source of inequality. About eighty percent of the people on earth live in nations that have practically no possibility of accumulating enough technological knowledge and infrastructure, on their own, to create any of the new technologies associated with technocapitalism.[67] Thus, the divide over fast accumulation is a formidable one. Its existence makes the vast majority of the world's population dependent on the "have" nations that can create the new technologies.

Among the twenty percent of the population that live in nations with some capacity to create new technology, only about five percent are in countries with the capacity to be at the vanguard of technocapitalism. This does not mean, of course, that they will be at the vanguard of the technologies of technocapitalism. It only means that they may have the potential to do so. The global hierarchy of technocapitalism is therefore radically skewed, with a relatively small number of nations presently in control of the technological knowledge and infrastructure required to create the new technologies associated with this new phase of capitalism.

This is not unlike the situation at the beginning of industrial capitalism—at the onset of the Industrial Revolution, in the late eighteenth century. Less than a handful of nations at that time had the requisite accumulation of resources to create the new technologies of industrial capitalism. One nation, Britain, was at the forefront of industrial capitalism, much as the United States is today at the vanguard of technocapitalism.[68] Nations that later accumulated the resources to enter that new

---

67   The divide over fast accumulation also has a geographical dimension. See Nigel Thrift, "Performing Cultures in the New Economy," *Annals of the Association of American Geographers* 90(2000): 674–92; Rodrigo Martinez, Juan Enriquez and Jonathan West, "The Geography of the Genome," *Wired* (June 2003): 160–61.

68   Britain's place at the forefront of industrial capitalism was closely related to its empire; see Hobsbawm, *Industry and Empire*.

era often depended on the British experience with its technologies and with its new mode of production (the factory system).

In a similar way, nations that can engage in fast accumulation are likely to rely on the American experience. The new sectors associated with technocapitalism, such as nanotech, genomics, bioinformatics, biopharmacology and others, have been grounded on much American research—much as the new sectors of industrial capitalism in the late eighteenth century, such as the steam engine and textile production technologies, that relied on early British know-how. In the context of technocapitalism, what is referred to here as "the American experience" actually refers to the experience of the new corporatism, of its systematized research regimes, and of its monopoly over intellectual property (in the form of patents), in the new sectors associated with technocapitalism. This does not mean, however, that nations able to generate the fast accumulation dynamics of technocapitalism will necessarily depend on the US or its corporations forever—it means that key aspects of the American experience with the new sectors and technologies may serve as stepping stones for others.

Related to the divide over fast accumulation is the global divide over *new technology*. This divide refers to the possibility of using the new technologies spawned by technocapitalism in an independent way, meaning without colonization by technocapitalist corporations (in the "have" nations). Such usage of the new technologies would be in the domain of corporations that are independent from the technocapitalist corporations that own the new technologies.

However, is it possible to think that a corporation anywhere that uses technologies *already owned* by technocapitalist corporations (in the "have" nations) will be truly independent? First, to use or develop the *already appropriated* technology, those "anywhere" corporations (mostly in have-not nations) would have to obtain a license from the corporate proprietor of the technology. Not doing so would subject them to lawsuits, international sanctions, trade barriers and other forms of persecution whenever they try to sell their products or services.[69]

A license may be rather expensive, and may be conditioned to the proprietor's acquisition of a stake in the corporation that uses it. Thus, any notion of independence begins to disappear quickly once the issue of intellectual property is broached. If the "anywhere" corporation waits until the technology becomes generic (thus having lost patent protection), then it cannot be considered to be using a "new" technology in any sense of the term. In so doing, the "anywhere" corporation would be little more than a hand-me-down applicator of a technology that was invented long before, and that would therefore not be at the cutting edge of its field.

The divide over new technology therefore revolves around corporate appropriation. This is the key to this divide, which is intimately related to the

---

69 Policing of corporate intellectual property in have-not nations is becoming a central priority of meta-national organizations, such as the World Trade Organization. See Peet, *Unholy Trinity*.

quest for power and profit. The divide over new technology is likely to become ever deeper as corporate intellectual property rights are enforced worldwide, more evenly and with greater effectiveness, using meta-national agencies such as the World Trade Organization. And it should not be overlooked that whenever international disputes arise over corporate intellectual property, the technocapitalist corporations with the largest repertories of intellectual property (typically in the "have" nations) will have substantial advantages on their side, not only because of their large repertories but also because they will have the most experience with disputes and litigation. The cards therefore seem stacked in favor of those (the "haves") at the top of the very skewed global hierarchy that technocapitalism imposes. Nations unable to engage in fast accumulation in any significant way are also bound to find themselves in the have-not end of the divide over new technology.[70]

In the context of fast neo-imperialism and most of all fast militarism, there is another divide. This divide involves *weapons* that will be closely associated with the new technologies spawned by technocapitalism. The techno-military-corporate complex, mentioned previously in this chapter, underlies this divide. With the weapons divide, a major aspect is force and domination of the have-nots by the haves. The tools used to impose this domination will be like no other war tools ever used, as noted earlier in this chapter.

The global divide over weapons is therefore also a global divide over fast militarism. As with the divide over fast accumulation, this global divide is very much skewed toward the "have" nations at the vanguard of technocapitalism. Those nations, and the United States in particular, will monopolize the new weapons created through the technologies spawned by technocapitalism. Much as heavy artillery, tanks or combat aircraft were an early monopoly of certain nations at the vanguard of industrial capitalism, so the weapons developed through biotech, nanotech, biomimetics, and other sectors associated with technocapitalism are likely to be the monopoly of nations and corporations at the vanguard of this new version of capitalism.[71]

Monopoly is another aspect of the global divide over weapons. Nations that create those new weapons will seek by all possible means to keep a monopoly over them. Sharing of such weapons by the haves with the have-nots is therefore out of the question, except in some very limited and fragmented ways, and only if a have-not nation becomes a surrogate—this will also likely extend to any sharing with "have"

---

70   Trying to join the very small group of nations that can support any of the sectors associated with technocapitalism has become a major priority for some nations. See Dennis Normile, "Can Money Turn Singapore Into a Biotech Juggernaut?," *Science* 297(August 30, 2002): 1470–73.

71   Their very high cost will likely contribute to that monopoly. See John Bellamy Foster, Hannah Holleman and Robert W. McChesney, "The U.S. Imperial Triangle and Military Spending," *Monthly Review* (October 2008): 1–19; Chalmers, *Sorrows of Empire*; Bacevich, *New American Militarism*.

nations. Since corporations are the key vehicle for creating and producing those new weapons, safeguarding appropriation for the "have" nations that possess this monopoly is a paramount objective. Thus, a very skewed global hierarchy for the creation and use of weapons will be part of the reality imposed by technocapitalism. The "haves" will control and use the new weapons, keeping a monopoly over them at all costs, while the have-nots will be denied access to them.

Another divide may also be considered, one that is cultural and ideological. This cultural-ideological divide is likely to set the stage for interventions against the have-nots in a vast array of areas, from socio-economic policies to finance, and military affairs. This divide will likely involve *competitism*. It is a divide between those who are considered to be "competitive" in the new global order imposed by technocapitalism and its corporations, and those who are not so regarded. The rules will, of course, be set by nations (and corporations) at the vanguard of technocapitalism, and they will likely be enforced through meta-national organizations.

The divide over competitism in many ways complements and reinforces the global divides over fast accumulation, new technology and weapons. After all, the have-nots who cannot make "progress" in the competitist game will, in the eyes of the haves, be those unable to sustain fast accumulation, or to use and create new technologies. Their place in the new global order imposed by technocapitalism and its corporations will be to become subservient to the haves. The divide over competitism is therefore linked to the other divides, and the other divides can in turn be linked to competitism. A failure to perform in the competitist game, and to bend to external corporate power, may trigger actions according to the relations of power that benefit the "have" nations.[72]

Conclusion

The globalization of technocapitalism is accompanied by inequalities that are deeply rooted in the character of this new era. The depth, the broad range and the pathological character of those inequalities reflect a level of distress and injustice that may surpass humanity's experience with prior versions of capitalism. The effects of those inequalities, which are based in the harnessing of technology and science to corporate power, are likely to impact most every aspect of human existence, of life and nature.

The inequalities between the haves and the have-nots are part of a larger phenomenon of eco-social distress. This phenomenon involves not only the pathologies and crises of technocapitalism and their effects on humanity, but also their damage to most every form of life, to the earth's ecosystems and to its

---

72   This sort of systemic integration and enforcement of inequality may become a major feature of the technocapitalist global reality, and may extend the systemic integration of prior versions of capitalism. See John Bellamy Foster, "A Failed System: The World Crisis of Capitalist Globalization and its Impact on China," *Monthly Review* (March 2009): 1–23.

environment. *The permanence of inequalities and injustices between the haves and the have-nots is thus one of the pathological outcomes of technocapitalism, of its apparatus of corporate power, and of its new vehicles of global domination.*

The new vehicles of domination are multi-dimensional. They comprise corporate, technological, scientific, military, organizational and cultural elements. *All of these elements of domination are part of the conceptual construct of fast neo-imperialism—a new systemic form of domination under the control of the "have" nations at the vanguard of technocapitalism.* This new neo-imperial power is closely associated with the phenomena of fast accumulation, with the new corporatism, with its need to appropriate and commodify creativity through research, and with its quest to obtain profit and power wherever and whenever it can.

Technocapitalism's roots in technology and science may therefore make its quest for domination and its inequalities deeper, farther-reaching and more systemic than those encountered in prior eras of capitalism. New global divides may thus emerge that are related to the vital phenomena sustaining technocapitalism and its globalization. These chasms between the haves and the have-nots involve fast accumulation, corporate power, new technologies, weapons and the cultural-ideological divide over competitism. Nurturing these divides are a multiplicity of vehicles that include meta-national organizations charged with setting rules, brain drain flows, corporate strategies pitting have-nots against each other, and a new kind of global military power based on the technologies of technocapitalism.

A question that emerges from this discussion is to what extent and for how long humanity can tolerate the new realities imposed by technocapitalism and its global apparatus of domination. Related to this question is the issue of resistance to an inherently unjust global order, and the forms that such resistance might take. These aspects—injustice, tolerance and resistance—are keys to social governance under technocapitalism. The depth of the inequalities, the social injustices, and the pathologies that accompany technocapitalism may thus call into question our current systems of governance, their capacity to address this unjust global order, and their possibility for checking new forms of social oppression.

Illusive Democracy

Democracy is a concept of governance that has long symbolized humanity's hope for justice and fairness. At the core of most every social and political upheaval in human history has been a desire for the kind of equity and justice that is commonly associated with democratic values. The global emergence of technocapitalism, however, promotes a form of public governance that negates those human aspirations.

Governance that places the interests of corporate power above those of the people fails the test of democracy and betrays the long history of human struggle for greater justice. Such governance, however it may choose to be called, cannot represent governance for the majority or for the interests of the majority. If it chooses to call itself democracy, it is a false democracy, or at best an illusion of democracy. Such governance might retain some of the trappings and motions of public democracy, but is in fact little more than a masquerade for governance that has little to do with democracy.

As technocapitalism and corporatism find it unavoidable to depend more on society, because of the need to reproduce creativity externally and because of the externalization of functions that decomposition entails, an important contradiction emerges. Corporatism's greater dependence on society, and its increasing loss of control over reproduction and over many previously internal functions, induce it to gain control over society's governance. But, instead of engaging with society and with the public interest in just and constructive ways, corporatism seeks to regain control by imposing its power on all of society. This imposition is nothing short of authoritarian, and reveals the pathological character of corporatism as it seeks to sustain its quest for power and profit.

The scope of this phenomenon is now global, and it is something through which technocapitalism and its corporate apparatus expand their reach. Neoliberal precepts are at the ideological heart of this corporate drive to control society's governance by any means, everywhere. Starting in the early 1980s, neoliberal ideas of governance began to spread around the world. Although their purported objective was to secure greater freedoms, the real effect of those ideas was to secure greater power for corporatism through the control of governance. The effects of this reconversion of governance are now all around us—they have turned democratic governance into an illusion, a masquerade that hides the manipulation of public governance by corporatism as it furthers its global quest for power and profit.

The character and effects of this global phenomenon will be explored in this chapter. The reconversion of governance involves global processes of redistribution and dispossession that favor corporate power at the expense of the majority of people in society, and at the expense of democracy. Such processes will be a central feature of the various components of this chapter. They are part and parcel of the reconversion of the state to serve corporate power, and of the deepening inequalities between nations and between social classes. As we will see, those inequalities are vital for technocapitalism and for its new corporatism to project their power around the world, and they are a major effect of reconversion. The global importance of fast neo-imperialism and its association with the reconversion of governance will also be considered, to see how technocapitalism and its corporate apparatus articulate new instruments of control over governance and society.

Corporatocracy versus Democracy

The globalization of technocapitalism is linked to a form of governance that is by and large antithetical to the fundamental essence of democracy. At the core of this form of governance is the overwhelming power of corporations over government at every level, in every possible form. This form of governance involves more than a collusion of corporate interests and public governance. It involves the *corporate domination* of public governance, institutions, and of most every kind of political organization, including the legislative, executive and judicial functions of government. Seemingly independent organizations, such as public foundations and regulatory agencies, are therefore within its reach.[1]

Corporatocracy is government for, by and of corporations, as opposed to government for, by and of the people. It is an authoritarian form of governance that is fragmented, flexible and sometimes also internally contradictory. These characteristics make it dynamic, variable and difficult to grasp. They are of great advantage to corporate power as it tries to disguise its domination of governance, institutions, culture and international relations.

Corporatocracies can operate behind the guise of representative democracy, with its facade of seemingly separate functions (executive, legislative, judicial) to set up what in reality is a masquerade of democracy. It can also be established through or behind openly authoritarian governance, as in the case of person-

---

1   Variants of this general definition can be found in the literature. For example, *corporatocracy* has been defined as "the powerful group of people who run the world's biggest corporations, the most powerful governments and history's first truly global empire" in John Perkins' "Introduction: New Confessions and Revelations from the World of Economic Hit Men," in Steven Hiatt (ed.), *A Game as Old as Empire: The Secret World of Economic Hit Men and the Web of Global Corruption* (San Francisco: Berrett-Koehler, 2007), p. 2. John Kenneth Galbraith's *The Predator State: How Conservatives Abandoned the Free Market and Why Liberals Should Too* (New York: Free Press, 2008) refers to this form of governance as the "predator state," or government that comes under the control of business interests and adopts corporate agendas as its own.

centered dictatorships, one-party political systems or absolute monarchies. Corporatocracy can operate through or behind totalitarian forms of governance, as in the case of planned economies run by corporate oligarchies. The outwardly democratic forms of governance, however, provide better cover and legitimacy for its apparatus of control.

In its democratic guises, corporatocracy's fragmented and flexible character makes its control over governance difficult to grasp. All the more so since the kind of corporate domination it embodies is generic, meaning that domination does not usually occur through one corporate actor, but through several or many.[2] Thus, the pool of corporate actors behind corporatocratic governance can change frequently, it can exhibit internal competition between the various actors as they jockey for greater influence, and it can dislodge some while new ones join the dance of domination.

The corporatocratic apparatus of governance is therefore a dynamic phenomenon that can change rapidly or present contradictory interests, paradoxical situations and even mutually hostile tendencies between the most influential corporate actors. It should not surprise, therefore, that many people can mistake the corporatocratic apparatus of domination for democracy, when in fact it is far from that. Its dynamic and flexible appearance can mislead and desensitize the public to its pathological hold over governance. Global media, largely controlled by large corporations, can cement this process of mass desensitization by trivializing opponents and spreading corporatist propaganda on an unprecedented scale.[3]

Regardless of its guises, corporatocracy turns the state into a tool of corporate power. Domination of the state is very important to corporate power because the state, be it outwardly democratic or dictatorial, has a monopoly over legality. The state thus becomes a very important tool for corporate power to legalize (and thereby legitimize) its actions, its means of control and its influence over society. The state also has a monopoly over violence since it can make war, sustain the techno-military-corporate complex, imprison or execute people, implement pervasive surveillance, and otherwise repress in a completely "legal" way those who might oppose corporatocratic governance.

---

2 Nonetheless, the richest corporations can have overwhelming influence over elections through the sheer weight of their contributions. For example, if Exxon Mobil (one of the richest corporations on earth) directs only two percent of its annual profit to political campaigns, the amount would be vastly greater than the total expended by Barack Obama's campaign in 2008, by far the most expensive political campaign in world history. See Doug Kendall, "Elections for Sale? If the Supreme Court Lifts Restrictions on Corporate Campaign Contributions, Watch Out," *Los Angeles Times* (September 8, 2009): A21. The US Supreme Court lifted restrictions on corporate political contributions in 2009.

3 See Robert W. McChesney, *The Political Economy of Media: Enduring Issues, Emerging Dilemmas* (New York: Monthly Review Press, 2008), and his *Capitalism and the Information Age: The Political Economy of the Global Communication Revolution* (New York: Monthly Review Press, 1998).

Corporatocratic governance is therefore contrarian to democracy. Democracy's core values of social justice, equity and collective wellbeing are undermined by corporatocracy. Democracy's social contract, which typically involves a redistribution of wealth from rich to poor and working people, a social safety net for the less fortunate, along with regulation of and limits on corporate power, is turned on its head. Institutions of governance that implemented democracy's social contract end up being rendered ineffective or dismantled, and are publicly denigrated by the corporate-controlled media.[4]

Corporatocratic governance thus fundamentally involves a redistribution of power and wealth to benefit corporatism. Wealth and political power are redistributed from the mass of the people, and most of all from the poor and the working people, toward corporate power and the rich segment of society associated with it. This reversal of the redistribution dynamic that accompanies democracy is a hallmark of corporatocratic governance. Corporate power, closely linked to the rich classes and corporate elites, thus becomes the great beneficiary of governance by dispossessing the poor, those who have to work to live, and practically everyone not closely connected to the corporatist apparatus. This is a systemic feature that applies throughout the global context of corporatocratic governance, in rich and poor nations alike.[5]

Neoliberalism provides the ideological foundation for corporatocracy. As with fast neo-imperialism, discussed in the previous chapter, neoliberal dogma justifies the imposition of corporatocracy on a global scale, sparing no nation and no instrument of governance that can be used to further corporate power and profit.[6] The neoliberal justification seems benevolent at first sight. Advancing human wellbeing is assumed to be most effectively achieved by maximizing corporate

---

4   Media corporations started to acquire diverse outlets (newspapers, television, radio) on a global scale starting in the 1980s. See Robert W. McChesney's *Corporate Media and the Threat to Democracy* (New York: Seven Stories Press, 1997).

5   Corporatocratic redistribution is consonant with the definition of "original" or "primitive" accumulation provided by Marx in his analysis of the rise of capitalism in the eighteenth and nineteenth centuries; see Karl Marx, *Grundrisse: Foundations of the Critique of Political Economy*, transl. M. Nicolaus (New York: Pelican, 1973). Among the scholars who subsequently explored the evolution of primitive accumulation, see Michael Perelman, *The Invention of Capitalism: Classical Political Economy and the Secret History of Primitive Accumulation* (Durham, NC: Duke University Press, 2000); Joan Robinson, *The Accumulation of Capital* (London: Macmillan, 1956). David Harvey refers to primitive accumulation as "accumulation by dispossession," noting how it differs from the generative (or non-distributive) form of accumulation; see David Harvey, "Neo-liberalism as Creative Destruction," *Geografiska Annaler* 88(2006): 153.

6   The spread of neoliberal dogma and its extrapolation as a form of governance is possibly the most important development in world politics since the late 1970s. See David Harvey, *A Brief History of Neoliberalism* (New York: Oxford University Press, 2005); William K. Tabb, *Economic Governance in the Age of Globalization* (New York: Columbia University Press, 2004).

or entrepreneurial freedom. The prescribed institutional context makes property rights, free markets, free trade, and the pervasive privatization of government activities its highest priorities in order to improve efficiency. Individual freedom of choice is the neoliberal siren song for the mass of the people, grounded in unfettered consumerism and orchestrated by corporate influence over most every aspect of life. Seemingly independent government functions that cannot be privatized, such as monetary management, or the financing of public projects that cannot turn a profit for corporatism, are nonetheless influenced by corporate priorities.[7]

Freedom is a strong propaganda camel to ride, but the camel ride of neoliberalism leads to mirages. In reality, the redistribution of political power and wealth that accompanies neoliberal policies takes away rights, economic security, social relations, benefits, and often even the personal freedoms of the mass of the people.[8] All too often, anyone not at the top of the corporate ladder, and those who do not own substantial corporate capital also end up in the losing end of this game of redistribution.[9] Greater individual choice and wealth for the masses thus become dreams that never materialize.

Dispossession, in a very real sense, is the outcome of this redistribution dynamic. Dispossession, for working people and the poor, of employee rights in the workplace, of the right to corporate-paid pensions, unemployment insurance, of access to health care, of the right to form unions, and for the poorer segment of the population the right to find affordable shelter and access to adequate schools.[10] A large portion of children also end up living in deprived conditions or poverty, with little or no access to the new technologies needed acquire skills. And much of the population can end up reaching old age to find they have little or nothing to show for a lifetime of work.

---

7   In the case of monetary policy, for example, the devaluation of a currency by reducing interest rates can benefit corporate power greatly by increasing exports, thereby raising corporate profits, while the mass of the people are shortchanged through higher prices for imported products and higher inflation. In the case of expensive public works that the private sector cannot finance because of low short-term returns, the projects are turned over to corporations to operate after they are built. Public Subsidies often also accompany such arrangements whenever operation becomes unprofitable for the corporate contractor.

8   Harvey, *Brief History*; Jamie Court, *Corporateering: How Corporate Power Steals Your Personal Freedom* (New York: Tarcher/Putnam, 2003).

9   Redistribution to benefit the rich comes in many guises. See David C. Johnston, *Free Lunch: How the Wealthiest Americans Enrich Themselves at Government Expense* (New York: Portfolio, 2007); John Krinsky, *Free Labor: Workfare and the Contested Language of Neoliberalism* (Chicago: University of Chicago Press, 2007); Loïc Wacquant, *Punishing the Poor: The Neoliberal Government of Social Insecurity* (Durham, NC: Duke University Press, 2008).

10   Rising economic insecurity for the vast majority of the population is another outcome; see Peter Gosselin, *High Wire: The Precarious Financial Lives of American Families* (New York: Basic Books, 2008); Wacquant, *Punishing the Poor*.

The dispossession dynamic of neoliberalism thus ends up making the mass of the population less socially secure, more economically unstable, more prone to illnesses and abuses that accompany socioeconomic anxiety, and more obligated to move ever faster in an economic treadmill of high debt and uncertainty.[11] A kind of collective psychosis based on insecurity and anxiety thereby becomes a societal feature, accompanied by existential fragility and emptiness, anti-social attitudes and a proliferation of fraud, as competitism generates interpersonal hostility and aggression in place of solidarity and constructive reciprocity.[12]

Dispossession and the New Corporatism

Technocapitalism, with its apparatus of fast neo-imperialism and global corporate power, is deeply entwined with this dynamic of dispossession. For the new corporatism and its research regimes, corporatocracy and all the avenues of power it opens are a bonanza. Limits on employee rights effectively make it easier to dispossess those who provide research creativity. Financial deregulation makes it possible to attract speculative capital to fund new research projects with very uncertain payoffs. Taking down regulations on corporate takeovers makes it possible for large technology corporations to take over other companies. The high debts incurred in those takeovers often translate into greater insecurity for employees in both the acquired and acquiring companies. Greater market power and higher profits through takeovers, along with debt, then help establish more control over employees through job insecurity. The lack of limits on executive pay allows high-level executives to raise their own compensation to hundreds of times the median salary and benefits of their employees, while reducing or eliminating company-paid pensions and health coverage.[13] Eliminating or reducing employee pensions and health care can help increase stock prices, that in turn raise the value of executives' stock options and provide more money for their bonuses and "golden parachutes."

---

11   Dispossession, increasing inequity and economic anxiety also have negative effects on public health; see Grace Budrys, *Unequal Health: How Inequality Contributes to Health or Illness* (Lanham, MD: Rowman and Littlefield, 2009).

12   Societal effects of this collective psychosis are often blamed on "materialism" by psychologists, without taking into account corporatocratic governance, the economic and social insecurity it generates, and their negative effects on human health and wellbeing. See Tim Kasser, *The High Price of Materialism* (Cambridge: MIT Press, 2002).

13   In 1970, the ratio of compensation of corporate chief executives to the median compensation of corporate employees in the US was estimated to be about 30: 1. By 2000, this ratio had risen to about 400: 1. See Harvey, "Neo-liberalism," p. 149; Task Force on Inequality and American Democracy, *American Democracy in an Age of Rising Inequality* (Washington: American Political Science Association, 2004); Ellen E. Schultz and Tom McGinty, "Pensions for Executives on Rise: Arcane Techniques, Generous Formulas Boost Payouts as Share Prices Fall," *Wall Street Journal* (November 3, 2009): C1.

This corporatocratic redistribution of power and wealth, grounded in neoliberal doctrine, supports technocapitalism's new corporatism and its globalization in four major ways. One of them involves aspects of redistribution that support the *corporate commodification of creativity*. The aspects involved are quite diverse and reflect wide-ranging effects of neoliberal policies that started to be implemented globally in the 1980s.[14] They comprise, for example, tax laws that support corporate research and development (R&D) through tax credits or deductions on employee compensation, operating expenses, and research hardware. Elimination of workplace rights makes it possible to commodify research creativity faster and with fewer roadblocks, such as regulatory inquiries, union disputes, the obligation to negotiate contracts, or requirements to provide paid vacations, sick leave, or time off for maternity and family care.

Corporatocratic support for the new corporatism thereby dispossesses those who provide creativity through commodification in myriad ways. Dispossession of employment security, of longstanding benefits of employment, of the possibility of contesting decisions made by corporate power, of having any say in the structuring of research strategies, or of being consulted whenever key decisions are made on aspects of their work, are but a few examples of this reality. [15] The impossibility of individual litigation against powerful corporate employers, because of its high cost and the lack of employee protections, make such dispossession quite feasible for corporate power.[16] Moreover, corporate influence over legislation makes it possible for corporate power to change the "rules of the game" in many ways.[17]

The dispossession dynamic noted before ties in strongly with the alienation of the providers of creativity from their creations, that is part and parcel of the commodification of creativity. This key feature of commodification, discussed in a previous chapter, is reinforced by the dispossession that characterizes corporatocracy. Those who provide creativity thus become disengaged not only from their creation but also from the possibility of democratically managing their

---

14 See Harvey, *Brief History*; David Hill (ed.), *The Rich World and the Impoverishment of Education: Diminishing Democracy, Equity and Workers' Rights* (New York: Routledge, 2009).

15 A corporate tactic that underscores the widespread lack of employee rights is to lay off the entire workforce of a company, and then "invite" selected individuals to "reapply" for their old positions or for new ones. See David Carr, "You're Gone. But Hey, You Can Reapply," *New York Times* (August 31, 2009): B1.

16 One of the results is greater employee dissatisfaction in the workplace. See *The Economist*, "Hating What You Do" (October 10, 2009): 70; Devorah Lauter, "French Experience Rise in Job Stress Beyond Usual Grumbling," *Los Angeles Times* (November 1, 2009): A26.

17 Employee safety violations, an important aspect of laboratory research, are among the most common examples. See Jessica Garrison, "Worker Safety Lost on Appeal: Cal-OSHA Penalties, Even for Violations Involving Serious Injury, are Repeatedly Reduced or Dismissed," *Los Angeles Times* (October 21, 2009): A1.

workplace. Dispossession thereby becomes a multifaceted phenomenon in the context of the new corporatism and the new reality created by corporatocracy.

From a broader perspective, corporatocracy also makes it easier to dispossess those who participate in any other process of corporate commodification. In the sectors that were symbolic of industrial capitalism, for example, the loss of employee rights is just as palpable, if not more so, than in the new sectors associated with technocapitalism and the new corporatism.[18] Corporations engaged in the commodification of nature also benefit greatly from the dispossession dynamic, as small farmers end up giving up their land to agribusiness corporations when they can no longer afford to purchase genetically engineered seeds for every crop and harvest.[19] The dispossession dynamic therefore casts a wide and deep net, snaring most everyone not directly connected with the upper echelons of corporate power, or with the ownership of substantial corporate capital.

A second way in which corporatocracy supports the new corporatism and its globalization is through redistribution involving the *corporate appropriation of creativity*. Such appropriation involves the corporate seizure of any intellectual property rights that result from the exercise of creativity, and the eventual rents (or revenues) obtained therefrom. This form of dispossession typically prevents those who exercise creativity from obtaining fair compensation for the results (in the form of patent rights, for example).[20] Dispossession here also involves the preemption of creativity providers' holding intellectual property rights over their creations, as opposed to the typical practice of turning those rights over to corporate employers as a compulsory condition of employment.[21] Invention patent awards, for example, are granted to individuals in the US, but corporate employers typically require employees to reassign to them the rights to all awards. Since

---

18   Worker abuse and the loss of employee rights seems widespread, especially in the US, where regulations are often violated. See Annette Bernhardt, Heather Boushey and Laura Dresser (eds.), *The Gloves-Off Economy: Workplace Standards at the Bottom of America's Labor Market* (Champaign: Labor and Employment Relations Association, University of Illinois at Urbana-Champaign, 2008).

19   See Marie-Monique Robin's documentary, "The World According to Monsanto" (Ottawa: National Film Board of Canada, 2008).

20   Published accounts of this problem are scarce, mainly because of the threat of lawsuits and blacklisting by corporations against employees who make their cases public. See "Letters: The Problem with Patents," *Science* 308(April 15, 2005): 353; J. Rodman Steele, *Is This My Reward? An Employee's Struggle for Fairness in the Corporate Exploitation of His Inventions* (West Palm Beach, FL: Pencraft, 1986). The systemic character of this particular facet of corporate dispossession is emphasized in Michael Perelman, *Steal This Idea: Intellectual Property and the Corporate Confiscation of Creativity* (New York: Palgrave Macmillan, 2002); Pat Choate, *Hot Property: The Stealing of Ideas in an Age of Globalization* (New York: Knopf, 2005).

21   Holding and hoarding such rights have become an important component of corporate strategy; see Anthony L. Miele, *Patent Strategy: The Manager's Guide to Profiting from Patent Portfolios* (New York: Wiley, 2000).

this is a standard requirement of employment contracts, refusal to abide leads to dismissal, lawsuits against the employee, and tacit blacklisting among employers.

Corporatocratic appropriation and dispossession thus transfer power (ownership of intellectual property) and wealth (rents from intellectual property rights) to corporate power (executives and shareholders). It is remarkable indeed to see how well accepted this form of dispossession has become. The public thinks nothing of it; indeed, the vast majority of the public may actually look upon it with favor, or at least with indifference. So desensitized have we become through the constant bombardment of corporate propaganda, infomercials, public adulation of corporate executives, and the corporate-controlled media's high praise of greed, clever exploitive schemes and get-rich-quick in-any-way mindsets, that we seem to take this sort of dispossession as a normal part of economic life.

For the new corporatism, emboldened through this convergence of public propaganda and corporatocratic support, appropriation now extends beyond the case of creativity providers. The ongoing appropriation of the global stock of genetic resources is an example. Biotech corporations and especially those in the agro-biotech, genetic engineering and biopharmaceutical fields are taking over life and nature. This corporate takeover occurs through the genetic decoding of any living organism to appropriate their unique codes of life, to modify or recreate them for commercial purposes.

This form of *corporate biopiracy*, meaning the exclusive takeover of life and nature by the new corporatism, is now worldwide in scope and scale. No plant or animal life anywhere in the world can be considered safe from this rapacious appropriation that involves rapid genetic decoding, securing patents on the decoded data, and then controlling the patent rights as any other form of corporate property. This research-driven process is now at the heart of many biotech companies that typify the new corporatism. Such companies are exclusively dedicated to genetic decoding and to selling or licensing the rights to the decoded data.[22] Their organizations have no production component and none of the ancillary functions that were typical of the corporations of industrial capitalism.

This corporate biopiracy, a form of appropriation that could not have occurred (scientifically speaking) in any prior version of capitalism, also involves dispossession. Dispossession of society's right to a common or collective resource. The appropriation of the earth's genetic resources thus turns into the *bio-dispossession* of a resource (plant and animal genetic stock) that is as much a part of the "commons" as air and water, or the atmosphere. Nature is thus appropriated under the legal and institutional mantle of corporatocracy, at a fast pace that leaves

---

22 See Betsy Morris, "No. 1 Genentech: The Best Place to Work Now," *Fortune* (January 2006): 79–86; Paul Rabinow and Talia Dan-Cohen, *A Machine to Make a Future: Biotech Chronicles* (Princeton, NJ: Princeton University Press, 2005); Ralph T. King, Jr., "Gene Quest Will Bring Glory to Some; Incyte Will Stick with Cash: Assembly-Line Sequencing Lets Firm Beat a Path to the US Patent Office," *Wall Street Journal* (February 10, 2000): A1.

little room or time for questioning and resistance. Corporatocratic governance makes sure that any such questioning and opposition is trivialized or censored.[23]

The third way in which corporatocracy supports the new corporatism and its globalization involves the *corporate manipulation of networks*. Corporate power's use and manipulation of networks is made possible by their dualistic character.[24] Networks can at times serve a liberatory purpose, helping bypass repressive control structures by providing direct contact, multiple alternatives, fluidity and speed. However, networks are also susceptible to seizure by corporate power to support its quest for greater profit and control.[25] Such seizure can be facilitated by corporatocracy whenever it dismantles anti-monopoly regulation, limits access (by allowing discriminatory pricing schemes, for example), censors interactions that oppose corporate interests, restricts network extent, or promotes hierarchical structures that lead to corporate control.

Examples of this unfolding phenomenon are most visible in the networks of the Internet and the Web, where some very large corporations exercise substantial influence. In Web searches, for example, one of the richest corporations in the world, Google, has managed to gain control of the vast majority of searches in what amounts to a form of monopoly.[26] Such searches are the most important entry point into the vast networks of the Web, and they provide a formidable strategic advantage to the corporation that seizes the gateway function they represent. With its unconventional culture that seems so clever and fluid, Google in many ways reflects the values and modus operandi of the new corporatism. Behind its monopoly over searches lurks a formidable worldwide information retrieval corporation that is diversifying to become the (Web-based) library of the world. This future online library of everything, for anyone anywhere in the world, plans

---

23   With corporate-controlled global media networks playing an increasingly important role in this process. See McChesney, *Political Economy of Media* and his *Corporate Media*.

24   See the chapter "Networks as Mediators," in Luis Suarez-Villa, *Technocapitalism: A Critical Perspective on Technological Innovation and Corporatism* (Philadelphia: Temple University Press, 2009). Networks are a major tool of global, corporate-driven capitalism as noted in Dan Schiller's *Digital Capitalism: Networking the Global Market System* (Cambridge: MIT Press, 1999). Another aspect of this dualism is the seizure of networks to neutralize political initiatives; see Jodi Dean, *Democracy and Other Neoliberal Fantasies: Communicative Capitalism and Left Politics* (Durham, NC: Duke University Press, 2009).

25   Attempts by major US telecommunication service corporations to ration access to the Internet through usage-based pricing (as opposed to flat-fee service) is an example; see Christopher Rhoads and Niraj Sheth, "Carriers Eye Pay-As-You-Go Internet," *Wall Street Journal* (October 21, 2009): B5.

26   Google's ascendance as the world's prime search engine has had considerable effects on businesses that depend on Web searches to attract customers. See John Battelle, *The Search: How Google and its Rivals Rewrote the Rules of Business and Transformed Our Culture* (New York: Portfolio, 2005); *The Economist*, "Clash of the Clouds" (October 17, 2009): 80–82; Ken Auletta, *Googled: The End of the World as We Know It* (New York: Penguin, 2009).

to comprise every single item published throughout humanity's history, including all hand-written manuscripts (incunabula) that preceded the arrival of the printing press.[27]

The case of Microsoft provides another example of how computer operating systems and the networks of the Internet can be manipulated by a corporate behemoth. A monopoly over computer operating systems became the key to a network-oriented monopoly that provided the only way to operate the hardware needed to access the Internet and the Web.[28] Aggressively eliminating challengers, Microsoft translated its early monopoly over computer operating systems software into a browser (Internet Explorer) monopoly that practically liquidated most every rival. The carcass of Netscape, an early browser (which preceded Microsoft's Internet Explorer), attests to Microsoft's formidable capacity to turn its operating software monopoly (Windows) into a browser monopoly.[29] A free e-mail service (Hotmail) and arrangements with hardware manufacturers to include Windows as a standard, pre-installed feature in every computer also helped consolidate Microsoft's monopoly.

Microsoft's operating software platform, Windows, was then turned into a trampoline from which innumerable online business applications, and new companies, were launched.[30] All of them dependent on Microsoft, of course, for any updates or new versions of the basic operating software upon which their

---

27 Google's universal library project has drawn concerns over its potential for becoming a tool of American cultural neo-imperialism. See Jean N. Jeanneney, *Google and the Myth of Universal of Knowledge: A View from Europe*, transl. T.L. Fagan (Chicago: University of Chicago Press, 2007).

28 As of May 2009, Microsoft controlled 95 percent of the computer operating system market (through its Windows software), as opposed to 3 percent for Apple Computer's Mac OS and 2 percent for Linux. As of January 2008, Microsoft controlled 94 percent of the market for business applications software (the MS Office Suite), as opposed to 4 percent for Adobe, 1 percent for Apple, and 1 percent for miscellaneous other providers. Through its monopoly on computer operating software (Windows), Microsoft controlled 67 percent of the browser market as of August 2009 (with its MS Internet Explorer), and 66 percent of the corporate e-mail market (as of January 2008). See Jeffrey M. O'Brien, "Microsoft Reboots," *Fortune* (October 26, 2009): 98–107; *The Economist*, "Clash of the Clouds."

29 By 2008, Netscape had practically shriveled into insignificance. Nonetheless, the early years of the Web held much promise for this pioneer of online searches, news and e-mail services. See Jim Clark and Owen Edwards, *Netscape Time: The Making of the Billion-Dollar Start-Up That Took On Microsoft* (New York: St. Martin's Press, 1999).

30 See Jennifer Edstrom and Martin Eller, *Barbarians Led by Bill Gates: Microsoft From the Inside, How the World's Richest Corporation Wields Its Power* (New York: Holt, 1998). Books that contain critical accounts of Microsoft, based on internal operations and inside knowledge, have become very scarce since the late 1990s. One potential reason is that employees are required to sign non-disclosure agreements on any internal aspect of the corporation, as a condition of employment. Violators of such agreements can expect expensive lawsuits that can drive them into bankruptcy, and their tacit blacklisting among software employers.

businesses were built. Failure to comply with Microsoft's demands and pricing schemes meant ruin or substantial losses and complications, as those dependent businesses found that the few alternatives available were either incompatible with their previous operational models, or required costly modifications with uncertain possibilities of technical support down the line.

The network-based redistribution of power to corporations thus presents another form of dispossession. Most of all, dispossession of choices for anyone who utilizes the network. In the case of Microsoft, for example, Internet users had practically no choice for operating systems (Windows) and very little choice in the case of browsers (Internet Explorer).[31] This lack of alternatives has been more poignant for business-related applications (such as payroll systems) since they were all based on the Windows platform. It therefore became impossible to avoid using a Microsoft-based product for any small or medium-size business that needed to digitize data. As the corporatocratic state failed to enforce anti-monopoly rules, Internet users were deprived of alternatives. This in turn lead to ever-higher profits for Microsoft, turning it into one of the world's richest companies. No matter how remote a place on earth, or how inscrutable a culture and society a people might belong to, they could not escape Microsoft's monopoly.

The fourth way in which corporatocracy supports dispossession is through the *corporate privatization of public functions*. This involves the privatization of any government activity or property that can be turned into a source of corporate profits and power. In the grand neoliberal scheme for society, no government activity is safe from privatization so long as corporate power can consider it potentially profitable. Thus, public education at all levels, agencies that oversee human health, public pension systems, and even postal services become targets for privatization. Similarly, rights to any public resource, such as land, water, air, the flora and fauna of any particular area, along with any public facility become "privatizable," whenever the corporate calculus of power happens to indicate they might turn a profit.[32]

Privatization of the commons, an important element of corporatocracy and of its neoliberal dogma, benefits the new corporatism in myriad ways. Any species of plant or animal life unique to an area that is public property, for example, can become a private domain. The corporation that acquires it can then treat all its life forms as its property. The genetic codes of all plant and animal life therein can be privatized as well, through decoding and the acquisition of patent rights over all such data. The patented genetic data can then be sold to other corporate entities,

---

31   Linux (Open Source) software is the only promising challenger to Microsoft's Windows and has had success in the server segment. For personal computing, however, Microsoft's early start and the immense variety of existing applications based on its Windows platform pose a formidable obstacle to any challenger. See Johan Söderberg, *Hacking Capitalism: The Free and Open Source Software Movement* (New York: Routledge, 2007).

32   See Harvey, *Brief History*; Becky Mansfield (ed.), *Privatization: Property and the Remaking of Nature-Society Relations* (Malden, MA: Blackwell, 2008).

such as biopharmaceutical or agro-biotech companies, to use in their research or in commercial products, such as biomedications or genetically engineered seeds.

Another example of privatization of collective resources involves ocean life. This new frontier of corporate exploration, intimately tied to biotechnology research, contains a vast diversity of life forms. Ocean life, which includes known and some as yet unknown species, is a prime target for privatization through corporate genetic decoding and patenting. Those life forms have much potential for corporate biomedicine, biopharmaceuticals, and for the corporate takeover of global ocean food sources. Similar to the takeover of food by corporate agribusiness and agro-biotech, privatization of ocean life can potentially generate new ocean-oriented Monsantos in the coming decades. This trend is already obvious in the case of corporate fisheries and the genetic engineering of fish to increase weight, improve survival in captivity, and modify taste or color in order to improve profits.[33]

The corporatocratic privatization of public functions also allows the new corporatism to acquire government science facilities and organizations around the world. The privatization of government laboratories, for example, usually opens them to foreign corporate control. Restricting such privatization to acquisition by domestic companies typically faces major obstacles as international organizations such as the World Trade Organization raise objections and the possibility of sanctions. Privatization of technological institutes and universities also opens the door to the new corporatism. Acquiring a technological university can be very beneficial to companies typical of the new corporatism, in the sense that they acquire access to sources of creativity and to repositories of accumulated technological knowledge.

The privatization of government-owned generic pharmaceutical companies in various nations, for example, also opens new vistas for the new corporatism. For biopharmaceutical corporations, the acquisition of those companies opens the possibility of access to a steady stream of revenues and potential profit. The revenue streams of those generic manufacturers can offset the high risk and uncertainty associated with bioengineered pharmaceutical products, which must undergo clinical testing that can result in failure rates as high as 8000 to one, with research expenses that can run into the hundreds of millions of dollars. Through this kind of privatization, corporatocracy turns government-owned companies created to provide low-cost (generic) medications to the poorer segment of the population, into corporate property that places profit over human wellbeing. As a result, the public (and most of all the poor and working people) are dispossessed of their access to low-cost medications.

---

33 Rögnvaldur Hanneson's *The Privatization of the Oceans* (Cambridge: MIT Press, 2006), provides insights on the emergence of exclusive rights of access (as a form of private property right) in the case of the world's fisheries, and how changes in the international law of the sea since the 1970s have made this possible.

For the governments that sell the generic pharmaceutical companies, privatization brings only a one-time benefit from their sale. Thus, governments forgo future, long-term revenue streams for the public treasury. The sale of such companies may also involve corruption, as companies vying to acquire them cajole, bribe or pay off officials to try to bias the sale process in their favor. Then, after privatization the acquiring corporations may have to bribe officials again in order to secure contracts for government purchases of medications, such that they can be made available (at subsidized government prices) to the poorer segment of the population. The game of patronage and corruption that often accompanies privatization thereby finds a way to perpetuate itself. With the spread of corporatocracy and of the new corporatism this trend has become a global phenomenon, with tentacles that lead to most every kind of government function or government-owned organization in existence.

Ideological constructs that support corporatocracy often argue that markets provide a better way to manage public functions than governments.[34] Lost in those arguments is the fact that markets are not the real force behind corporatocratic governance. Corporate power is the real force, regardless of how fragmented, fluid or flexible it may be. The supposed "free play" of markets that would result from privatization is usually a fantasy, a mirage that does not take into account the reality after privatization, and the larger processes of redistribution and dispossession of which it is part. In any case markets, even when they work without much manipulation, are corporate in letter and spirit and are vehicles for greater inequality.

Global Inequality and Corporatocracy

The undermining of democracy that the shift toward corporatocracy represents is a worldwide phenomenon. No longer confined to certain rich nations that viewed corporate-driven neoliberal policies as potential stimulants of economic growth, corporatocratic governance is spreading to every corner of the earth. No nation, people or government on earth, no matter how poor or how remote, can consider itself immune to this advancing phenomenon.

The worldwide spread of corporatocracy is part and parcel of the globalization of technocapitalism and its new corporatism for two important reasons. One is the pressing need to increase long-term growth in rich nations. The new sectors associated with technocapitalism provide the only long-term hope for growth, as the old industries of industrial capitalism decline or move to lower cost nations. Growth driven through financialization, as noted earlier in this book, has been

---

34 An argument of neoliberal propaganda. See Harvey, *Brief History*; Susanne Soederberg, Georg Menz and Philip G. Cerny (eds.), *Internalizing Globalization: The Rise of Neoliberalism and the Decline of National Varieties of Capitalism* (New York: Palgrave Macmillan, 2005).

ephemeral and dangerous. The growth that financialization delivered was generated through dangerously high and unsustainable debt, extreme risk, and reckless financial speculation that led to bankruptcies and massive government bailouts.[35] Thus, the only long-term hope to generate well-paying jobs and high value exports lies with the sectors associated with technocapitalism.

Corporatocracy helps keep this hope alive by removing barriers to profit and power, that stand in the way of the new corporatism in its takeover of life, nature and human existence. In rich and poor nations alike, corporatocracy is therefore a fundamental component of the advance of technocapitalism and its corporate apparatus. The new corporatism cannot feel safe if corporatocracy is confined to rich nations, since it increasingly depends for its profits and power on the rest of the world. Of particular importance are the sources of creativity, which are now increasingly global as brain drain flows and the outsourcing of research intensify. Access to those global sources of creativity require the sort of governance that corporatocracy provides: greater freedom of action for corporate power to assert itself, and state-supported redistribution to benefit corporate interests above everything else.

This global reality brings up the second reason why corporatocracy is of vital importance to the globalization of technocapitalism and its corporate apparatus. Corporatocracy provides the means to sustain and increase the global divides between rich and poor nations upon which technocapitalism and the new corporatism depend. Those global divides, discussed in the previous chapter, are grounded in deep inequalities between "have" (rich) and have-not (poor) nations that are part and parcel of the globalization of technocapitalism.

The need to sustain or even increase global inequalities between the haves and the have-nots is vitally important for corporate power. This is where corporatocracy comes into the picture. Corporatocratic governance provides the means to sustain and expand those inequalities by redistributing power and wealth from the have-nots toward the haves, most of all toward the corporations (in "have" nations) that are deeply associated with the globalization of technocapitalism. This dynamic also comprises a class dimension between the haves (the rich upper class, closely linked to corporate power) and the have-nots (the poor and working classes) that must be taken into account. The richer class of society is a direct beneficiary of redistribution since it typically owns substantial corporate capital, and therefore has direct influence on corporate decisions. Regardless of whether it is viewed from a class or nation-based perspective, this phenomenon of inequality and corporatocratic redistribution is fundamental to our understanding of technocapitalism and its global projection.

---

35 Nonetheless, governments tried to re-start financialization as the prime means to recovery. See John Bellamy Foster and Robert W. McChesney, "Monopoly-Finance Capital and the Paradox of Accumulation," *Monthly Review* 61(October 2009): 1–20.

Redistribution through Global Corporatocracy

Corporatocracy's support for global inequality through the redistribution dynamic has three important features. One feature involves *corporate welfare*, or the provision of government subsidies to corporate power. The subsidies come in many forms and guises.[36] They can involve, for example, tax credits for expenses directly related to research, such as purchases of laboratory hardware, experimental materials, research unit payrolls, or construction of research facilities. Another form of subsidy comes through funding for projects of the techno-military-corporate complex, which is typically quite substantial and can be one of the largest components of government budgets.

Corporate welfare can also involve bailouts of corporations deemed essential to national economic stability. Needless to say, such "stability" is all too often linked to the permanence of corporate power (the status quo) in times of crisis. Although mega-banks were the most visible beneficiaries of this kind of corporate welfare in recent times, the survival of some very large industrial corporations has often depended on this form of subsidy. It is also quite possible that some of the larger corporations associated with technocapitalism will benefit from this kind of corporate welfare in the future, most of all those closely connected to the techno-military-corporate complex. Corporate welfare may thus be provided under the justification of maintaining national security, whenever the corporations in trouble are linked to the creation of military technology.

Corporate power also often influences the level of corporate welfare through manipulative schemes. Should the level of welfare provided by public governance be insufficient, corporate power can come up with machinations to induce greater support. A common strategy is to pit governments against each other, to make them compete for corporate investment in their jurisdictions. This competitist game often involves payoffs to government officials if doing so can secure a higher level of corporate welfare. Such payoffs sometimes serve as a tool for potential blackmail down the line, if the paid-off officials renege on promises, or sell themselves to a higher bidder. Thus, corruption can be part of the game of corporate welfare and can lead to scandals when the loyalty of officials wanes.

Redistribution through corporate welfare involves taking resources from the public treasury to support corporate priorities. Since government resources are finite, what is given as corporate welfare reduces the resources that can be devoted to public needs. Those public needs come in many forms, but it is not hard to see that of all the myriad items in any government budget, resources that would go to meet the needs of the poor and working classes are most likely to be affected.

---

36   Corporate welfare is possibly the most obvious example of how public governance is co-opted by corporate power. See David J. Sirota, *Hostile Takeover: How Big Money and Corruption Conquered Our Government* (New York: Crown, 2006); Ted Nace, *Gangs of America: The Rise of Corporate Power and the Disabling of Democracy* (San Francisco: Berrett-Koehler, 2005).

The poor and working people are typically those with the least amount of political power in any contemporary capitalist society.[37] Even in so-called representative democracies where elections are not manipulated, the votes of the poor and the working classes usually count for little. Fragmentation of their political loyalties and votes, through a variety of parties that typically compete with (and often damage) each other, typically saps their power to have much influence on governments' allocation of resources.

Corporate interests, on the other hand, usually coalesce and consolidate their political power through strong parties, that can have a chance to win and implement corporatocratic agendas. Money is not an obstacle for such parties, as might be expected, since the value of corporatocratic governance is usually quite high to corporate power and justifies vast, media-rich propaganda campaigns. The propaganda campaigns are often orchestrated by political spin specialists who run global consultancies, and have accumulated substantial know-how in the management of campaigns. The ascent to political power of their corporate-backed clients is their prime objective, and their all-encompassing campaign strategies usually leave no stone unturned in their effort to win elections and discredit opponents.[38]

A second feature of corporatocracy's support for inequality involves the *reduction of risk and uncertainty for corporate power*. This second feature, often linked to the first (corporate welfare), also involves a redistribution of political power from the have-nots in society (the poor and working classes) to the haves (corporate power and the rich classes). Reduction of risk and uncertainty to corporate power thereby usually leads to an increase in risk and uncertainty (and greater social injustice) for the public at large (and most of all for the poor and working people).

Increased risk and uncertainty to the people occurs whenever the public resources available to make them more economically secure are reduced in order to lower corporate risk. In the context of technocapitalism, diminishing employment rights, such as the right to corporate-paid pensions, health care, vacations and leaves, the right of creativity providers to retain control over the results of their creativity, and the right to contest corporate decisions, for example, reduce corporate risk at the expense of increasing it to those who exercise their creativity for corporate employers. Increased risk to those who work or exercise creativity involves greater economic insecurity, and more difficulties in defending themselves against corporate abuse. For corporate power, risk is therefore reduced by making it easier to commodify creativity, appropriate its results, and obtain surplus value.

---

37 See Wacquant, *Punishing the Poor*.

38 See *The Economist*, "The Globalization of Spin: Marketing Maestros" (May 24, 2008): 109; James Harding, *Alpha Dogs: The Americans Who Turned Political Spin into a Global Business* (New York: Farrar, Straus and Giroux, 2008).

For the new corporatism, corporatocracy's power to lower risk in any area related to research (or to its outcomes) is of paramount importance. The vehicle for corporatocracy to reduce corporate risk in research is governments' monopoly over regulation and "legality." Examples of this vehicle can be found in any government that has internalized neoliberal precepts. Loosening up or dismantling regulation is a typical tool.[39] This is particularly important for corporate entities engaged in food- or medication-related research, as in the case of many biotech, agro-biotech or biopharmacology corporations.

Lifting or loosening up regulation is often carried out by appointing former corporate lobbyists or executives as regulatory agency heads. Corporatocratic transformation can thereby occur from within. Internal frameworks for regulation involving review, testing and approval can be dismantled or diluted. Agency scientists who question or oppose the new reality can be sidelined or disciplined.[40] Unproven assumptions that can make a great difference in testing can be enthroned as internal policy in order to facilitate approval of corporate products.

An example of this reality was the assumption that genetically engineered plants or crops will develop, or have the same effects over the long-term, as non-engineered ones. This assumption preempts long-term testing of new genetically engineered seeds, which is typically costly and very time-consuming. Adopting this assumption as a cornerstone of regulatory testing and approval saved many billions of dollars for agro-biotech corporations such as Monsanto.[41] At the same time, the use of this assumption allowed such corporations to start reaping billions of dollars in profit immediately after approval of new genetically engineered seeds. For the public, the use of this assumption introduced greater uncertainty and risk, since the question of long-term effects of engineered crops on eco-systems, the environment and possibly also human health, remains unanswered.

Another way to reduce corporate risk and uncertainty involves vacating government's responsibility to safeguard the public interest, in the purchase of corporate products or services. Pricing policies that benefit corporations at the expense of the public treasury and the public interest, particularly for research-intensive products and services, are a common vehicle. In the US, for example, an expansion of the Medicare program to include coverage for prescription medications was designed in such a way that the federal government basically denied itself

---

39   A prime target of deregulation in the US has been anti-monopoly laws; see David O. Savage, "Antitrust Law Losing Its Teeth: The Supreme Court Has Relaxed Rules Against Price Fixing," *Los Angeles Times* (March 19, 2007): A1. The financial crisis that started in 2007 was partly a consequence of deregulation; see Susan Pulliam and Tom McGinty, "Congress Helped Banks Defang Key Rule," *Wall Street Journal* (June 3, 2009): A1.

40   In particular, "whistleblowers" (scientists who denounce agency collusion with corporations whose products it must regulate). See Jennifer Levitz, "Whistleblowers are Left Dangling: Technicality Leads Labor Department to Dismiss Cases," *Wall Street Journal* (September 4, 2008): A3.

41   See Robin, "World According to Monsanto."

the prerogative to negotiate prices or demand discounts.[42] Thus, the government virtually guaranteed monopoly pricing to biopharmaceutical companies whenever they supply their products to the Medicare program. Rapidly rising medication prices over time at the expense of the public and the public treasury, and higher budget deficits, were some of the results. A major future consequence will likely be the reduction of benefits to Medicare recipients, thereby dispossessing the neediest recipients of their access to affordable medications.

The third feature of corporatocracy's support for inequality involves the *global redistribution of creative talent*. This redistribution comprises the previously discussed global brain drain flows toward rich nations. Corporatocracy supports this phenomenon and its underlying inequities by creating immigration laws that stimulate the brain drain flow while at the same time limiting the employment and residency rights of immigrant researchers. The best-of-all-possible worlds scenario it creates for corporate power, and especially for the new corporatism, is all too palpable in nations that are at the vanguard of technocapitalism.[43]

In the US, for example, where the vast majority of PhD-level engineers and scientists employed in technology corporations are immigrants, a complex system of laws regulates residency and employment visas that is tailored to support corporate interests above all else.[44] Immigrant researchers without permanent residency who are abused by their corporate employers, and seek to change employment, have little real recourse in court against either their employer or the immigration authorities. The cost of legal representation alone is prohibitive, not to mention the long periods of time that typically elapse before a court decision can be rendered. Then, deportation can often occur before any such decision is issued, thus preempting any legal challenges or the serving of individual justice.

Another vehicle for corporatocracy to support the brain drain phenomenon is through the global flows of graduate students in science and technology fields. Again, the US with its vast and diverse repertory of universities, and its leading role in the technocapitalist dynamic provides a good example. Foreign students who pursue graduate education in the US in science and technology fields are usually better prepared than their American-born counterparts.[45] Moreover, the public costs of their primary, secondary and prior university education (along with

---

42   See Galbraith, *Predator State*; Melody Petersen, "Paying for Pills," *Los Angeles Times* (October 10, 2009): A33.

43   See Susan Hockfield, "Immigrant Scientists Create Jobs and Win Nobels," *Wall Street Journal* (October 20, 2009): A19; *The Economist*, "Give Me Your Scientists: Restricting the Immigration of Highly Skilled Workers Will Hurt America's Ability to Innovate" (March 7, 2009): 84.

44   See Michael P. Smith and Adrian Favell (eds.), *The Human Face of Global Mobility: International Highly Skilled Migration in Europe, North America, and the Asia Pacific* (New Brunswick, NJ: Transaction, 2006); *The Economist*, "Give Me Your Scientists."

45   Teresa B. Bevis, *International Students in American Colleges and Universities: A History* (New York: Palgrave Macmillan, 2007); Hockfield, "Immigrant Scientists."

the public costs of their upbringing and health care, for example) were paid for by their home nations. Once in the US, and most of all after they complete their graduate degrees, those highly qualified individuals are often hired by American technology corporations and can obtain permanent residency.

The United States thereby acquires a formidable advantage in the global panorama of technocapitalism. To a great extent, this global flow of students, combined with the immigration of scientists and engineers, may account for its current position at the forefront of technocapitalism. The inadequacy of American primary and secondary education in science and technology is thus greatly offset by the arrival of students from other nations.[46] By making it easy for foreign students who hold a degree from an American university in a science or technology field to stay, US laws help satisfy the corporate need for new creative talent. At the same time, those laws preempt global competitors from having access, in their home ground, to the kind of talent they need to establish a foothold in the new scenario of technocapitalism.

In poor nations, corporatocracy can facilitate the global redistribution of creative talent by making emigration easier. This can involve, for example, withdrawing any requirement that those who study abroad return home after completing their degrees, or repay any of the public support they received for their education if they fail to do so. Similarly, lifting restrictions on the emigration of creative talent, by forgoing any individual reimbursement of the cost of public education or other public support (such as health care) to each emigrant (or to their nations of destination) is another way to facilitate brain drain flows. Governments that have tried to impose such restrictions in the past have been branded as xenophobic by the corporate-controlled global media networks, ignoring the high costs that the emigration of creative talent imposes on have-not societies, and the tacit subsidy that such emigration provides to the "have" nations that receive it.

Corporations in the "have" nations are the main beneficiaries of such flows and subsidies, since they are the prime employers of immigrant talent. By influencing immigration and residency legislation to their advantage through corporatocratic governance, they ensure themselves an abundant flow of talent at lower cost than they could obtain from home sources. Moreover, the social class dimension of such flows, which often involve middle class individuals in the context of the

---

46 See National Center for Education Statistics, *National Assessment of Educational Progress: The Nation's Report Card* (Washington: NCES, 2009), available at http://nces. ed.gov/nationsreportcard/ (accessed October 15, 2009); Robert Tomsho, "U.S. Math Scores Hit a Wall," *Wall Street Journal* (October 15, 2009): A3; *Wall Street Journal*, "Education: Why We're Failing Math and Science" (October 26, 2009): R5. The large number of foreign students in American universities (about 700,000 in the fall of 2008, by far the largest of any nation in the world in absolute terms) partly makes up for this systemic deficiency. See *The Economist*, "University Students Abroad: And is There Honey Still for Tea?" (November 21, 2009): 59.

nations of origin, also provides an additional incentive to corporate power.[47] Such emigrants are more likely to work harder and avoid conflict with their corporate employers, thus providing a malleable population whose talents and creativity can be more easily commodified.

Failed Governance

Corporatocracy represents a failure of democracy. Notions of justice, equity and public participation that are fundamental to democratic governance are turned on their head. Dynamics of redistribution that have long been considered a vital component of democratic governance are reversed, in order to favor corporate interests, the corporate elites, and the wealthier segments of society.

At the core of corporatocracy's failed governance is a *reconversion of the state* to legalize, orchestrate and implement a redistribution of power and wealth from the public at large toward corporate interests, and toward those who own substantial corporate capital.[48] This reconversion of governance is accompanied by a process of dispossession of power, of economic security and of social benefits from the vast majority of the population. Dispossession involves a loss of political power and public trust, along with greater risk and uncertainty for the majority of society, and the curtailment (if not the collapse) of access to collective resources. At the same time, such dispossession increases corporatism's political power, reduces its risk, enhances its profits, and consolidates its influence over public governance.

For technocapitalism and for the new corporatism, corporatocracy is fundamentally important in the quest for greater profit and power. The global ascendance of corporatocracy and of the neoliberal precepts that underpin its logic have opened new frontiers for this new version of capitalism and for its corporate apparatus. As corporatocratic governance increasingly becomes "normal" governance, the new reality it creates helps sustain the new corporatism's appropriation of creativity, life, nature and human existence. In many ways, therefore, corporatocracy is very important for the commodification of creativity,

---

47 For the international migration of talent, socioeconomic class is a very important aspect. Although meritocracy is often cited as a powerful attraction in the rich nations that receive such migration, social class-based arrangements pervade both migration and employment of highly skilled immigrants. See Stephen J. McNamee and Robert K. Miller, *The Meritocracy Myth* (Lanham, MD: Rowman and Littlefield, 2009).

48 See Nace, *Gangs of America*; Sirota, *Hostile Takeover*. An effect of reconversion is the destruction of what some authors refer to as the public sphere of governance, or the public interest. See Lawrence C. Soley, *Censorship, Inc.: The Corporate Threat to Free Speech in the United States* (New York: Monthly Review Press, 2002); Carl Boggs, *The End of Politics: Corporate Power and the Decline of the Public Sphere* (New York: Guilford, 2000).

for the appropriation of its results, and for the sustenance of the corporate research regimes upon which this new version of capitalism depends.

In the context of technocapitalism, corporatocracy's importance for the new corporatism and its globalization is associated with two fundamental phenomena. One of these phenomena is the *split between the commodification and the reproduction of creativity*, discussed earlier in this book. Because of this split between commodification and reproduction, it is practically impossible for corporate power to control the reproduction of creativity. This fundamental aspect of technocapitalism stands in stark contrast with the situation under industrial capitalism, when both commodification and reproduction were under the control of corporate power. This contrast is largely due to the very different character of the most important resources of technocapitalism and of industrial capitalism. Under industrial capitalism, the main resources were tangible and could thereby be controlled physically through production and distribution. In the context of technocapitalism, however, the most important resource, creativity, is *intangible and qualitative*, and depends on external social mediation for its reproduction.[49]

This split between commodification and reproduction that is a major characteristic of technocapitalism greatly increases risk and uncertainty for corporate power, as the possibility of controlling reproduction largely vanishes. The reproduction of creativity thereby becomes a social function, external to the corporate domain, and is mediated through social relations, cultural influences, and the (also external) accumulation of knowledge. As a result corporate organizations, and in particular the new corporatism, are more vulnerable to external social factors and relations over which they have little control. Corporatism must perforce become more social, and thus attempts to regain some control by exercising more influence over society through public governance.

Therein lies one of the roots of corporatocracy. To try to gain some control over the social medium of reproduction, corporatism ends up exercising greater control over society's governance. And, although control over reproduction escapes its grasp given the large-scale, diffuse and dynamic nature of social relations, of their mediation, and of the greater sociocultural context, control over public governance does not. In this sense, corporatocracy is the result of corporatism's effort to assert its power, and of the effort to acquire some measure of control over the larger domain of society, in which the reproduction of creativity is embedded. From this effort to exercise greater control over society arises corporatocracy's pathologies, among which dispossession and redistribution for the benefit of corporate power are most noticeable.

The second phenomenon driving corporatism's search for control over society is the ongoing *decomposition of corporate functions*, discussed earlier in this book, and the growing importance of external networks and social relations for corporate

---

49   See the Chapter "Creativity as a Commodity", in Suarez-Villa, *Technocapitalism*, pp. 31–55.

operations.[50] Corporatism thereby loses power and control over its activities, as functions are externalized. The external parties are quite diverse and can involve research subcontractors, myriad suppliers, and service providers, for example. This phenomenon affects both the new corporatism and the older, conventional corporate organizations associated with industrial capitalism (and with the so-called post-industrial or services-based capitalism). In many ways, decomposition means that corporations cannot consider themselves to be separate from society, looking solely after their own narrow interests in isolation from society.[51]

Corporatism's growing influence over governance is a response to this situation. In many respects, corporatocracy's ascendance is a result of this quest for influence and control. After all, if decomposition shifts functions and power out of the corporate domain, it is logical for corporate power to pursue greater control over society and over its governance. The loss of control, and the greater uncertainty that decomposition entails is thereby offset by a quest for control over the external, that is, over society and its governance. Governance becomes the easier target in this game of control, since its structures are static and provide access to politicians and officials whose political fortunes can be influenced or engineered to serve corporate priorities.

Corporatism's quest for influence cannot limit itself to national governance, however. Because corporatism depends so much on worldwide flows, its quest for influence is global. In the case of the new corporatism, its dependence on global flows of creative talent, research outsourcing, accumulated knowledge, and venture capital means that its quest for influence over governance seeks the establishment of corporatocracy everywhere in the world. Similarly, the old, established sectors associated with industrial capitalism also seek to set up or sustain corporatocracy wherever their supply chains, labor needs and raw material sources are significant.

The failure of corporatocratic governance is therefore global in scope and reach. Three aspects associated with corporatocracy's global ascendance attest to its failure, and pathological character, as a new mode of governance. The first aspect involves the relations of power that corporatocracy imposes on society.

---

50 See Suarez-Villa, *Technocapitalism*, "Decomposing the Corporation," pp. 86–122.

51 The fallacy that society benefits most when corporations look solely after their own interest has been a major precept of neoliberalism and of neo-conservatism. Its theoretical core is grounded in neoclassical (mainstream) economics. The foremost exponent of this fallacy was Nobel laureate economist Milton Friedman, by far the most important academic propagandist of neoliberalism. His work had much impact in the spread of neoliberalism and of corporatocratic governance around the world since the 1980s. One of the early adopters of Friedman's (and the Chicago School's) prescriptions was the Pinochet regime in Chile during the 1970s. See Harvey, *Brief History*. A major and much neglected aspect of neoliberalism is its close relationship with neoclassical economics. Stephen A. Marglin's *The Dismal Science: How Thinking Like an Economist Undermines Community* (Cambridge: Harvard University Press, 2008), exposes the negative effects of that relationship on the public interest.

Through its hegemony over governance, corporatocracy turns public governance into a *commodity* at the service of corporate interests. The kind of commodification that corporatism implements day in and day out, whether in research, production or services, is thereby extrapolated to public governance. And since commodification is something that corporatism knows well and can control internally, how could this be otherwise? After all, what works to sustain control within the corporate domain should work to establish control over public governance, so the rationale of corporatism goes.

The commodification of public governance that corporatocracy represents thereby turns government into a commodity at the service of corporate power. Rather than serve the public interest, this commodification of governance serves the interests of corporate power, turning most any public human endeavor that has a potential for profit into a tool of corporatism. The symptoms of this new reality of governance are now all around us. No activity that comes under some purview of public governance can be considered immune to the effects of this commodification. In health care, for example, where privatization has made inroads around the world, corporate profits come before the public's health. Health care is thereby turned into a commodity with human health becoming a secondary concern. Similarly, in agriculture corporate profits and power are the utmost priority, whereas feeding humanity and providing healthy food become secondary concerns.

In culture, government all too often becomes a partner in the amputation of identities that accompanies the corporate colonization of public culture. As a result, the trivial and ephemeral gain overarching importance.[52] Culture thereby becomes a commodity, with corporatism denigrating histories and ways of life that cannot be force-fitted into its narrow quest for profit and power.[53] Public information, a tool for public awareness and solidarity, is also commodified and turned into a corporate-controlled vehicle for corporatism's propaganda and spin

---

52   See Bernd Hamm and Russell Smandych (eds.), *Cultural Imperialism: Essays on the Political Economy of Cultural Domination* (Orchard Park, NY: Broadview Press, 2005). The amputation of identities that accompanies the corporate colonization of public culture can be associated with the voracious corporate quest to appropriate any and all forms of culture and creative talent, that can lead to profit. Media corporations, for example, now try to anticipate every possible future stream of profit by dispossessing amateur performers of the right to be compensated. See Dionne Searcey and James R. Hagerty, "Lawyerese Goes Galactic as Contracts Try to Master the Universe: From Stage to Pickle Shop, These Terms Cover All Rights for All Time in All Worlds," *Wall Street Journal* (October 29, 2009): A1.

53   Adorno's views on the corporate appropriation of pop music seems relevant to this point. See Theodor W. Adorno, *Night Music: Essays on Music 1928–1962*, transl. W. Hoban (Chicago: Seagull, 2009). More generally, Adorno noted how the standardization of popular culture became an essential commodity to capitalism, harnessed for the benefit of greater profit and also for greater social control. See Gerhard Schweppenhäuser's *Theodor W. Adorno: An Introduction*, transl. J. Rolleston (Durham, NC: Duke University Press, 2008).

campaigns.[54] Those campaigns, which are now more subtle than ever, tie into the commodification of culture noted previously, and they are also a vehicle for political propaganda favoring candidates who can advance the corporatocratic agenda. Public images and opinions are thus engineered through the corporate colonization of public information and the commodification of culture.

In technology and science, which are deeply associated with technocapitalism and with its experimentalist ethos, government-supported research is turned into a tool of corporate power. Research and inquiry for the sake of knowledge, or for the enjoyment of discovery thereby become either untenable or secondary to the corporate quest for profit and power.[55] Human emancipation, a longstanding objective of publicly-supported scientific research, becomes incompatible with corporate priorities. Such emancipation involves a loss of control for corporate power, increasing its risk and uncertainty, and creating another roadblock to greater profit. Government's support for, and the regulation of, scientific research for human emancipation and wellbeing are thereby shortchanged. Regulation over

---

54 During the national debate on health care reform in the US, for example, a vast and rich propaganda campaign by pharmaceutical and biotech corporations, and by the corporate-run health insurance and managed care sectors, fiercely attacked Canada's government-run health care system. See, Michael M. Rachlis, "A Canadian Diagnosis: Caricatures of Its 'Socialized' Medicine Are Used to Keep Corporations –Not Patients– Healthy," *Los Angeles Times* (August 3, 2009): A19. Some of the fiercest corporate opponents to a publicly-run health care program were the chief executives of companies (such as Eastman Kodak and Verizon Communications) that were laying off tens of thousands of employees (Kodak: 22,000, Verizon: 16,000, both by December 31, 2009), who would be left without any access to health care. See David Lazarus, "Business Leaders' Health Care Stand Takes Chutzpah: CEOs' Stand Places Profits Before People's Lives," *Los Angeles Times* (November 1, 2009): B1.

55 Daniel S. Greenberg's *Science, Money, and Politics: Political Triumph and Ethical Erosion* (Chicago: University of Chicago Press, 2001), shows how readily and enthusiastically scientists forsake the standards and values they claim to uphold (such as scrutiny of research methods, critical evaluations of research results, and respect for the integrity of data), when they seek to further their interests by obtaining money or gaining political influence. One-third of US university scientists, for example, admitted to engaging in practices and behaviors considered unethical by their university officials; see Brian C. Martinson, Melissa S. Anderson, A. Lauren Crain and Raymond DeVries, "Scientists' Perceptions of Organizational Justice and Self-Reported Misbehaviors," *Journal of Empirical Research on Human Research Ethics* 1(2006): 51–66; Antonio Regalado, "Ethics of U.S. Scientists May Be Shaky, Poll Says," *Wall Street Journal* (June 9, 2005): A1. Self-serving data analyses, poor research project design and miscalculations are thought to affect a majority of published scientific research claims, according to some analyses; see Neal S. Young, John P. A. Ioannidis and Omar Al-Ubaydli, "Why Current Publication Practices May Distort Science." *PLoS Medicine* 5(2008): http://www.plosmedicine.org/article/info: doi/10.1371/journal.pmed. 0050201 (accessed November 4, 2009); John R.L. Hotz, "Most Science Studies Appear to Be Tainted By Sloppy Analysis," *Wall Street Journal* (September 14, 2007): A7.

research thus becomes accessory to corporate power, and is enlisted to legitimize corporate priorities.

A second aspect of corporatocracy's failed governance is its reinforcement and deepening of *inequalities*. The deepening of inequalities has a global dimension that encompasses both nations and social classes. Deeper inequalities are a result of the redistribution and dispossession phenomena discussed earlier in this chapter. Reconverting the state to redistribute power and wealth from the people to corporations is possibly the most egregious case of inequality generation.[56] In many ways, it reflects a reversal of twentieth century trends that brought about social security and unemployment compensation programs, pension systems, universal health access, and progressive taxation. The dispossession of rights to social benefits and collective goods that accompanies such redistribution casts a wide net that snares not only the poor and working classes, but also the middle class and most anyone not closely connected to the corporate elite or the ownership of substantial corporate capital.

The deepening of inequalities created by corporatocracy is far from coincidental or unintended. Corporate power and control are enhanced by greater inequity whenever it results in lower costs, especially in employment, which

---

56   The inequality generated through three decades of neoliberal policies is staggering. In the US, for example, one percent of the population (the richest) controlled more wealth in 2007 than the bottom 40 percent (the poor and working classes). Real hourly wages for US workers rose only one percent between 1979 and 2007, even though worker productivity in the US rose by 60 percent over the same period. American workers also worked more hours during this period than their counterparts in all other rich nations (including Japan). At the same time, American workers' health insurance and pension plans were practically "phased out" by most employers, while economic insecurity became a major problem even for highly skilled professionals. See Schultz and McGinty, "Pensions for Executives"; Steven Greenhouse, *The Big Squeeze: Tough Times for the American Worker* (New York: Knopf, 2008); Vanessa O'Connell, "Lawyers Settle for Temp Jobs," *Wall Street Journal* (June 15, 2011): B1. In contrast, the top-earning American hedge fund manager made 3.7 billion dollars in total compensation during 2007, an amount equal to the total worth of one of the richest men in the world in the mid-1970s (J. Paul Getty); see Thomas Frank, "Our Great Economic U-Turn," *Wall Street Journal* (May 14, 2008): A23. The effects of this pattern of rising inequality on children is staggering. One study, for example, estimated that about 50 percent of all children in the US would be dependent on food stamps (a welfare program for the poor) at some point in their childhood; see Paul H. Wise, "Children of the Recession," *Archives of Pediatrics and Adolescent Medicine* 163(2009): 1063–64; Liz Szabo, "Study: Half of U.S. Kids Will Receive Food Stamps," *USA Today* (November 2, 2009): www.usatoday.com/news/health/2009-11-02-food-stamps_N.htm (accessed November 3, 2009). Moreover, the vast majority of the US's lowly skilled labor force is made up of undocumented immigrants who have practically no rights and are vulnerable to exploitive schemes. See John Bowe, *Nobodies: Modern American Slave Labor and the Dark Side of the New Global Economy* (New York: Random House, 2007).

is the vehicle through which corporate power obtains creative talent.[57] In the calculus of corporate power, people in greater need usually translates into a more pliant workforce, easier corporate appropriation of creativity, and also greater internal flexibility to make decisions or execute strategies. In many ways, this is an important consolation to corporate power for its lack of control over the reproduction of creativity, and for the loss of control that the decomposition of internal corporate functions entails.

The third aspect of corporatocracy's failed governance is a most pernicious one: its *association with neo-imperialism*. Imposition, aggression and the will to dominate are at the heart of neo-imperialism. In the case of fast neo-imperialism, discussed in the previous chapter, the game of global domination is fundamentally based on the corporate appropriation of creativity, the accumulation of knowledge and technological infrastructure, and the use of systematized research regimes (a key feature of the new corporatism) as exploitive vehicles and tools of domination. Corporatocracy thus comes into play in this game of global domination as a vehicle to establish the laws, the enforcement apparatus, and the legitimacy of those vehicles of domination.

It should not surprise, therefore, that a major objective of fast neo-imperialism is to establish corporatocratic governance whenever and wherever campaigns of conquest happen to be carried out. Fast militarism thereby comes into the scene, whenever aggression is executed. Military conquest for its own sake is pointless, and fast neo-imperialism has no real reason for being, unless the imposition of corporatocracy is part of the end game of conquest. Military conquest that seeks "regime change," to use a term from the jargon of twenty-first militarism, is therefore useless unless it can set up corporatocratic governance when weapons fall silent.[58] This fundamental objective of fast neo-imperialism and of its militaristic apparatus must not be overlooked, whenever the imposition and global spread of corporatocracy are considered.

An objective for fast neo-imperialism and its militaristic dimension, therefore, is the imposition of corporatocratic control over society whenever "regime

---

57 The deepening of inequalities has long been downplayed or ignored by pro-corporate authors and journalists, and by the vast majority of corporate executives. Academia has not been spared, as an American academic who frequently writes on entrepreneurship and creativity, tacitly advocates for greater inequality as *the* remedy to achieve higher economic growth and innovation; see Richard Florida, "The Rise of the Mega-Region," *Wall Street Journal* (April 12, 2008): A9. Recent writings by that academic advocate greater concentration of wealth (and government resources) in 40 global mega-regions that he claims "power the global economy," are home to one-fifth of the world's population, account for two-thirds of global economic output, and provide 85 percent of all global innovation.

58 Early twenty-first century American military expeditions made this point clear. See John Bellamy Foster, *Naked Imperialism: The U.S. Pursuit of Global Dominance* (New York: Monthly Review Press, 2006); Ray Kiely, *Empire in the Age of Globalization: US Hegemony and Neoliberal Disorder* (London: Pluto, 2005).

change" is attempted. The imposition of corporatocratic control, however, requires pervasive monitoring of all human social activities. Surveillance over society thus becomes an important element of corporatocracy, justified through government's monopoly over violence and "legality." Corporatocratic governance thereby creates surveillance societies as part of its apparatus of power.[59] After all, what benefit could corporatocracy provide to corporatism if it cannot effectively control and impose the new order on society?

Related to corporatocracy's establishment of surveillance societies is the privatization of prison systems.[60] A corporate-run prison system thus emerges, whereby a nation's judicial system also becomes a commodity of corporatism. Through corporatocracy and privatization, the judiciary function of governance can become an appendage of corporate power. Prisoners thus become the "customers" of prison corporations. Such corporations, in order to turn a tidy profit, must keep their facilities full of "clients" and can, if necessary, resort to co-opting the judicial system—most of all the judges who impose sentences.

The judicial system, as the provider of "clients" through sentencing criteria and punitive guidelines, thus becomes an accessory to corporate power that must be given "incentives", such that "customers" can be readily conveyed to the corporate-run prison network. Incentives can involve payoffs to judges, or changing the rules of the game in sentencing so that more "clients" are landed in prison even for minor offenses.[61] Since recidivism is usually quite high, once those

---

59   Although corporatocratic propaganda wants everyone to believe that pervasive surveillance protects liberty, much the opposite is usually the case. The imposition of surveillance societies is closely associated with the erosion of civil liberties and of individual freedom. One of the most common justifications for pervasive surveillance, whenever it is questioned, is the "if-you-have-nothing-to-hide-you-have-nothing-to-worry-about" argument. Anthony C. Grayling's *Liberty in the Age of Terror: A Defence of Civil Society and Enlightenment Values* (London: Bloomsbury, 2009) considers such arguments to betray hard-won civil liberties and individual rights, partly because of their assumption that authorities will always be benign, that they will not identify opposition views and behaviors as unacceptable, that they will always identify "bad people" precisely and correctly, and that they will never expand their surveillance power and capabilities to engage in repression. Nonetheless, pervasive surveillance has received considerable backing from those who favor corporate power and corporatocracy. See Adam L. Penenberg, "The Surveillance Society: We Routinely Sacrifice Privacy for Convenience and Security. So Stop Worrying. And Get Ready for Your Close-Up," *Wired* (December 2001): 157–60.

60   The privatization of prison systems in the US led to the creation of large and profitable corporations that are intimately tied to the judicial system and to legislation. See Donna Selman, *Punishment for Sale: Private Prisons, Big Business and the Incarceration Binge* (Lanham, MD: Rowman and Littlefield, 2009); see Michael A. Hallett, *Private Prisons in America: A Critical Race Perspective* (Urbana: University of Illinois Press, 2006); Wacquant, *Punishing the Poor*.

61   In the US, two judges received 2.6 million dollars in kickbacks from a private prison corporation, for sending juveniles to its prisons. In exchange for the kickbacks, the judges provided the private prison corporation with 1.3 million dollars per year of public

"clients" land in prison it is practically guaranteed that most will return after they are released. In the United States, for example, as many as two-thirds of all ex-prisoners are re-arrested within three years after release, and the vast majority of them are returned to prison. There are close to two million prison "orphans" in the US today, that is, children with one or both parents in prison. Perhaps it should not surprise, then, that the United States, where the corporate prison system is firmly established, has more prisoners per capita than any other nation, and by far now holds the world's largest number of prisoners.[62]

These examples of corporatocracy's corruption of public institutions, of its injustices and of its pathological character, may provide an idea of its failure as a system of governance. Corporatocracy's systemic failure, the inequalities and injustices it generates, and its pernicious association with neo-imperialism and militarism, raise disturbing questions for humanity. To what extent is this new global order inevitable, given its vast, corporate-provided resources for control and oppression? In a global order where injustices and pathologies are imposed systematically through corporatocracy, can this system of governance be reversed or overturned? And, how and to what extent can effective means of resistance be created to oppose its pathologies, and its depredation of human values, life and nature?

Conclusion

The globalization of technocapitalism is closely associated with the ascendance of corporatocracy. Based on neoliberal precepts, corporatocracy has become a "normal" mode of governance. In various forms and with greater or lesser intensity, corporatocratic governance can now be found most everywhere. *Through its reconversion of the state to serve corporate power, corporatocracy makes the global spread of technocapitalism and of its new corporatism a viable phenomenon.*

The ethos of corporatocracy, to place corporate priorities above the needs of the people, puts it in direct conflict with the fundamental idea of democracy. The purposes of government functions and institutions that were created to serve the public interest are thereby turned on their head. Notions of fairness, and of the

---

funds. The sentencing of juveniles was part of a scheme to keep the private prison facilities full in order to direct more public funds to the prison corporations, and thereby increase their profits. In the vast majority of cases, the accused juvenile had no lawyer (the incidence of such situations was said to be 10 times the state average for Pennsylvania), and sentencing typically took one minute-and-a-half to three minutes. See Thomas Frank, "Lock 'Em Up," *Wall Street Journal* (April 1, 2009): A21.

62   The US, with less than 5 percent of the world's population, has about 25 percent of all prisoners on earth. See *The Economist*, "A Nation of Jailbirds: Far Too Many Americans are Behind Bars" (April 4, 2009): 40.

importance of equity and social justice for human wellbeing are discarded, as corporatism takes over most any aspect of government that can lead to greater power and profit. This reconversion of governance to serve corporate power, over and above everything else, has nefarious consequences for humanity, with pathologies that are bound to become important features of the twenty-first century.

Policies meant to advance corporatocracy around the world are now central to the prescriptions dispensed by the most influential meta-national organizations. Most any economic, social or political problem elicits the imposition of those policies as a precondition for receiving loans, investment, or maintaining government solvency. Corporatocracy therefore seems inescapable for most any nation that solicits international help to deal with its problems. Also, from within, political movements orchestrated by powerful corporate interests that seek to impose their agenda on society have become commonplace. One result is the ascendance of corporate-financed parties and politicians, that gain power through campaigns orchestrated by global political spin consultants hired to advance corporatocracy at any cost, anywhere, by any means.

Corporatocracy's reconversion of the state involves a redistribution of power and wealth from the mass of the people, and most of all from the poor and working classes, toward the corporate elites and the richest segment of society. Redistribution is accompanied by a dispossession of the people from a wide spectrum of rights, individual, social, economic, political, environmental and ecologic, in order to benefit corporatism and increase its influence over society's governance. These twin phenomena of redistribution and dispossession result in greater and deeper social, economic and political inequalities. Those inequalities have now taken up a global dimension, as corporatocratic governance spreads around the world. The chasm between the corporate elites, the rich classes who own substantial corporate capital, and the mass of the people thereby grows and creates a new reality, that is as socially unjust as it is depredatory of human dignity, of life and of nature.

The inequalities generated through redistribution and dispossession are greatly beneficial to corporatism. *In the context of technocapitalism and of its globalization, those inequalities support the new corporatism's urgent need for more creative talent, aggressive intellectual property rights, lower research costs, and for its appropriation of a wide range of bioresources, including the genetic codes of every living organism on earth.* Growing brain drain flows, widespread research outsourcing, more expansive intellectual property regimes, greater influence over regulation, and the corporate appropriation of collective resources are some of the effects associated with those inequalities, which are now global in scope and scale.

Those global inequalities involve deepening divides between nations and between social classes. At the level of classes, they increase not only the technological divide between haves and have-nots, but also the wealth divide between those who own substantial corporate capital or are part of the corporate elite, and those who are not. At the international level, inequalities increase the brain drain flows toward rich nations upon which the new corporatism depends, they open new lower-cost frontiers for research outsourcing, and they facilitate the corporate takeover of collective resources that can support research. Those chasms and inequities are thus closely associated with brain drain flows, with the dispossession of those who provide creative talent, and with the public's dispossession of any collective resources sought by corporatism.

At the root of the global corporate quest for influence through corporatocracy, are two fundamental phenomena of technocapitalism. *One of these phenomena is the split between the commodification and the reproduction of creativity, which results in the loss of corporate control over reproduction. The second phenomenon involves the decomposition of corporate functions through external networks, which also entails a loss of corporate control.* In both phenomena, control is externalized from the corporate domain toward society, its networks, social relations, and culture. Corporatocratic governance thus becomes the logical vehicle for corporatism's quest for regaining control, a form of control that is societal in scope and scale, and that seeks to make up for the loss of internal control that accompanies technocapitalism and its globalization.

Is There Any Alternative?

The global reach of technocapitalism and of its corporate apparatus poses major problems for humanity. Technocapitalism, corporate power, and corporatocratic governance involve conquest on a global scale. It is a form of conquest unlike any humanity has previously experienced, because of the fundamental influence that technology and science play in it, and because of corporatism's capacity to colonize our relationships with society, life and nature. This key feature of technocapitalism and of its globalization must be kept in mind, as we confront the social pathologies imposed by this new version of capitalism.

The technologies associated with technocapitalism and with its globalization pretend to have an unprecedented degree of autonomy from society. Their social character and socially-grounded sources, of which creativity is most precious, their technical complexities, and their effects on humanity, life and nature are abstract and difficult to comprehend. This means that the social pathologies that are being imposed on us, their effects on human existence, on life and on our planet may be difficult to oppose.

The incipient globalization of technocapitalism, of its corporate apparatus, and of its pathologies require new visions for social action. A vision that understands technocapitalism and its globalization as an intrinsically social phenomenon is necessary. Technocapitalism, its globalization, and the new technologies it is spawning, do not therefore involve solely the exercise of control over science and nature. *The social domain must be taken into account because technocapitalism, its globalization and its corporatism are a result of human creativity, which in the context of technocapitalism is inherently social.* This most vital resource of technocapitalism must, after all, be reproduced through social mediation.

In the context of technocapitalism, therefore, technological efficiency considerations are entwined with the social dimension. Those who believe greater efficiency to be the sole purpose of technology will not recognize this argument, because acknowledging it will undermine their belief, and because it is much easier to deal with technology solely in terms of efficiency criteria. This belief is now entrenched in neoliberal dogma, in corporatocratic governance, and in the neoclassical economic precepts that support neoliberalism. Taking efficiency into account without considering the social dimension, or the social character of creativity that makes efficiency possible in the first place, however, is unreal in the context of technocapitalism.

This book therefore opposes the dominant view that assumes technology and science, and greater efficiency, will by themselves generate new forms of social, economic and political management. Or, that those new forms of management will necessarily be positive for humanity, life, nature, and for public governance.[1] In the practice of neoliberalism, such "management" necessarily depends on corporatocratic governance. As we saw in the previous chapter greater inequality, dispossession of the majority of the people, and redistribution of wealth and power to benefit corporate interests, are the outcomes of neoliberal "management" of society.

The global implementation of technocapitalism, and of its neoliberal ethos, cannot therefore occur without a political system—corporatocracy—that takes over the state. It is a takeover that is orchestrated by corporate power, by its elites, and by the richer classes associated with those elites. The state is thereby placed at the service of corporate power, to serve corporate interests and priorities above everything else. This reality therefore contradicts the empty fantasies of neoliberalism that advocate a withering of the state and of state power.[2] A shrivelled state is no more useful to technocapitalist corporatism than a ship without a hull is to a sailor.

A state is essential to sustain technocapitalism and its corporatism, forcefully if necessary, if redistribution of power and wealth to benefit corporate interests— and the accompanying dispossession of the mass of the people—are to occur. Any withering of the state is therefore unrealistic in the context of technocapitalism, because perpetrating the injustices that accompany corporatocracy requires making the state a surrogate. The state's monopoly over violence and "legality" are therefore a precious asset to the corporatocratic agenda to redistribute power, dispossess the public, and deepen inequities.

---

1   The adverse effects of technology and science on humanity are all too often ascribed to the nature of technological innovations (or to their efficiency), rather than the social, economic and political system in which they occur. Thus, for example, a well-known author writing on biotechnology noted that this field's advances may decimate our humanity, as if biotech innovations occurred in a social vacuum [see Francis Fukuyama, *Our Posthuman Future* (New York: Farrar, Straus and Giroux, 2002)]. Taking science and technology's social, economic and political grounding, biologist Richard Levins had long before summed up how and why most of technology and science's social dysfunctions occur, noting that "the irrationalities of a scientifically sophisticated world come not from failures of intelligence but from the persistence of capitalism;" see Richard Levins and Richard Lewontin, *The Dialectical Biologist* (Cambridge: Harvard University Press, 1985), p. 208.

2   In reality, neoliberal policies have actually strengthened state power in many places where they have been applied; see, for example, David Harvey, *A Brief History of Neoliberalism* (New York: Oxford University Press, 2005). Implementing and sustaining injustice require force and state legalism, and a weakened state would not have the capacity to enforce neoliberal programs. However, privatization of governmental functions might give the impression that the state can be dismantled, when what actually occurs is that corporate power takes up more of the societal functions of state power. See John Kenneth Galbraith, *The Predator State: How Conservatives Abandoned the Free Market and Why Liberals Should Too* (New York: Free Press, 2008).

This means that technocapitalism, its globalization, and the new technologies associated with them cannot be treated as extra-political entities, governed by "natural" laws of supply and demand, or solely through efficiency criteria. Treating them as extra-political entities is unreal in terms of the imposition of corporate interests over society. To treat technocapitalism, its globalization, and its corporate apparatus as extra-political entities will mean not only greater injustices but also greater social alienation. Thus, new forms of democratic governance are needed that can be responsive to the socially mediated domains of global technocapitalism, of its corporatism, and of its vital resources.

Neo-Imperialism, Nations and Class

On the question of democratic governance and technocapitalism's globalization, an important contradiction surfaces. While technocapitalism and its corporatism acquire a *global* scope, the control of its corporate apparatus is nonetheless strongly *national*.[3] This nationally-grounded control over technocapitalism is today rooted in the United States, given its place at the vanguard of technocapitalism, and to a significant extent in Japan and the richer nations of Western Europe. The technocapitalist corporations of this mega-triad (the US, Western Europe and Japan) are therefore in control of technocapitalism's global reach, and of its association with fast neo-imperialism and with corporatocracy.

The globalization of technocapitalism does not therefore abolish neo-imperialism, in the sense that national domination over others (and the world) are very much a part of this new era. This kind of globalization has not generated a system that is both nowhere and everywhere, transcending all boundaries, as the neoliberal propaganda promulgates. It is, by and large, a nationally-grounded system of global domination based on the hegemony of one nation, accompanied by a small group of other rich nations. Thus, the center-periphery dichotomy of neo-imperialism has not been surpassed. Much to the contrary, it is quite important for understanding technocapitalism's global reach.

The kind of neo-imperialism associated with technocapitalism—fast neo-imperialism—has major roles to play in this panorama of global conquest. One role involves helping monopolize access to global resources, especially creative talent and its worldwide brain drain flow. As discussed earlier in this book, fast neo-imperialism's association with these flows, and with the global inequalities that support them, is of vital importance to the globalization of technocapitalism. In addition, fast neo-imperialism takes up the longstanding imperialist role of securing access to natural resources in order to benefit corporate power. This second role

---

3   The contradiction between neo-imperialism's nationally-grounded power and the global reach of its domination was addressed in Samir Amin's *Beyond US Hegemony: Assessing the Prospects for a Multipolar World*, transl. P. Camiller (London: Zed, 2006), and in his review of "Empire and Multitude," *Monthly Review* (November 2005): 1–12.

is vital for corporatism to secure the resources that consumerism requires, even when this works to the detriment of nature on earth. Technocapitalist corporatism does depend on consumerism, much as industrial capitalism did, only now it is a new version of consumerism attuned to the highly sophisticated technologies of technocapitalism.

Fast neo-imperialism also serves to preempt any national powers from defying the new global order imposed by the mega-triad, and most of all by the United States.[4] Whenever such defiance occurs fast neo-imperialism, its associated new militarism, and "regime change" that imposes corporatocratic governance, are brought into play. These three elements also provide power and flexibility to the United States to pursue its interests alone, whenever it is suitable to do so, or to seek the mega-triad's assistance whenever this can yield better results. This sort of flexibility is very important in a world where taking rapid action are of prime strategic importance. As noted earlier in this book, the new technologies spawned by technocapitalism and by the techno-military-corporate complex make it possible for such action to be more effective and intrusive than ever.

Beyond the debate over the continuing importance of nation-states and of neo-imperialism, this book rejects the neoliberal argument that social classes are or have become irrelevant.[5] Social class struggles and inequalities are entwined with neo-imperialism and with the global brain-drain flows of creative talent as never before.[6] The edifice of brain drain flows and immigration upon which technocapitalist corporatism depends so much would be severely damaged without class differences

---

4 See John Bellamy Foster, *Naked Imperialism: The U.S. Pursuit of Global Dominance* (New York: Monthly Review Press, 2006); Harvey, *Brief History*. The close association between US global military hegemony and the global spread of neoliberalism deserves attention. Achieving greater social justice on a global scale may hinge on the unraveling of that association; see Samir Amin, *The World We Wish to See: Revolutionary Objectives in the Twenty First Century*, transl. J. Membrez (New York: Monthly Review Press, 2008).

5 Neoliberals have attacked social class cleavages by trying to turn the poor into property owners; see Hernando de Soto's *The Other Path: The Invisible Revolution in the Third World*, trans. J. Abbott (New York: Harper & Row 1989). Their projects, in many cases supported by funding from the World Bank and other international organizations, have had little impact because of larger problems connected to the nature of capitalism in most poor nations around the world. The redistribution that corporatocracy undertakes through the privatization of public services, in particular, can be devastating to poor people and to any effort to turn the poor into property owners.

6 Even in nations with relatively dynamic economies, social class issues and struggles have remained at the forefront of national debates. See Paul Burkett and Martin Hart-Landsberg, *Development, Crisis, and Class Struggle* (New York: Palgrave Macmillan, 2000); Stephen A. Resnick and Richard D. Wolff, *Knowledge and Class* (Chicago: University of Chicago Press, 1987); William I. Robinson, *A Theory of Global Capitalism: Production, Class and State in a Transnational World* (Baltimore: Johns Hopkins University Press, 2004).

and inequities. Social class cleavages are, after all, an important driver of the global flows of talent that corporate power depends on, in its quest to appropriate.

Related to the neoliberal fallacies about the supposed irrelevance of nation-states and social classes, it has often been claimed that neoliberal (or corporatocratic) globalization constitutes objective "progress." In reality, such "progress" only applies to corporate power and to its global quest for markets and greater profit, as well as for the richer classes who own corporate capital. For the vast majority of the people such "progress" is a mirage. The wide-ranging dispossession and redistribution that favors corporate power and the richer segments of society are the very opposite of progress, and lead to a sort of global apartheid, between nations and between social classes.

In the global apartheid created by neoliberal "progress," inequalities and injustices need to be preserved if the new global order imposed by technocapitalism is to survive and thrive. This kind of global apartheid is one of the outcomes of the globalization of neoliberal dogma, of its corporatocracy, and of the apparatus of state power that supports the globalization of technocapitalism. This global apartheid created by corporatocracy cannot be corrected from within, as some apologists argue. Reform and correction from within are practically ineffective because of the vast power of co-optation and corruption that corporatocracy wields.[7] Moreover, the corporatocratic state's monopoly over "legality" ensures that those who stray from the circumscribed space assigned to opposition are repressed or submitted to the priorities of the state.

Opposition to neoliberal apartheid and to its corporatocratic state apparatus should therefore be carried out *outside* the system. Opposition from outside may have a greater chance of success, unshackled from the priorities of corporate power and from its corporatocratic state agent. External opposition to the system may also provide opportunities to make use of some of the new technologies spawned by technocapitalism, against the very technocapitalist system that created them. Such opposition must necessarily engage creativity in all its forms and dimensions, to overcome the social alienation and the fragmentation of human existence through which corporatocracy wields its power.

Defragmenting

The fragmentation of society and of human existence an important tool of domination for corporatocracy and corporate power. Fragmentation is in multiple dimensions, at the global level, at the macro-societal scale, at the level of communities, groups, and also individually in our lives and daily routines, is a formidable vehicle for corporatocratic conquest. Fragmentation's value for corporatocratic conquest

---

7 This condition is quite obvious in the American case with its two-party political system. See Thomas Frank, "A Low, Dishonest Decade," *Wall Street Journal* (December 23, 2009): A19; Galbraith, *Predator State*.

rests on its capacity to prevent unity of purpose among the various components of society, and to pit those components against one another. Dividing society in order to allow powerful interests (internal or external) to conquer has been one of the oldest strategies for domination since humanity's earliest days.

Fragmentation has been characteristic of capitalism since its earliest days, and it is also a major feature of the technocapitalist era. It is more intense under technocapitalism because of its deep reliance on technology and science, and because of their power to intrude upon and transform most everything we do, and most every form of life. Among its pathologies is *social alienation*, a result of the atomization of the social fabric and of our daily lives. For corporatism, such alienation is a wonderful vehicle to take consumerism to new heights, profiting from the sense of social disengagement and the psychological insecurities alienation creates.[8] Social alienation thereby becomes a means to foster unfettered and wasteful consumption, and the mountain of debt that accompanies this phenomenon, as a means to obtain greater profit and control over society.[9] In this manner, fragmentation and social alienation serve the needs of corporate power and corporatocratic governance, as consumerism, heightened psychological and economic insecurity, and debt dependence keep the vast majority of the population on a treadmill of collective anxiety. This widespread panorama of anxiety and insecurity leaves no time to reflect on the larger social context of corporate domination in which we are embedded.

Another example of how fragmentation and social alienation cement corporatism's power over society involves political organization. Fragmenting political opposition in order to impose a political order, particularly an unjust and

---

8   One example reflecting the insecurity that accompanies contemporary consumerism is that of product warranty extensions, which are widely promoted and sold to consumers whenever they purchase most any appliance. Those warranty extensions are said to generate about 15 billion dollars annually for American corporations, yet the vast majority of the products involved rarely malfunction within the covered period, and when malfunctions occur the vast majority of repairs usually cost less than the price of the warranty extensions in the first place. Poorer consumers (who can least afford the prices of warranty extensions) are the ones who most frequently purchase them. See Tao Chen, Ajay Kalkra and Baohong Sun, "Why Do Consumers Buy Extended Service Contracts?," *Journal of Consumer Research* (2009): http://www.journals.uchicago.edu/doi/abs/10.1086/605298; *The Economist*, "The Psychology of Warranties: Protection Racket," (November 21, 2009): 66.

9   The medicalization of normalcy by pharmaceutical corporations is an example of how corporate power's quest for greater profit and power opens up new frontiers for consumption. See *The Economist*, "Sex and Pharmaceuticals: Arousing Interest" (November 21, 2009): 82.; Daniel Costello, "Healthcare: Two Drugs Might Have No Benefit," *Los Angeles Times* (March 31, 2008): C1; Rhonda L. Rundle, "Competitive Squeeze: Industry Giants Push Obesity Surgery," *Wall Street Journal* (March 31, 2008): A1; Marcia Angell, *The Truth About the Drug Companies: How They Deceive Us and What to Do About It* (New York: Random House, 2004); H. Gilbert Welch, Lisa Schwartz and Steven Woloshin, *Overdiagnosed: Making People Sick in the Pursuit of Health* (Boston: Beacon Press, 2011).

exploitive one, is a strategy as old as politics. Such fragmentation is easier to achieve when social alienation is widespread, leading to political apathy for a large portion of the population, and to a fragmented opposition. A split opposition has been a major vehicle to monopolize power, and to submit those who oppose it, throughout history. In the context of technocapitalism and of corporatocracy, such submission is likely to be deeper and more intrusive than for any prior form of capitalist governance, particularly when corporatism controls the main functions of governance, public services, consumption, education, food, health care, and the media.

Fragmentation now intrudes into most every human activity, no matter how esoteric or far removed those activities may be from most peoples' daily existence. In academic research, for example, fragmentation has made deep inroads during the past four decades. Pervasive *reductionism* and micro-empiricism are now characteristic of academia, and are entwined with the larger panorama of societal fragmentation. Reductionism in research and teaching, along with an overwhelming emphasis on micro-empiricism, narrow specialization, and the replacement of education by training, banish broad (big-picture) perspectives.[10] Such perspectives are now more necessary than ever to understand fragmentation's multifaceted character, and the relations of power that sustain it, yet they are conspicuously missing from academia. Through reductionism, knowledge ends up becoming fragmented as well, compartmentalized into the narrow niches that corporatism finds convenient to set up, in order to subordinate it to the overarching quest for profit.

How far reductionism has penetrated the psyche of academia and research, and how much it is associated with fragmentation, can be seen throughout the academic spectrum of disciplines, in the natural sciences, in the social sciences, and even in the humanities. In virtually all academic disciplines today, reductionism has become essential for most any work to be published. Practically all professional fields today are greatly affected by reductionism, to the point that it is often impossible to find broad, big-picture analyses of situations, problems and outcomes. In the health sciences, for example, research that narrowly targets a problem in order to come up with a testable hypothesis all too often ends up

---

10 The narrow approaches to problem-solving that are so typical of reductionism (supported by micro-empiricism) often fail to take into account the complex, larger influences affecting the problem being studied. Understanding complexity is all too often the key to unraveling the mysteries of most phenomena. Richard Levins' work has shown how it is practically impossible to understand fully the causes and features of most scientific problems without a good grasp of the social, economic and political context in which they occur. Levins, the founder of the human ecology program at the Harvard School of Public Health, noted in a recent article that "problems have to be solved in their rich complexity; the study of complexity itself becomes an urgent practical as well as a theoretical problem" in science. See Richard Levins, "Living the 11th Thesis," *Monthly Review* 59 (January 2008): 34; extensive discussions of this and related topics can be found in Levins and Lewontin, *Dialectical Biologist,* and their *Biology Under the Influence: Dialectical Essays on Ecology, Agriculture, and Health* (New York: Monthly Review Press, 2007).

missing vital aspects of the general context in which the problem occurs, its side effects, and in some cases even its more important causal associations.

Objectives

For what ends should we then pursue defragmentation, and why is it important to do so in the context of global technocapitalism? *One objective of defragmentation is to overcome social alienation, a most common feature of our time, and one that has long been closely associated with capitalism.* Social alienation is becoming ubiquitous, and it is no longer confined to workplaces or specific social environments. It is global in its reach and scope at the macro level, and at the individual level it increasingly pervades both trivial and vital human activities, across cultures, nations and social classes. Supported by technocapitalism's intimate association with technology and science, alienation reaches deeper into human societies, affecting attitudes about our existence, about nature, and about life. Anti-social attitudes and actions, aggressive competitism that all too often harms even those who practice it, oppressive management, existential emptiness, and destructive hedonic decision patterns are some examples of its effects. This form of alienation in turn fosters fragmentation, in what becomes a mutually reinforcing cycle of social pathology. A result of this deeper and wide-ranging form of social alienation is a crisis of human existence, that involves not only humans but also nature and most forms of life.[11]

The pathologies social alienation creates are now becoming more visible around the world. One of them involves the destruction of nature in the quest for ever greater (and more indebted) consumption, to sustain corporate profits and power. Global environmental destruction, at multiple levels and in various dimensions, is one of the symptoms of a collective pathology of social alienation. Another example of social alienation is what can be referred to as the loss of the commons, or the loss of collective resources (natural, societal and human) to corporate power and profit. This loss, or public dispossession, of a collective resource is part and parcel of corporatocratic governance, as discussed in the previous chapter. Dispossession of the commons is entwined with social alienation, becoming both outcome and source in a dialectical sense.

Dispossession of the poorer segments of society in order to redistribute wealth and power to corporate elites, and to the richer classes, is also related to our alienation from society. The indifference (if not opposition) that all too often greets those who seek to make us aware of this kind of injustice shows how deeply alienation has taken hold. This is more palpable when corporate interests are aggressively advocated by individuals with little or no personal (or class) linkage to corporate wealth and power. It is all the more perplexing when such interests actually damage the advocate's own social wellbeing. Confusion about

---

11   In the sense provided by Richard Levins' eco-social distress syndrome; see his and Lewontin, *Biology Under the Influence.*

one's interests therefore seems to be one of the many symptoms of contemporary social alienation. More evidence on the depth of social alienation can be found in widespread apathy and ambivalence toward some of the most serious issues ever faced by humanity. At no other time in human history can one find social and environmental problems of the magnitude that we find today, yet the level of resignation is perplexing given the crises we are likely to face in coming decades.

A second objective of defragmentation is to overcome the pathological intrusion of technocapitalism and of its corporatism into human existence, and into life and nature. Technocapitalism threatens to monopolize our existence, partly through the routines that we follow in our daily lives.[12] This intrusion involves a sort of *programmed (but self-induced) regulation* of our existence that is deeply entwined with our daily routines. Soon to be aided by genetic manipulation and biopharmaceuticals, this kind of control over humanity on a global scale may become one of the most unfortunate features of the twenty-first century. Programmed (self-induced) regulation of human existence will of course target our behavior, most of all our attitudes and habits, such that we contribute more effectively to the corporate quest to maximize profits and power.

The same sort of programmed regulation is already being applied to nature. If a certain crop takes too long to grow, does it not enhance corporate agro-biotech's profits if its growth is accelerated, reducing the time from planting to harvest? Reductions of those time windows greatly increase corporate profits, by allowing crops to be rotated more quickly or to have several harvests of one type of crop during the time it took to grow one. If soil quality should limit this possibility, more potent fertilizers can be introduced, to generate more profit for the corporate entities that produce them. The introduction of bioengineered seeds has made this situation a reality.[13] Corporate propaganda touts the importance of this manipulation of nature, claiming that reductions in planting-to-harvest time will banish famine and hunger forever from the planet.

Programmed regulation, whether it occurs in humans or nature, is an example of the manipulation the world faces as the new corporatism wields its power, using its deep grounding in technology and science. It is a manipulation that

---

12   This may be understood in the sense provided by Henri Lefebvre's *Critique of Everyday Life*, transl. J. Moore (London: Verso, 2008), but magnified through the use of technology and science, including such new tools as behavior modification through pharmaceuticals (already occurring) as well as (in the near future) genetics and biopharmaceuticals. For the corporate entities involved, those new tools promise to become among the most profitable ever, as their use spreads globally, opening new markets and sources of profit.

13   See Marie-Monique Robin's documentary, "The World According to Monsanto" (Ottawa: National Film Board of Canada, 2008); Dominic Clover, *Monsanto and Smallholder Farmers: A Case Study on Corporate Accountability*, IDS Working Paper (Brighton, UK: Institute for Development Studies, University of Sussex, 2007). The nations where global agro-biotech and agribusiness corporations have made the deepest penetration are often those where wide-ranging neoliberal policies were implemented.

has no prior historical precedent, in terms of its depth, its global scope, and its potentially wide-ranging consequences. This deep and extensive manipulation of life, nature and human existence constitute the most formidable platform for corporate domination ever witnessed. This is greatly assisted by the vast influence that corporations have over governance, international relations and military power. In many respects, such manipulation of life, nature and human existence impose a new reality that is global, multi-faceted, and very difficult to oppose by the conventional means used in the past.

Elements

What elements of technocapitalism might then be considered for defragmentation, and why is it important to take them into account? One obvious point of departure is *fast accumulation*, a fundamental societal element of technocapitalism. As may be recalled from an earlier chapter, fast accumulation provided the means for technocapitalism to emerge. Two fast accumulation modes, in particular— the accumulation of tacit and of codified knowledge—were especially important. These two modes, which are essential for the global advance of technocapitalism, hold promise for resisting its pathologies. Another mode, the accumulation of infrastructure, particularly of the elements that are closely related to the generation of tacit and codified knowledge, also deserves our attention.

Reclaiming the crucial modes and processes of fast accumulation can thus become a prime objective of defragmentation. The fast accumulation modes closely associated with the emergence of technocapitalism are inherently social, and are thus deeply embedded in the larger societal milieu. Because of their social character, these accumulation modes are vital for, and greatly influence, the reproduction of creativity. The social relations in which they are embedded are also largely out of the control of corporate power, even though they are often affected by corporate schemes. The vital accumulation modes have a global projection, as discussed in earlier chapters, which is entwined with the emerging worldwide scope of reproduction, and with the rapid diffusion of knowledge that is so characteristic of technocapitalism. Their global projection can also facilitate relations and actions that are outside the domain of corporate power.

Reclaiming vital institutions through which fast accumulation operates should be an important objective for defragmentation. One such institution is *the university*. Reclaiming the university as a major societal institution, reversing its corporatocratic governance, and reconstituting it as a major element of social and political awareness can be part of defragmentation.[14] The university, as a

14 Corporatocratic governance has made inroads in universities around the world, but most notably in the US (and from the US, by imitation, to many other nations). This goes beyond greater dependence on corporate donations (for buildings, endowed professorships, research grants, scholarship funds, and the like). It now includes, for example, the assimilation of corporate management practices in every aspect of university administration,

source and repository of codified and tacit knowledge, is closely related to the fast accumulation modes upon which technocapitalism depends. The university is also a component of the infrastructural accumulation mode, because of the vital role that educational infrastructure plays in the technocapitalist dynamic. Given the university's vital role for fast accumulation, any effort that seeks to advance defragmentation must necessarily take it into account.

In addition to its vital role for fast accumulation, the university fulfills other important societal functions. A university education, for example, is considered to be a basic social right in many nations around the world. Universities are where the world's future leaders will mature educationally, and where their social and political awareness will be honed. The political and professional classes of entire nations depend on the university to renew their ranks, and to address pressing societal problems. The university also has a vital role in charting multiple agendas that can address the pathologies generated by technocapitalism and its corporate apparatus.

Another element of technocapitalism that can help defragmentation is *the network*. Reclaiming networks as vital social vehicles for human interaction and awareness, and to resist the social pathologies of corporatocracy and technocapitalism, can also become a major objective of defragmentation. Networks, however, are all too often dualistic.[15] They can serve oligarchic interests, by introducing hierarchies and nodes of control that favor the strong over the weak. Or, they can bring together diverse and fragmented elements that contest oppressive power. In that second role, they can be a vehicle for unity, promoting collective coalescence for network participants.

Networks can therefore be a vehicle for defragmentation, to the extent that they unify diverse interests and help call attention to pressing issues. The power of networks for defragmentation is associated with their worldwide scope and

---

the allocation of resources to academic units based on revenue yields and other markers similar to those used in corporate organizations, with little or no regard for the educational necessity of a particular discipline, the large-scale hiring of temporary faculty with no job security (similar to the corporate trend to rely more on temporary workers), setting up obstacles to union organizing, and eroding the independence of academic decision-making from corporate influence. See Jennifer Washburn, *University, Inc.: The Corporate Corruption of American Higher Education* (New York: Basic Books, 2005); Marc Bousquet, *How the University Works: Higher Education and the Low-Wage Nation* (New York: New York University Press, 2008); Bernard Wysocki, Jr., "Ivory Power: Once Collegial, Research Schools Now Mean Business," *Wall Street Journal* (May 4, 2006): A1; Benjamin Johnson, Patrick Kavanagh and Kevin Mattson (eds.), *Steal this University: The Rise of the Corporate University and the Academic Labor Movement* (New York: Routledge, 2003); Rebecca Buckman, "The Golden Touch of Stanford's President: How John Hennessy's Silicon Valley Connections Reap Millions for the University—and Himself," *Wall Street Journal* (February 24, 2007): A1.

15   See Luis Suarez-Villa, *Technocapitalism: A Critical Perspective on Technological Innovation and Corporatism* (Philadelphia: Temple University Press, 2009), pp. 72–8.

the fact that they can simultaneously bring together many people with diverse interests. Networks that help defragmentation must therefore be global in scope and scale, if they are to have a significant impact as instruments of resistance against the pathologies of technocapitalism. Global networks with the capacity to defragment our social environment can only work effectively outside the control of corporate power, however.

Working outside the control of corporate power, global networks that serve as vehicles for defragmentation must be open and inclusive.[16] This means that any agenda for network-based defragmentation should be flexible, in order to be able to deal not only with diversity within the network, but also with the flexible character of corporatocracy and of corporate power. Corporatocracy and corporate power tend to be dynamic, metamorphosing quickly in order to dominate and control, and this characteristic must not be lost sight of. An effective network-based opposition to fragmentation must therefore have the capacity to understand these characteristics, and it must be able to act and adjust quickly whenever there is a need to do so.

Defragmentation, in sum, must strive to unite the elements of human existence, of life and nature that capitalism splits. This is an urgent concern in the context of technocapitalism and of its globalization. Technocapitalism's deep association with technology and science, its advancing globalization, and its increasing capacity to manipulate aspects of human existence, life and nature make defragmentation an urgent concern. Such manipulation of human existence, life and nature was largely out of the reach of previous versions of capitalism. The globalization of corporatocracy and the collapsing of restraints that accompany technocapitalism, have made this manipulation and its fragmentation of human existence a source of our alienation. Uniting the diverse constituencies that are vulnerable to corporatocratic injustice, and to corporate domination and dispossession, is a central concern of defragmentation.

---

16   The rapid global spread of Open Source networks in many fields can provide some insights. See Samir Chopra and Scott D. Dexter, *Decoding Liberation: The Promise of Free and Open Source Software* (New York: Routledge, 2007); Andrew Lih, *The Wikipedia Revolution: How a Bunch of Nobodies Created the World's Greatest Encyclopedia* (New York: Hyperion, 2009); Mark Magnier, "Cyberspace Gumshoes Afoot," *Los Angeles Times* (November 23, 2008): A12; *The Economist*, "The Internet and Government: Leaks and Lawsuits: Lawyers and Governments Battle Over Free Speech on the Internet" (March 8, 2008): 62; Justin Lahart, "Taking and Open-Source Approach to Hardware," *Wall Street Journal* (November 27, 2009): B8; *Economist Technology Quarterly*, "An Open Source Shot in the Arm?" (June 12, 2004): 17–19. The diverse scope of these references, which encompasses software, encyclopedias, criminal investigation, whistleblowing, computer hardware and medicine, indicate the versatility of Open Source networks and their potential for defragmentation.

Transformative Emancipation

Emancipation has been central to humanity's hope for justice and fairness since the earliest times. In the context of global technocapitalism, emancipation should be an objective in our opposition to the pathologies and injustices of this new version of capitalism. Freedom from corporatocracy, from manipulation by corporate power, from their nefarious influence, and from their social injustices is as worthy an objective today as those of past struggles for justice, fairness and human dignity.

In the context of technocapitalism, of the new corporatism and of their globalization, however, it is clear that the centuries-old human yearning for emancipation from injustice must take up a new vision. Social emancipation must also *transform*. Freedom from oppression, the ages-old objective of emancipation, must transform the relations of power in society if emancipation is to have any permanence. The fluid and dynamic character of technocapitalism, of corporatocracy and of the new corporatism, and their capacity to re-establish their domination by multiple means, make it necessary for transformation to accompany emancipation.

In that sense, therefore, *transformative emancipation* must aim to change society. This means that it is not enough to liberate, or to understand how liberation can occur, but that it is also necessary to change society if emancipation is to last. Changing society means that the social relations of power must necessarily be transformed, such that those interests that oppress, that manipulate, exploit and generate pathologies can no longer do so. In the context of technocapitalism this is a fundamental need, given the fluidity, the dynamism, and the overwhelming capacity of this new version of capitalism to reconfigure itself nationally and globally. Unless this fundamental aspect is understood, and becomes an integral part of any agenda for praxis, the achievements of emancipation will be fleeting.

Fallacy of Determinism

Transformative emancipation is contrarian to *determinism*, or the notion that technology (or technocapitalism, for that matter) has an autonomous functionality that can be explained without reference to social influences, such as corporate power, or to social mediation in the reproduction of creativity. Technology is therefore not simply social through the uses it is put to, as determinism assumes. Technology is inherently social, in the sense that it is greatly influenced by the research agendas set by corporate power, by social struggles against its effects, and by social mediation over creativity, among other aspects.[17] Social processes

---

17 Many examples of social influences, especially those involving public resistance and their impact on technological development, occurred during the past five decades. See Martin Bauer, *Atoms, Computers and Genes: Public Resistance and Socio-Technical Responses* (London: Routledge, 2008).

and relations of power have major influence on technology because through them creativity is reproduced, and because corporate power decides the agendas that create technology, and controls the research regimes that commodify creativity. Social processes thus create technology's functions in a dialectical sense, as opposed to determinism's assumption that social processes only adapt to those functions.

Transformative emancipation is also contrarian to the deterministic notion that technological development follows a linear trajectory, from less advanced to more sophisticated forms.[18] Instead, the trajectory of technological development is complex and dialectical, and is influenced by social processes and the prevailing relations of power. Thus, the development of technology is not unidirectional. It can follow various trajectories and reach higher levels of sophistication in more than one track. The relations of power also influence which trajectory is taken. In the context of technocapitalism, corporate power therefore influences the trajectory of development as well as the technical considerations that affect development, and these (the trajectory and the technical considerations) in turn affect corporate decisions.

The end results of technology adoption and diffusion are not inevitable, as determinism assumes, but are influenced by corporate power (itself a socially grounded phenomenon) and by society. Determinism fallaciously assumes that technological adoption and diffusion are largely inevitable, by working backwards and extrapolating the abstract rationale of outcomes into the past. The abstract rationale (determined ex post) is then viewed as the cause of the development of any particular technology. This manufactured sense of causality, extrapolated ex post, is applied to every technology. Left out of the deterministic, unidirectional trajectory and its abstract (ex post) rationale is the very important influence that corporate power has in setting the research agendas that create the technology, and its role in shaping technological development. In the context of technocapitalism, those research agendas and the shaping of technological development are geared toward enhancing corporate power and profit above everything else, often at the expense of the very functionality that determinism touts and cherishes.

Perspective on Constructivism

Transformative emancipation disagrees with *social constructivism*, to the extent that constructivism neglects the larger social panorama, its political economy,

18 Extrapolated to the global level and to the development of have-not nations, determinism assumes that they will travel the same technological road to modernity as the "have" nations. The error of the deterministic vision is noted by Andrew Feenberg in his "Subversive Rationalization: Technology, Power, and Democracy," in Andrew Feenberg and Alastair Hannay (eds.), *Technology and the Politics of Knowledge* (Bloomington: Indiana University Press, 1995), pp. 3–22, and also in Feenberg's *Critical Theory of Technology* (New York: Oxford University Press, 1991).

technocapitalism (and capitalism, in general), and their influence over technology and science as vehicles of exploitation and alienation.[19] All the more so, in view of the reality and the pathologies that this new version of capitalism imposes globally. Moreover, social constructivism's contemporary emphasis on reductionism and microempiricism, to the neglect of the larger social panorama, is a roadblock to our understanding of technocapitalism, the overarching importance of corporate power, their manipulation of technology and science, and the social pathologies they create.

However, transformative emancipation does converge with the general perspective of social constructivism in two important ways. The first point of convergence involves the notion that the nature of the problems addressed technologically often changes in the trajectory toward a solution. This is what some social constructivists who specialize in the study of technology and science refer to as "interpretive flexibility."[20] In the context of technocapitalism, corporate power looks after those changes in its overarching quest for greater profit and power.

Changes that are considered to increase corporate profit and power, or to have a better chance of doing so, are those likely to be pursued. This aspect is built

---

19 Considerations of corporate power over science, how it shapes science and research, along with other aspects of contemporary capitalism that influence science and scientists, were missing from society-science studies. Instead, much emphasis was placed on the study of controversies in science, the micro-level ethnographic details of how scientists work, and how they come to conclusions that differ from those of other scientists doing much the same work. See Bruno Latour's *Science in Action: How to Follow Scientists and Engineers Through Society* (Milton Keynes, UK: Open University Press, 1987), and his and Steve Woolgar's *Laboratory Life: The Social Construction of Scientific Facts* (Beverly Hills, CA: Sage, 1979). Later macro-level emphasis on the democratization of science has also tended to exclude the role of corporate capitalism (and of capitalism, generally speaking); see Latour's *Politics of Nature: How to Bring the Sciences Into Democracy*, transl. C. Porter (Cambridge: Harvard University Press, 2004). Their approach nonetheless broke apart the deterministic view of science and technology that prevailed through the 1970s. Avoiding political economy and radical social criticism, however, made their efforts incomplete, limited their social scope, and ignored the earlier and important questioning of science's role in society pioneered by John D. Bernal, *The Social Function of Science* (New York: Macmillan, 1939) and John B.S. Haldane, *Dialectical Materialism and Modern Science* (New York: Labour Monthly, 1942). One result is that the work of scientists such as Richard Levins (see his and Lewontin's *Dialectical Biologist*) has also been ignored in their work.

20 See Trevor Pinch and Wiebe Bijker, "The Social Construction of Facts and Artefacts: Or How the Sociology of Science and the Sociology of Technology Might Benefit Each Other," *Social Studies of Science* 14(1984): 29–42; also referred to in Feenberg, "Subversive Rationalization", p. 7. Many production technologies used in the factories of industrial capitalism shared many elements but were put to different uses. Many uses often had the effect of de-skilling the workers that operated them, compared to alternative uses they could be put to. See Harry Braverman *Labor and Monopoly Capital* (New York: Monthly Review Press, 1974); David F. Noble, *Forces of Production: A Social History of Industrial Automation* (New York: Knopf, 1984).

into corporate strategy nowadays, whenever research is taken into account. It acquires paramount importance given the high cost of research in certain sectors, such as biopharmacology, where the research costs of a single product can exceed one billion dollars. Clearly, the nature of problems addressed technologically by corporate power *has* to change, and often does, as the scope of those problems are adjusted (through research agendas) in order to increase profit and power.

A second point of convergence is the constructivist notion that there are various potential solutions and actors (in a social sense) for any technological problem. Those actors are assumed to make their decisions by selecting among technologically viable solutions. In the context of technocapitalism, the "actors" are corporate. Corporatism and corporate power are the main actors, and all too often the only real actors, overwhelmingly so wherever corporatocratic governance exists. Corporate power, as the main or only actor, also influences greatly which solutions become available, since it sets research agendas in the first place. Those "solutions" do not drop from the sky, they do not come out of anonymous black boxes, and they are not created by entities that are autonomous from social influence, or from the relations of power that prevail.

In this regard, constructivism assumes that the technological system available at any given time is flexible, and can be adapted to meet social necessities. From the standpoint of transformative emancipation, however, those necessities tend to be defined by the relations of power that prevail, and by the decisions that are made by those who hold the power. The reality imposed by technocapitalism and its corporate apparatus, therefore, try to ensure that the technological system is heavily biased to benefit corporate power above everything else. The flexibility of the technological system is not in question, therefore. Rather, it is the bias which technocapitalism introduces as it takes advantage of that flexibility, in order to favor corporate power above everything else. The technological system is thus potentially flexible alright, but such flexibility is manipulated and made to serve the interests of technocapitalist corporatism. In this sense, the technological system available at any given time becomes socially grounded, as it is manipulated by the relations of power that prevail over society.

Democracy and Praxis

Beyond transformative emancipation's position vis-à-vis determinism and constructivism, its emphasis on *praxis* is fundamental. Transformative emancipation's central concern is change through praxis. Social change in the interest of social justice is a core objective. This is a dialectical process, in which people transform themselves and society through their practice: the practice of emancipation, and the practice of changing technocapitalist society to achieve social justice.

Creativity has a major role to play in this dialectical process. Change through praxis must involve creativity in the simultaneous transformation of circumstance, and in most every human action that pursues emancipation. This transformation through practice must aim to change contexts and to redefine the prevailing relations of power in society. Defragmentation, which is also part of this process, must involve creativity in the process of emancipation and in the practice of radical democracy. In other words, *democracy as praxis* is a major objective of transformative emancipation, as opposed to the ossified form of "democracy" that has been taken over by corporate power and turned into corporatocracy. Radical democracy, democracy as praxis, must operationalize democratic decision-making in every domain of human action: in schools, in workplaces, the home, recreation, and in the ways we relate to life and nature.

Operationalizing democratic decision-making in every domain of human action can be guided by several considerations. These considerations can be placed at the core of transformative emancipation through the practice of democracy. One of these considerations is *solidarity*, based on a recognition of humanity's common yearning for justice and fairness. The objective of solidarity here converges with those of defragmentation and of radical democracy: coalescing to find alternatives to exploitive, corporatocratic governance, that can lead to greater social justice and a more humane society.

In the context of technocapitalism, the road toward a more humane society must target the satisfaction of human needs, as opposed to the satisfaction of the needs of corporate technocapitalism. The satisfaction of the needs of corporate technocapitalism involve commodifying creativity in any form and by any means such that profit can be extracted, placing it over and above people's needs, and promoting excessive consumption to generate ever greater corporate profit and power. The pathologies that are being created by the needs of corporate technocapitalism are a result of this condition, and they are likely to be hallmarks of the twenty-first century. We can see their effects in the deepening social alienation of human existence, the demeaning of life and the destruction of nature.

Another consideration for transformative emancipation and radical democracy involves the *reclamation of the commons*. The common resources of humanity, whether in governance, public services, nature or life, rightfully belong in the public domain and should be accessible to all. Their damage, closure, curtailment or destruction at the hands of corporate power and corporatocracy harm the public interest. In this regard, and also with respect to governance in general, the public interest must be placed above that of corporatism. Until and unless this can be accomplished, real democracy will be out of reach.

In the context of technocapitalism, reclaiming the commons takes up greater importance, not only because of the overwhelming power of corporatism and because of its authoritarian character, but also because of the abstract and highly complex nature of the technologies that are used to manipulate and colonize nature, life and human existence. The knowledge to understand the character of those technologies, and the pathologies that corporatism creates through them, are more out of reach of the public's understanding than any prior tool of capitalism. The practice of real democracy, radical democracy, must seek to accumulate and mobilize the intangible resources (such as creativity and knowledge) that can reclaim the commons for the public domain, by helping us understand these new technologies and their effects.

Reclaiming public governance and the commons for the public interest is therefore a vital component of the struggle for transformative emancipation. In the context of technocapitalism and of its globalization, this struggle now takes up a different scope from past struggles for democratization. Four decades ago, many people around the world were greatly concerned with either the power of the state and its bureaucracy (mostly targeting the Soviet model), or about oppression by authoritarian, right-wing military regimes (the Pinochet regime in Chile being among the most blatant examples). Concerns and voices for democratization were targeted at one or the other of these models, or both, and their dismantlement was viewed as the uppermost priority for global democratic action.

Today, however, corporate power and corporatocracy come to the fore as the prime sources of authoritarian oppression. The Soviet bloc, long ago dissolved, and the vanishing of most right-wing military regimes have given way to a new, more clever, sophisticated form of authoritarian power, the power of corporatism and of corporatocracy. It is a different form of oppression, no doubt, from those of the earlier models noted above, because it operates through so-called "democratic" institutions, and because it is engineered to rule through the trappings of representative democracy, consumerism and technological novelty. Its oppressive power is far more subtle and uses the guise of "choice" at the personal level, even when in fact collectively there is *no* choice, or when the so-called choices that are made available have little difference between each other. We have thus been launched into the global neoliberal utopia of technocapitalist corporatocracy, under the authoritarian control of corporate power, on a scale which neither the powerful bureaucratic states nor the right-wing dictatorships of the twentieth century could reach.

How far we have come along this road is manifest in how we have internalized *competitism* as a prime cultural, economic and social objective. The culture of competitism now reigns supreme globally, grounded in neoclassical economic theories legitimized through Nobel prizes, and in the ever more powerful reach of business training and management schools.[21] It pushed aside and denigrated

---

21   Diffused largely through works such as Michael Porter's *Competitive Advantage: Creating and Sustaining Superior Performance* (New York: Free Press, 1985) and his *The Competitive Advantage of Nations* (New York: Free Press, 1990). Porter, an endowed professor at Harvard Business School, where he created the Institute for Strategy and Competitiveness, is considered to be the world's best-known authority on competition and corporate strategy. Among Porter's disciples are two of the world's foremost consultants on competition and corporate strategy, George Stalk, Jr., and Robert Lachenauer, authors of "Hardball: Five Killer Strategies for Trouncing the Competition," *Harvard Business Review* (April 2004): 62–71, and of (with John Butman) *Hardball: Are You Playing to Play or Playing to Win?* (Boston: Harvard Business School Press, 2004). Their work exemplifies the mindset of contemporary corporate consultants and executives on competition and competitive strategy. Perhaps it should not surprise that many corporate executives,

concerns about solidarity, social justice, alienation, social pathologies and the destruction of the commons, as the tidal wave of neoliberalism and corporate power of the past three decades swept away all restraints. The utopia of global corporate and market capitalism, based on neoclassical economic precepts and business school indoctrination, thus placed competitism, or the need to be competitive by any and all means, as the prime function of human existence.

Breaking down competitism as a form of authoritarian control over human existence is therefore another consideration for transformative emancipation. Competitism is now part of a collective psychosis in many societies around the world. It is deeply entwined with widespread social alienation, economic insecurity, the redistribution of power and wealth toward the corporate elites and the richer classes, the dispossession of the poor and working people that such redistribution entails, and the ideological justification of all these pathological symptoms. Competitism is therefore far from socially useful emulation, the kind that strives for constructive improvement at multiple levels, in the societal, group and personal spheres.

The enshrinement of competitism and of its intellectual premises in competition theory in neoclassical economics, in business school indoctrination, and in the neoliberal guidebook to development, has turned this cultural trait of corporatism and corporatocracy into dogma. Peoples, nations and social classes anywhere in the world who "fail" to live up to the expectations of corporate power, of neoliberal dogma, and of corporatocracy cannot but find themselves required to adopt competitism as their uppermost economic and social policy objective. The meta-national organizations that lend, channel investment, or punish those who defy the global corporatist utopia enforce the dogma of competitism, threatening with financial isolation those unwilling to comply.[22]

The multiple spheres of action that transformative emancipation must deal with create major challenges. Taking into account the context of technocapitalism, transformative emancipation must break down our dependence on corporate power, by searching for and implementing non-corporate alternatives to satisfy most every human need, and to address how we relate to life and nature. In this path, transformative emancipation must necessarily enlist creativity in every possible form and measure. The main resource of the technocapitalist era and of its corporate apparatus must therefore be turned away from corporatism, and against the social pathologies that this new version of capitalism imposes.

---

consultants and business academics see strong analogies between war, militarism, and corporate competitiveness. See C. Kenneth Allard, *Business as War: Battling for Competitive Advantage* (Hoboken, NJ: Wiley, 2004).

22 See Richard Peet, *Unholy Trinity: The IMF, World Bank and WTO* (London: Zed, 2009); Harvey, *Brief History*; Lori Wallach and Patrick Woodall (eds.), *Whose Trade Organization? A Comprehensive Guide to the WTO* (New York: New Press, 2004).

Creativity as a Global Public Resource

Turning creativity into a public resource is a potential outcome and also a source, in a dialectical sense, of transformative emancipation. As a public resource, creativity can become a vehicle for emancipation. Its social character places it at the core of most every human activity today. The fundamental importance of social mediation for reproducing creativity makes this most precious resource of technocapitalism era socially grounded, as discussed in an earlier chapter. This aspect makes it vital to enlist creativity in the struggle for emancipation.

Enlisting creativity in the struggle for emancipation, and turning it into a public resource, must go beyond the empowerment of those who provide creativity.[23] As a public resource with a global scope, creativity transcends individual and corporate contexts to become part of the commons, owned by no one and belonging to everyone. For creativity to become a collective resource, it must necessarily be both source and product of transformative emancipation. All of the elements of transformative emancipation must therefore be brought into the struggle for turning creativity into a collective resource. Breaking down our dependence and domination by corporate power, reclaiming the commons, vanquishing competitism, satisfying human needs, nurturing solidarity, and establishing real democracy that serves the public interest all require creativity (broadly conceived) in order to succeed. In this effort, broad perspectives that can help us understand technocapitalism as a systemic phenomenon must take precedence over narrow, reductionist views of the obstacles that must be overcome.

As a public global resource, creativity must provide alternatives to fast neo-imperialism and its schemes of domination. Fast neo-imperialism is antithetical to the possibility of turning creativity into a public resource, and any collusion between creativity and this new form of imperialism would negate transformative emancipation. Turning creativity into a public resource in order to support neo-imperialism would also negate defragmentation. Although turning creativity into a public resource to support neo-imperialism might conceivably occur, given technocapitalism's dynamic capacity to metamorphose, this would undoubtedly deepen its pathologies.[24] This possibility should not be underestimated, even if

---

23   Empowerment of those who provide creativity is an important aspect in this regard; see Suarez-Villa, *Technocapitalism*, pp. 161–64.

24   One of the most blatant examples of how collective creativity can become a tool for neo-imperialism is provided by the American military's use of Open Source software (Linux) to run supercomputers that will coordinate military operations, such as those involving radar surveillance, targeting imagery, tactical deployment, and other military applications. See, for example, *The Economist*, "Military Use of Consumer Technology: War Games; Consumer Products and Video-Gaming Technology Are Boosting the Performance and Reducing the Price of Military Equipment" (December 12, 2009): 89–90; Nathan Hodge, "Killer App: Army Tests Smartphones for Combat," *Wall Street Journal* (June 3, 2011): A2.

it occurs at the margins of corporate power. The opportunity it might provide to buy time for technocapitalism and corporatocracy to reinvent their apparatus of domination makes it all too likely to happen.

Turning creativity into a public resource must necessarily start with the phenomena of *fast accumulation*. The new modes of accumulation that are closely associated with the emergence of technocapitalism are particularly important: the accumulation of tacit knowledge and of codified knowledge. These accumulation modes, discussed in an earlier chapter, provided the platform that allowed technocapitalism and its new corporatism to emerge. In the context of the evolution of capitalism, these accumulation modes played as important a role as the accumulation of capital did in the emergence of industrial capitalism.[25]

Disengaging these accumulation modes from the domination of corporate power, and from corporatocracy, should be part of the struggle for turning creativity into a collective resource. Disengagement here involves reclaiming public or collective control over these accumulation modes. A key social institution to reclaim, which is fundamentally important for these accumulation modes and for creativity's condition as a collective resource, is *the university*. As noted earlier, universities are societal repositories (and sources) of tacit and codified knowledge. The fact that university governance has copied corporatocratic governance, essentially installing mini-corporatocracies in most universities around the world, makes reclaiming this social institution all the more pressing.[26]

The university's contribution to turn creativity into a collective resource is potentially a most important one, therefore. A point of departure in this struggle is to redefine the social purpose of the university, to articulate what this vital institution should be in terms of the common good and of the public interest. At the same time, an effort should be made to define what the university should *not* be. The university should not be and cannot be a corporate business. The university should not be a "brand," knowledge should not be treated as a commodity, students should not be considered "clients" or "products," faculty should not be considered "assets" (or hired labor), and the educational experience should not be thought of as a production process (or, in neoclassical economists' parlance, a "production function"). Digital diploma corporations must be recognized for what they are—

---

25   See Eric Hobsbawm, *The Age of Capital: 1848–1875* (London: Weidenfeld and Nicolson, 1975); Joan Robinson, *The Accumulation of Capital* (London: Macmillan, 1956).

26   Governance of universities increasingly mimics the corporatocratic governance of society. For example, the redistribution of rights (such as those related to free speech, collective decision-making, salary scales, cost-of-living adjustments, and the setting of teaching loads) from faculty to university executives is in some ways similar to the redistribution of political power from the poor or working classes to corporate elites, that is typical of corporatocratic governance. See Bousquet, *How the University Works*; Washburn, *University, Inc.*; Johnson, Kavanagh and Mattson, *Steal this University*.

providers of training rather than education.[27] Most of those corporations trade their shares in stock markets and place profit maximization above any real interest in education.[28] These digital diploma mills are but a small sample of the iceberg that is to come if the university is not reclaimed for society.

Beyond the new accumulation modes and the university's role in reclaiming creativity as a public resource, there is another important aspect to consider: *intellectual property*. A redefinition of intellectual property rights that can provide global criteria is needed, if creativity is to be turned into a collective resource. Property rights have been at the core of capitalism since its earliest days. Ownership (through property rights) of any resource that is to be commodified is essential in order for the capitalist enterprise to extract exchange value, surplus value, profit, and to be able to exploit any resource. In the heyday of industrial capitalism, property rights were mostly related to tangible resources, with corporate power controlling both the commodification and the reproduction of those resources. Those rights constituted the backbone of control over commodification, over the labor process, and over most any transaction. The fact that corporate power could control *both* the commodification *and* the reproduction of those resources was very important for securing appropriation, and for manipulating industrial and services production regimes.[29]

In the context of technocapitalism, the most important kind of ownership right corporate power can have is the intellectual property right. This kind of property right, whether in the form of a patent, trademark or copyright, for example, provides the platform upon which the corporate commodification of creativity occurs. In

---

27   David F. Noble, *Digital Diploma Mills: The Automation of Higher Education* (New York: Monthly Review Press, 2001). The Pentagon and the various branches of the US military are the most important clients of digital diploma corporations. The global deployment of US military forces, with bases in over 70 nations, make the service that those corporations provide a necessity given the Pentagon's promises to its recruits to help with their "education." Providing organizational training for military purposes is another purpose of the Pentagon's use of digital diploma corporations.

28   For-profit online diploma companies are said to enroll about ten percent of all university-level students in the US, and they are also the only educational sector that has significantly expanded student enrollment; see Anya Kamenetz, "Universities Inc.," *Fast Company* (December 2009): 52–4. Speculation and profiteering have become rampant in this sector, with private equity companies (hedge funds) buying up bankrupt conventional (brick- and-mortar) colleges and universities in order to use their names as a front to attract online customers. In the case of the Apollo Group (owner of the University of Phoenix, an online diploma company that has one of the largest enrollments in North America), the compensation of recruiters was tied to their performance enrolling new students. See Dawn Gilbertson, "Apollo Group Settles Suit for $78.5 million," *Arizona Republic* (December 15, 2009): http://www.azcentral.com/arizonarepublic/business/articles/2009/12/14/20091214biz-apollo1215.html.

29   See Hobsbawm, *Age of Capital*, and his *Labouring Men: Studies in the History of Labour* (London: Weidenfeld and Nicolson, 1964).

contrast with industrial capitalism, however, corporate power cannot control both the commodification and the reproduction of this most precious resource. As noted earlier in this book, the intangible nature of creativity and its qualitative character make its reproduction fundamentally social, since it is achieved through social mediation out of the control of corporate power. This fundamental aspect, which is one of the most salient features of technocapitalism, means that any property right that provides ownership over creativity or its results should be questioned. Since the reproduction of creativity is fundamental for corporate power to commodify this most important resource of the technocapitalist era, and to extract value, and since such reproduction is primarily social—that is, subject to social influences and mediation—any rights to the exercise of creativity must *also* be considered social. This means that the corporate appropriation of creativity, or of its results, inherently involves the confiscation of a collective resource.

Social mediation, which is fundamental for the reproduction of creativity, therefore provides the grounds to consider creativity a collective resource. Because of the social mediation required to reproduce it, creativity must be considered part of the commons. Fundamentally, then, corporatism's appropriation of creativity through intellectual property rights involves the expropriation of a public resource. The privatization of creativity in this manner, using corporate property rights to prevent the collective sharing and use of this most precious resource is socially unjust. In many ways, this form of expropriation is not much different from the sort of dispossession of public resources that corporatocracy undertakes to benefit corporate power, as noted in the previous chapter. Such dispossession, through privatization and the granting of exclusive property rights to corporate power, is one of the central tenets of neoliberal doctrine.[30]

Intellectual property laws that grant corporate power the right to appropriate the results of creativity are therefore socially unjust. In view of the fundamental importance of social mediation for reproducing creativity, and of the inherently social nature of creativity, those laws allow corporate power to dispossess society from a collective resource. Moreover, the granting of exclusive intellectual property rights seems obsolete, being a legacy of twentieth century industrial capitalism—and of the time when corporate power could control both commodification and the reproduction of its vital resources internally. The fact that in the context of technocapitalism such control vanishes with the reproduction of creativity, should allow us to contest the corporate appropriation of this most precious resource.

Turning creativity into a public resource also depends greatly on reclaiming governance to serve the public interest. This aspect must have a global scope if it is to succeed against the worldwide onslaught of corporatocracy and of corporate influence. Reclaiming public governance must address the unjust character of corporatocracy, its capacity to redistribute and dispossess, and its monopoly on legality. A major issue involves finding ways to reverse the redistribution of wealth and power to benefit corporate elites and the richer classes connected

30   See Harvey, *Brief History*.

to them. Another issue involves overturning the dispossession of the poor and working classes through redistribution, which is part and parcel of corporatocratic governance. Reclaiming the commons, the collective resources of society, must also be part of the struggle to turn creativity into a public resource, and to regain governance that serves the public interest.

Beyond these issues, turning creativity into a public resource must also involve global coordination. Coordination at all possible levels, especially on phenomena that transcend borders and cultures. Redressing to poor nations the brain drain loss of talented individuals, which amounts to a subsidy of sorts to rich nations, is one necessity. In particularly, the *creativity subsidy* that such brain drain flows entail must be fully understood and dealt with, and the corporations and nations that exploit those flows need to be held accountable.

The creativity subsidy provided by poor nations to global corporations and to rich nations is one of the most egregious injustices of our time. This kind of subsidy not only perpetuates the global inequalities and the exploitation of creativity upon which technocapitalism and its corporatism thrive, but they also foster a new kind of imperialism—fast neo-imperialism—discussed earlier in this book. Through this subsidy, the global relations of power between rich nations at the vanguard of technocapitalism, and poor nations, are asymmetrically structured to favor the former.[31] The most important sectoral beneficiaries of this subsidy are the global technocapitalist corporations, for which this subsidy is a key element in their commodification of creativity. The subsidy's support for commodification also allows corporate power to sustain the techno-military-corporate complex that is at the core of fast neo-imperialism. This exploitive connection is part of a mutually reinforcing cycle of domination that is now global in scope, and involves the most sophisticated technologies and the richest corporations of our time.

Research, an activity that is strongly linked to the global creativity subsidy noted before, also deserves attention. Research is to technocapitalism what production was to industrial capitalism. For industrial capitalism, the factory system and its labor processes provided the organizational platform for the commodification and reproduction of resources. Under technocapitalism, systematized research regimes provide the organizational platform for the corporate commodification of creativity. Research thereby becomes the key activity of technocapitalist corporatism. It is an activity that is structured and organized through the systematized research regime, much as production activities were structured through the factory regimes of industrial capitalism.

Turning creativity into a public resource must therefore involve research as an economic and social endeavor, to limit the control of corporate power and of

31 Sustaining this asymmetrical global relationship seems to be part of the foreign policies of some of the richest nations on earth, notably the US. See Foster, *Naked Imperialism*; Amin, *Beyond US Hegemony*; John Nichols and Robert W. McChesney, *Tragedy and Farce: How the American Media Sell Wars, Spin Elections, and Destroy Democracy* (New York: New Press, 2005).

corporatocracy. This is a formidable project that must enlist creativity (broadly defined) to breach the obstacles created by corporate power. Building research organizations that are *not* corporate, and through which creativity can be freely shared and engaged in the public interest, is a necessary element of praxis. The practice of democracy that is at the core of transformative emancipation must therefore encompass this vehicle. The creation of non-corporate research organizations as vehicles for collective creativity can, for example, involve research cooperatives and networks that operate in the public interest. These organizations might operate in any of the sectors closely associated with technocapitalism, such as biopharmacology, bioinformatics and nanotechnology, to deal with urgent societal needs.[32]

Internally, the practice of democracy in non-corporate research organizations must incorporate social solidarity and sharing as guiding principles, as well as service to the public interest. Creating an intrinsic (non-pecuniary) reward dimension out of the reach of corporate domination is another important aspect. Turning creativity into a public resource thus also becomes an organizational challenge, to the extent that new non-corporate research organizations must be created. In contrast with corporations, these organizations would not be set up to commodify creativity, but to share and provide this precious quality as a public resource. In many ways, these organizations would help or be involved in the reproduction of creativity, by supporting the sharing of ideas and by serving as collective clearinghouses of tacit knowledge needed to undertake research. Any property rights would be collective, belonging to no one and to everyone. Corporate appropriation would thus be replaced by collective sharing and usage for the common good, where creativity can be exercised for its own sake and also for the public interest.

The principles of social solidarity and sharing must transcend national boundaries. Only a non-corporate organizational ecology of research organizations that is truly global in scope and reach can hope to turn creativity into a collective resource. This poses a major challenge, in the sense that common goals and

---

32 Non-corporate research organizations may, for example, address health problems more creatively and more effectively than conventional pharmaceutical corporations. By sharing and collaborating around the world with similar organizations, without the overarching imperative to appropriate research results, they may dynamize not only our knowledge of disease but also medical delivery. Today, less than fifty percent of all known human diseases cannot be treated, and medications designed for those that can be treated work less than fifty percent of the time. Although pharmaceutical corporations typically use this situation to argue for greater freedom to appropriate research results (by extending patent validity, for example), the key to more effective medications and treatments may lie in cooperative, non-proprietary research organizations embedded in global networks. In this regard, the overarching corporate pharmaceutical emphasis on intellectual appropriation may be a hindrance to the advancement of human health. See Jerome Kassirer, *On the Take: How America's Complicity with Big Business Can Endanger Your Health* (New York: Oxford University Press, 2005); Angell, *Truth About Drug Companies*.

guidelines of governance must be articulated broadly. A broad articulation of those goals must be inclusive and dialectical, to allow dynamic responses to the fluidity of technocapitalist corporate domination, and to counter its capacity to metamorphose and generate new schemes of exploitation.

The twenty-first century is witnessing the global spread of a new form of capitalism with potentially disastrous consequences for humanity. Although much about this new version of global capitalism remains unknown, it is important for humanity to explore new avenues of resistance to its pathologies. The reversal of its injustices and pathologies may depend on how well we understand this new phenomenon, its corporate agents, and its effects on human existence. How well we turn that understanding into organization and action may decide whether the twenty-first century becomes a century of hope or a greater source of exploitation and injustice.

We are now at the crossroads of what may be a new trajectory for humanity, given technocapitalism's use and abuse technology and science, the overwhelming power of its corporations, its capacity to legitimize such power, and its quest to impose it on the world. The crises that we have witnessed in recent times may be a prelude to the maelstrom of crises and injustice that await us, if effective means are not enlisted to contest this new version of capitalism. Hopefully, this book will make us more aware of the daunting prospects we face, the extraordinary asymmetry in the relations of power we confront, and the need to mobilize our minds and hearts to resist an unjust new global order.

Index

creativity subsidy, 232, *see also* brain drain
flows
crises, 18, 22, 23, 25, 26, *see also*
capitalism; financialization;
neoliberalism
culture, 200, 201, *see also* corporate
power; fast neo-imperialism
cyber-warfare, 171, *see also* fast neo-
imperialism; fast militarism;
software

decomposition, *see* fast decomposition;
networks
defragmentation, 213–20, *see also*
social mediation; solidarity;
transformative emancipation
democracy, 177–82, 224–27
as praxis, 224–27, *see also*
corporatocracy; neoliberalism
deregulation, 15, 16, 194, 195, *see also*
neoliberalism; financialization
determinism, 221, 222
development, *see* innovation; research;
systematized research regimes
digital diplomas, 229, 230, *see also* higher
education; massification of higher
education; universities
disengagement, 76, 77, 92, 93, 116–18,
122, *see also* commodification
dispossession, 17, 182–90, 216, 217,
see also corporate welfare;
corporatocracy; neoliberalism;
redistribution
domination, 32–34, 97, 149–52, 178,
179, 211–15, 228, 229, *see*
also corporatocracy; fast neo-
imperialism; neo-imperialism
drug companies, *see* pharmaceutical
corporations

economic insecurity, 19–22, *see also*
corporatocracy; neoliberalism
eco-social distress syndrome, 153–59
features of, 153–56, 159
education, *see* higher education;
massification of higher education;
universities

emancipation, *see* transformative
emancipation
espionage, *see* corporate espionage
exchange, 77, 78, 85–89, 92, 93, *see also*
commodification
exchange value, 85, 92, 93, *see also* market
value
experience, 69, *see also* fast accumulation;
intangibles
experimentalism, 27–32, 118, 119, 110–24
and productionism, 118, *see*
also corporatism; research;
technocapitalism
experimentation, 74, 118–24, 142, 143, *see*
also research

factory production regime, *see* industrial
capitalism; productionism
fast accumulation, 43, 63–65, 80, 147, 148,
172–74, 218, 219, 229
and commodification, 44–49
consequences of, 58–63
definition of, 43
and fast decomposition, 100
and globalization, 43–45
and neo-imperialism, 159, 160
new modes of, 44–49, *see also*
accumulation
fast decomposition, 98, 102, 107–10, 143,
198, 199, 206, 207
and corporate control, 108–10
definition of, 99, 100
and networks, 102–107
and reproduction, 99–101
and systematized research regime,
110–24, *see also* commodification;
corporate organization; networks
fast invention and innovation, 61–63, *see*
also systematized research regime
fast militarism, 167–71, 174, 175, 203,
204, 211–13, *see also* fast
neo-imperialism
fast neo-imperialism, 159–62, 174–76,
203, 204, 211–13, 228, *see also*
techno-military corporate complex
fast research regime, 110–24, *see also*
commodification; systematized
research regime